W9-CHC-863

The Autobiographical Novel of Co-Consciousness

The Florida James Joyce Series

University Press of Florida
Gainesville / Tallahassee
Tampa / Boca Raton
Pensacola / Orlando
Miami / Jacksonville

Galya Diment

The Autobiographical Novel of Co-Consciousness

Goncharov, Woolf, and Joyce

99 98 97 96 95 94 6 5 4 3 2 1

Diment, Galya.
The autobiographical novel of co-consciousness: Goncharov, Woolf, and Joyce / Galya Diment.
p. cm.
Includes bibliographical references (p.) and index.
ISBN 0-8130-1304-6 (acid-free paper)
1. English fiction—20th century—History and criticism. 2. Autobiographical fiction—History and criticism. 3. Goncharov, Ivan Aleksandrovich, 1812–1891. Obyknovennaia istoriia. 4. Woolf, Virginia, 1882–1941. To the lighthouse. 5. Joyce, James, 1882–1941. Ulysses. 6. Consciousness in literature. 7. Point of view (Literature) 8. Split self in literature. I. Title.
PR888.A8D56 1994
823'.91209—dc20 94-8385

The University Press of Florida is the scholarly publishing agency for the State University System of Florida, comprised of Florida A & M University, Florida Atlantic University, Florida International University, Florida State University, University of Central Florida, University of Florida, University of North Florida, University of South Florida, and University of West Florida.

University Press of Florida
15 Northwest 15th Street
Gainesville, FL 32611

To the memory of my mother,
and to my father

We make out of the quarrel with others, rhetoric,
but of the quarrel with ourselves, poetry.
W. B. Yeats

in each such separation there is a tendency toward reunion
James Joyce

Contents

Foreword

It is particularly fitting that Galya Diment's *The Autobiographical Novel of Co-Consciousness: Goncharov, Woolf, and Joyce* should be the first volume in the new James Joyce series at the University Press of Florida. The series seeks new ways of looking at Joyce, as well as approaches that set him within the largest possible cultural framework, thus focusing on James Joyce both at the *center* of a cultural phenomenon and at the varying peripheries. The paralleling of Joyce and Virginia Woolf along numerous lines has become a trademark of modernist analogies, yet Diment finds a fresh line of investigation in their quasi-autobiographical perspectives. In Woolf's case, she explores a most unusual and convincing juxtaposition.

The inclusion of Ivan Goncharov, on the other hand, adds a far more exotic dimension, crossing numerous boundaries of time and place—as well as of literary format and style—and yet succeeds in building important bridges between the classic realist novel of nineteenth-century Russia and the modernist novel of twentieth-century Britain and Ireland. The Goncharov/Woolf/Joyce field of play allows for diversity in arrangement, moving the perspective beyond chronology and influence, as Diment finds her own lines of inquiry and points of contact, while the historical extension beyond her three subjects includes other peripheral but related analogies. Diment defines her own terms and suggests her own theoretical bases in a psychological examination unrestricted by existing dogmas. *The Autobiographical Novel of Co-Consciousness: Goncharov, Woolf, and Joyce* is offered by the series as a fresh and imaginative contribution to comparative literary criticism.

Bernard Benstock
Series Editor

Preface

My interest in duality probably predates even my interest in literature and is largely autobiographical—but we all have our share of dualities and I obviously do not have to detail my experience with it—except for one aspect that has a direct bearing on this book. I was born into Russian culture but have spent most of my adult life living in American; Russian literature was my first youthful passion, while English literature became my strong mature love. As a result, I became a comparativist, a specialist in both literatures, and this explains both the nature of this book and the choice of its subjects.

The initial impulse for the research presented here was my reverence for two writers—James Joyce and Virginia Woolf—and my admiration for two novels—*Ulysses* and *To the Lighthouse.* I read *Ulysses* several years before I became acquainted with Woolf's novel. I do not remember connecting the two right away but I do remember feeling that *To the Lighthouse* was almost as "complete" and thus as satisfying as *Ulysses,* which until this very day remains for me (and undoubtedly for very many others) the measuring stick for literary perfection.

While I was preparing for my Ph.D. exams in 1983, everything somehow came together. I remember rereading Goncharov's *A Common Story,* by no stretch of imagination a literary equal to Joyce's and Woolf's novels, and being struck by a realization that *Common Story's* nephew and uncle may be unexpected, seemingly illogical precursors of Joyce's Stephen and Bloom, who are fictional portraits of their creator as a young artist and as a mature everyman.

The book is based on my 1987 dissertation, which has undergone numerous revisions. Back then—living in a state of blissful scholarly innocence—I did not realize yet what I know fully well now: it takes a truly brave and discerning publisher to bring out a book with such seemingly strange bedfellows as Goncharov, Woolf, and Joyce. I commend the University Press of Florida—and am most grateful to them—for being such a publisher. Its editor-in-chief, Walda Metcalf, has been throughout the whole process as helpful as she has been enthusiastic and supportive, while Heather Blasdell, who copyedited the manuscript and readied it for publication, truly impressed me by the rare combination of genuine expertise, high professionalism, and sensitivity to the author's vanity.

My most profound thanks go to Robert P. Hughes and Alex Zwerdling, both of the University of California at Berkeley and codirectors of my dissertation, for the generous guidance and advice they gave me at that early stage of the present manuscript. Their Berkeley colleagues Simon Karlinsky, Eric Johannesson, Olga Hughes, and Hugh MacLean also gave me valuable feedback on the earlier version of the manuscript. I am also grateful to Paul Neumarkt, the editor of the *Journal of Evolutionary Psychology,* for reading and commenting on chapter 3; to Vladimir E. Alexandrov of Yale University, Peter Barta of Texas Tech University, and my colleague James D. West for doing the same for the chapter concerning Andrei Bely; to Karl D. Kramer, also my colleague at the University of Washington, who has helped me rework the manuscript by letting me bounce ideas off him; and, finally, to the University Press of Florida readers who gave me extremely useful suggestions for final revisions.

Some of the Ivan Goncharov material has appeared in the *Slavic and East European Journal* as "The Two Faces of Ivan Gončarov: Autobiography and Duality in *Obyknovennaja Istorija,*" and I thank AATSEEL of the USA Inc. for the permission to use it.

My very special thanks go to my family: my husband, Rami, who is always splendidly patient and helpful, and my daughters, Mara and Sasha, who, even though not as patient as their Dad, have been every bit as loving and supportive.

Unless otherwise noted, all translations from Russian of primary and secondary sources are mine. I have used the Library of Congress system of transliteration except in the case of well-known Russian names, which I have rendered in their familiar spellings.

G. D.

Why all this fuss and bother about the mystery of the unconscious? What about the mystery of the conscious? What do they know about that?

James Joyce, as quoted by Frank Budgen

Introduction: Divided They Stand

This book is about uses and expressions of autobiography and duality in three novels: Ivan Goncharov's *A Common Story,* Virginia Woolf's *To the Lighthouse,* and James Joyce's *Ulysses.* It is about a distinct fictional genre, an alternative to the traditional autobiographical bildungsroman, which Goncharov, Woolf, and Joyce mastered and perfected. It is also about the "mystery of the conscious" as it makes its presence felt in the three writers' sophisticated and subtle treatment of their inner conflicts through two well-developed, fully dimensional, very "unsupernatural," and perfectly active parts of a fictional "split self."

"The first novelist to use duality consciously in order to reveal the mental struggle of his characters was Goethe," writes Clare Rosenfield in "The Shadow Within."[1] But before Goethe's *Wilhelm Meister* (1777) there was Cervantes' *Don Quixote* (1605), which featured a duo of an emotional and idealistic protagonist and his pragmatic and down-to-earth servant and consort. There were also Swift's *Gulliver's Travels* (1726) and particularly his "Voyage to the Houhynhnms," a work on which psychoanalytical critics have been feasting for many years. One does not even have to be a Freudian to be tempted to see Gulliver and the Houhynhnms, who "are endowed by nature with general disposition to all virtues," as the ego and the ego-ideal, respectively, and Gulliver and the Yahoos, who "are cunning, malicious, treacherous and revengeful,"[2] as the ego and the id. There is likewise plenty of conscious duality in Defoe's *Moll Flanders* (1722), whose heroine at different points of her life is poor and rich, a whore and a loyal wife, a criminal and a "penitent." And what is the marriage of Mr. B. and Pamela in Richardson's *Pamela;*

or, Virtue Rewarded (1740) if not an attempt at reconciliation between Mr. B.'s "dark" passion and Pamela's common, as well as moral, sense?

No, Goethe did not introduce duality in novels, but neither did Goncharov, Woolf, or Joyce. Why, then, should I feel compelled to make *these* particular writers the subject of my book? A comparative study of several authors from different cultures and eras often runs the risk of being seen as random, especially when it features such an unlikely combination as two giants of English modernism, about whom so much has been written, and a relatively obscure Russian writer who, while highly esteemed in Russia for his 1859 novel *Oblomov,* does not enjoy the same name recognition in the West as do Tolstoy, Dostoevsky, or even Turgenev. But, as this book will show, the choice is anything but random.

Though Goncharov, Woolf, and Joyce did not invent duality in literature, in a crucial sense they *reinvented* it. Theirs was a special way of projecting inner conflicts onto multiple fictional selves, and it differed markedly from the classical tradition of the doppelgänger. I have borrowed Morton Prince's term "co-consciousness" to define Goncharov's, Woolf's, and Joyce's approaches to inner duality where the writers fictionalize what appear to be equally *conscious* sides of their complex personalities. I strongly believe that it is this co-consciousness that provides the most telling distinction between two different approaches to the theme of inner duality—the "divided-they-stand" approach of the writers discussed in this study, and the "divided-they-fall" approach of the celebrated masters of the double. The extent to which this concept of "simultaneous consciousness" is psychologically valid presents an interesting question which is discussed at some length in chapter 3. Yet in our investigation of Goncharov, Woolf, and Joyce, the problem of the validity of the concept of co-consciousness from a psychological point of view is largely secondary to what really matters: that those were the terms in which the authors themselves—writers, not psychologists—saw their duality and reconstructed it in their novels.

In this process of reconstruction Goncharov, Woolf, and Joyce also reinvented the autobiographical novel. Mikhail Bakhtin once suggested that there exist but two kinds of novels: non-bildungsromane that "know only the images of the ready-made hero" and bildungsromane where "the hero himself, his character, becomes a variable . . . [and] changes in the hero acquire a plot significance."[3] But as we will see later, having two protagonists as surrogates for their younger and older selves allowed Woolf and Joyce to create yet another kind of a novel, a viable alternative to the traditional autobiographical bildungsroman. Thus *Ulysses* and *To the Lighthouse* circumvent the long but selective chronological span of a bildungsroman in order to compress the action into a much shorter yet, in many ways, much more complete "moment of being." They do that, however, without sacrificing the highest achievement of classical novels of education—the changeable quality of their protagonists. The same technique enabled Goncharov to parody the very essence of the bildungsroman, so fashionable in his time, by replacing the traditional upward spiral of a character's development with a closed and vicious circle.

That Goncharov, Woolf, and Joyce cohabit the same study on duality in literature does not really seem all that surprising if one reflects on the conflicted nature of the periods that formed the three writers' sensibilities. The 1840s in Russia and the first quarter of the twentieth century in England and the rest of Western Europe were characterized by strong reactions against a previously dominant cultural tradition and the slow maturation of a new one. Many of the essential dichotomies so graphically expressed in the three novels that will be discussed here appear to have stemmed, at least partially, from the contradictions of the transitional period in which the novels were written. Consequently, the struggle to reconcile opposites, which is an omnipresent human pursuit in any era, may have been even further intensified for Goncharov, Woolf, and Joyce (as well as for many of their contemporaries in Russia and Western Europe), who often found themselves first shaped and then split by two rather antagonistic sets of cultural values.

One such opposition involved emotion and reason. This opposition, as we will see later, was central to both Goncharov's and Woolf's novels. For Goncharov, whose literary activity began in the 1840s, an era marked by a renewed spirit of pragmatism and utilitarianism among Russian intelligentsia, the "heart or head" dichotomy became synonymous not only with two different approaches to life but also with two different artistic movements: romanticism and realism. By the time Woolf came to the scene in England, this juxtaposition of feeling (subjectivity) versus reason (objectivity) was once again a hotly debated issue, a cultural commonplace, and a metaphor for the new confrontation between two artistic schools: realism and modernism. Therefore Woolf's own struggle to reconcile "sense and sensibility" within herself should not be totally divorced from the general plight of her generation. Likewise, Joyce's interest in the opposition between body and soul, which is as central to *Ulysses* as the opposition between head and heart is to *A Common Story* and *To the Lighthouse,* originated not only in the writer's own re-evaluation of the concepts of Christianity but also in the growing secularization of the cultural period he helped to define.

In 1908 Sigmund Freud remarked that the "psychological novel in general probably owes its peculiarities to the tendency of modern writers to split up their ego by self-observation into many component-egos, and in this way to personify the conflicting trends in their own mental life in many heroes."[4] Freud may be indirectly responsible for the fact that it seems so peculiar to feature Goncharov, Woolf, and Joyce in the same study. One is often tempted to assume that psychologically complex fiction with a sophisticated and subtle treatment of inner conflicts, which Woolf and Joyce came to practice in the first half of this century, had become possible primarily due to the heightened awareness of the "divided consciousness" that grew out of the era of Freud's *Ego and the Id.* "Not until Freud revealed the importance of the irrational in man," writes one critic, "have we been willing to admit the possibility that each of us has within us a second or a shadow self dwelling beside the eminently civilized, eminently rational self, a Double who may at any time assert its anti-social tendencies."[5]

But the rich nineteenth-century tradition of duality and the double in literature had preceded Freud by many years, and there did exist other prominent psychologists (several of whom are discussed in this book) who influenced writers throughout the nineteenth century. Unlike his various disciples and followers, Freud himself was quite aware that he did not set any trends when it came to literary manifestations of duality: the novels to which he refers in the quote cited above had obviously been written prior to the time his influence could have possibly affected them. Thus crediting Freud with originating a meaningful discussion of duality is about as erroneous as crediting Goethe with the first conscious use of duality in literature.

As a subject for contemplation, duality is of course as old as it is broad and vague. It was most likely our ancestors' tendency to project the tensions of their inner beings onto the outside world that led them to populate their folklore with numerous creatures of contradictory natures: mortal and divine, human and animal, feminine and masculine. From the very outset of the written tradition, there have been plenty of literary practitioners who felt torn apart by opposing impulses or conflicting desires, and who found ways to externalize those self-divisions by injecting them into their works. Such attempts often resulted in the endless sets of juxtaposed characters whom we have come to recognize as heroes and villains, where the villains, as has often been observed, frequently appear more convincing and realistic than their counterparts. That a well-drawn villain often represents his creator's darker side may strike many as a naive and simplistic idea, but it has definitely drawn strong support from some influential literary minds. Thus William Blake—himself no stranger to duality—firmly believed that "[t]he reason Milton wrote in fetters when he wrote of Angels and God, and at liberty when of Devils and Hell, is because he was a true Poet and of the Devil's party without knowing it."[6] "He drew Shylock out of his own long pocket," Joyce's Stephen Dedalus says of Shakespeare,[7] and D. H. Lawrence insisted that the character of the Grand Inquisitor was, "of course, Dostoievsky himself, in his thoughtful, as apart from his passional and inspirational self."[8]

Writers' frequently held belief in the essential duality of "a true Poet" has been shared by literary critics, one of whom observed that "many famous pairs of fictional characters are so closely linked that, like Dr. Jekyll and Mr. Hyde, they can be regarded as component parts of one person."[9] The existent critical literature on duality in fiction usually displays a healthy awareness of the scope of the problem. With the exception of C. F. Keppler, who made an attempt to generalize "the literature of the second self" by defining and describing the second self's six major appearances,[10] and Robert Rogers, whose psychoanalytic study of the double in literature also groups the instances according to major categories,[11] most critics steer away from generalizations and seem to prefer to curb their ambitions and limit the area of investigation. Thus, a substantial number of works focuses either on some of the most famous instances of the doppelgänger in Western literature (such as Hoffmann, Poe, Stevenson, Dostoevsky, and Maupassant),[12] or on a particular period of a nation's literature when literary expressions of duality appear to have been especially numerous. Among the latter works, by far the most sensitive and generous approach to the problem can be found in Masao Miyoshi's *The Divided Self: A Perspective on the Literature of the Victorian* (1969), while Karl Miller's richly eclectic study of the tradition of duality in Anglo-American culture of the past two hundred years, *Doubles: Studies in Literary History* (1985), is the most suggestive. Works on the German romantics, on the other hand, seldom seem to go much beyond the original treatment of the subject in Ralph Tymms's *Doubles in Literary Psychology* (1949).[13]

But whereas in one's investigation of the doppelgänger in literature it may be wise to limit the material, limiting methodology to only one particular approach is often unjustifiable. It stands to reason that any study of a split personality in literature should avail itself of relevant works in psychology, and yet the predominance of strictly psychoanalytical interpretations of literary duality is somewhat disturbing. Clifford Hallam in his 1980 attempt "Toward a Definition of *Doppelgänger*" concludes that "concerning the relationship between the literary Double and psychoanalytic criticism, the vast majority of available evidence suggests that any Double figure in prose fiction . . . can in most cases be understood more fully, more clearly and, in crucial ways, more convincingly by depth psychology." He supports his observation as being "borne out by the mass of scholarship, since any serious treatment of the doppelgänger motif in recent decades is almost invariably informed by psychoanalytic theory,"[14] but in doing so, he unfortunately confuses quantity with quality.

Bigger is, of course, not necessarily better, and while it is true that in the present state of the field several of the more important works on duality have been written from a psychoanalytical point of view, it is by no means certain that the strictly psychoanalytical approach to the theme of the double is necessarily the best informed one. For the truth is—and there is hardly a student of literary duality who does not acknowledge it[15]—the relevant "mass of scholarship" is still so small and spotty that any generalization on what works best is premature. It is my firm belief, for example, that the "divided" autobiographical selves in the present study *cannot* "be understood more fully" or "more convincingly" by "depth psychology" alone. "Freud's is not a psychology of the healthy mind," C. G. Jung quipped once,[16] and his simplistic generalization actually captures one of the main deficiencies of Freud's theory when applied to such works as *A Common Story*, *Ulysses,* and *To the Lighthouse.* It is a tendency to tolerate the splits as an inevitable yet not life threatening condition which immediately strikes one as a crucial feature of Goncharov's, Woolf's and Joyce's literary treatment of split personality.

But the most severe deficiency of a purely psychoanalytical approach to duality in fiction lies, in my opinion, in its tendency to reduce works of art to semiclinical "cases," thus ignoring the strong evidence that the fictional split self often functions not only as an expression of a writer's inner conflicts but also as a very powerful and conscious artistic tool. One of the considerable artistic effects of using doubles of any sort lies in their ability to underscore the artificial nature of the work (where, unlike in real life, such a physical expression of one's duality is possible) and thus to aid their creators in achieving a larger degree of artistic distance. In the cases of Goncharov, Woolf, and Joyce, this use of two fictional alter egos appears, in fact, to have been crucial in securing a stronger buffer of detachment between the writers and the immediacy of the autobiographical materials they chose to incorporate into their novels.

A few words should be said about the book's arrangement. The sequence of chapters was not dictated by simple reasons of chronology, which explains why a chapter on *To the Lighthouse,* published in 1927, precedes the one on Joyce's *Ulysses,* published in 1922. The reason I start with Goncharov's *A Common Story* is because of its relative simplicity when compared to the other two novels. Being by far the most transparent of the three in its use of a split autobiographical self, Goncharov's novel also conveniently serves in chapter 3 as a vehicle for discussing Prince's theory of co-consciousness as well as some of the larger theoretical issues pertaining to the subjects of autobiography and artistic expressions of duality. I conclude the study of the three main texts with *Ulysses* because

I believe that it is in this novel that the co-conscious split autobiographical self has found its perfect home.

Finally, though I do not know of any other works that can quite equal these three in their innovative, consistent, and versatile expression and use of co-conscious autobiographical selves, there are, to be sure, other novels that employ somewhat similar techniques and approaches. Chapter 10 focuses on several such novels, among them Cervantes' *Don Quixote,* Samuel Richardson's *Pamela,* and, more extensively, Andrei Bely's masterpiece *Petersburg,* a novel that is concerned more with the mystery of the "superconscious" than it is with the "mystery of the conscious," yet possesses many remarkable affinities with *A Common Story, Ulysses,* and *To the Lighthouse.*

Sudden changes are at the very core of my personality. I can never be the same for two weeks in a row. If on the surface I do appear to be stable and true to my regular habits, it is merely because of the immobility of forms in which my life is cast.

Ivan Goncharov

1

Goncharov and the Russian Autobiographical Tradition

A Common Story (*Obyknovennaia istoriia*, alternately translated as *The Same Old Story*) may be "transparent," but the fact that it *is* an autobiographical novel is one of the better-kept secrets in Russian, Soviet, and even Western criticism, where there exists a long-standing tradition of viewing Ivan Goncharov as a cool-headed writer who created broad, realistic epics with maximum objectivity. The tradition started with Vissarion Belinsky, who characterized Goncharov's artistic temperament as "pure talent" with no emotions,[1] and grew in strength throughout subsequent generations of critics. But this prevalent view is only half-right. For while no one should dispute Goncharov's desire to objectify his fictional presentations, the picture of Goncharov as nothing but an impersonal artist depicting generalized social types is distorted. Goncharov's novels are, in fact, much too subjective to be treated merely as "objective epics"[2] or "monumental epic panoramas."[3] Leon Stilman's 1948 argument with the "Belinsky" trend in Goncharov criticism still rings true today. "Goncharov," wrote Stilman in "Oblomovka Revisited," "was least of all an annalist of social transition. His work is remarkable for lack of historical perspective. His chronology is purely subjective: it is a chronology of reminiscence."[4]

Goncharov's authorial calmness can be, in fact, as misleading as his personal one. Thus in a chapter appropriately called "The Man and the Mask," Alexandra and Sverre Lyngstad aptly characterize Goncharov as a man whose "dominant persona" and "impassive exterior" concealed "many contradictions" and "deep tensions."[5] But although the Lyngstads do note Goncharov's essential dualism, often revealed in strong tensions between his private and public selves, they, like many other critics, stop short of pursuing the theme of duality into Goncharov's novels, perhaps out of fear that by doing so they may "blur the distinction between the man and the artist."[6] The fear is legitimate, yet one's best critical intentions become a handicap when they obscure the true nature of a writer's work.

It was not until late in life that Ivan Goncharov felt like reminiscing about his early years. He was born on a large estate in Simbirsk (now called Ulyanovsk), a reasonably sized but hopelessly provincial Volga town which Goncharov forever associated with lazy sleepiness. The year of his birth varies, depending on which of his several *curricula vitae* we read. In 1859, in a short autobiography submitted for a literary magazine, he alleged that he was born either in 1813 or 1814 ("I don't remember the exact year").[7] In 1874, in another autobiography written for similar purposes, he stated, this time with no hesitation, that "I. A. Goncharov was born in 1814."[8] Only on occasion, as in a brief autobiographical note submitted to the city of Simbirsk, where his birth records were kept, did Goncharov feel compelled to divulge the truth—for he was born not in 1813 or 1814 but in 1812, a year so significant in Russian history that it would be hard to imagine that he could possibly forget it. And most likely he never did. He simply did not like to talk about his age, just as one of his first fictional characters, Piotr Aduev, does not like to talk about his: "not on account of petty vanity, but in accordance with well thought-out calculations, as if he wished to insure his life at a premium."[9]

Ivan Goncharov's father, a well-off merchant, was thirty years older than his second wife and died when Goncharov was seven. The boy was raised by his poorly educated and strong-willed mother with the help of his godfather, Tregubov, a retired Navy captain, who lived in the Goncharovs' household as a tenant and acted as a surrogate father. Their home library was small and eclectic, and the boy, often left with little guidance, read without any discrimination. Later in life Goncharov would often draw a direct connection between this childhood experience and his intellectual deficiencies. His years at a merchant school, where he was sent by his mother and godfather, did little to improve his education. It was only at the age of nineteen, when he pleaded with his elders to be allowed to go to Moscow University, that he first began to fill in the gaps and acquire systematic education. Three years later, now a university graduate, Ivan Goncharov returned to his sleepy hometown; but within a year, despite his mother's tears and pleadings, he fled Simbirsk to embark on what he hoped would be a prestigious political and literary career in St. Petersburg. Instead, for the next ten years, he had to settle for working in a boring minor bureaucratic position and writing for a handwritten literary magazine run by the prominent Maikov family (which included several generations of famous artists, critics, and poets) and read mostly by the contributors themselves.

It was the fourth decade of the nineteenth century, and small Petersburg bureaucrats were far more often the stuff of literature than its creators. Some of Goncharov's contemporary writers, Gogol among them, had by necessity to find minor posts in governmental departments, but they generally quit those jobs soon after they were published. It seems that at first Goncharov had a similar intention. His first significant magazine publication—the translation from French of several chapters from Eugène Sue's *Atar-Gull*—was achieved rather painlessly in 1832, when he was still a student. Thus encouraged, he was hoping to do the same for his own, mostly poetic, works—the same poetic works that he was to ridicule later by attributing them to Aleksandr Aduev and letting the protagonist's uncle pitilessly take them apart. He also wrote prose but its quality never satisfied him, and he destroyed most of his early writings. The short stories he spared appeared in the same handwritten magazine, and only one of them, the Gogolesque "Ivan Savich Podzhabrin," was published in Nekrasov's *Sovremennik* (*A Contemporary*) in 1848, following the success of *A Common Story.*

Thus it should not come as a surprise that by 1843 Ivan Goncharov was all but ready to abandon his dreams of being a writer. Determined to give himself one last chance, he settled on writing a novel about two old landowners who fall under the beneficial influence of the countryside and become better people. But the novel went nowhere and he soon concluded that the life of *starosvetskie pomeshchiki* (old-world landowners), so masterfully described by Gogol, was for him a very hard subject, and that he "had seen and observed too little of life yet"[10] to write about almost anything else. The truth was that though this relative inexperience could have contributed to Goncharov's problems, he was by no means a youngster. At thirty-one, Ivan Goncharov was six years older than Gogol at the time of his "Mirgorod" stories. Whether Goncharov believed his explanation or just used it as a convenient excuse, he must have been troubled by the larger implication of this inability to keep up with his influential contemporary.

That implication was, of course, that he was not another Gogol. Most of all, he lacked "the sympathetic imagination," which enabled Gogol to grasp and penetrate a life or mentality quite dissimilar to his own. "[People say] 'Describe such and such an event, such and such a life, take up this or that problem, this or that hero or heroine.' I cannot, I do not know how," Goncharov confessed later while summarizing his literary career. "*All that has not grown up and matured within me,* that I have not seen and observed, by which I have not lived, is foreign to my pen" (his emphasis).[11] In earlier prose attempts, notably "Podzhabrin," Goncharov could follow in Gogol's footsteps mostly because, like the author of the "Petersburg Tales," he had had enough opportunity to observe his fellow bureaucrats and enough wit to ridicule their tastes and manners. But for his first novel he needed more than that. Lacking confidence not only in his ability to describe someone else's life but also in his basic writing skills—"I write 'painfully and laboriously'" ("Ia pishu 'gorestno i trudno'"),[12] he often complained, echoing one of Pushkin's gypsies—Goncharov must have felt he was faced with the choice of either abandoning his literary career or writing about what he knew best: his own life and "that which adhered to it."[13] Yet the choice was not at all easy since there was no strong tradition of published Russian autobiographical writings to encourage his undertaking.

Russia was a relative latecomer to the world of European literature. When talking about the history of autobiography in Russia it is important to bear in mind that the first European Christian autobiography, St. Augustine's *Confessions,* was written more than five hundred years before Russia was even Christianized and that the first "poetic" autobiography, Dante's *Vita Nuova,* was composed at least three centuries before great Russian poets stopped being largely anonymous creators of military epics and folkloric tales. In later years, the gap between Medieval Russian autobiography and that of Western Europe may have been widened even further by the Mongol rule, which lasted for nearly 250 years: it only stands to reason that literature at the time of a foreign and, in this case, "infidel" rule, would be more concerned with the fate of the whole "tribe" and its Christian faith than with that of a single individual.

Yet strong as those factors may have been, neither Russia's late arrival in the literary arena nor its experience with foreign dominance seems to have impeded the early development of autobiography nearly as decisively as the particularly strong emphasis that early Kievan Christians placed on humility. At the time when the rest of Europe and their own Byzantine teachers still worshipped the unforgiving, autocratic image of God, the Russians chose to pay special attention to the kenotic aspect of Christ. Thus the early Kievans (apparently causing some consternation among the Greeks) ruled that martyrdom can be synonymous not only with perishing for one's faith but also with dying humbly, thus clearing the way for Princes Boris and Gleb, who had meekly submitted to their death in a fratricidal power struggle, to become the first Russian saints. If we remember that Russia was one of the last European countries to part with paganism, and that there was only a short period of less than thirty years between the Christianization of the Kievan state (988) and the assassination of Boris and Gleb (1015), such a quick and drastic turn in ideals—from the heroic warrior to the submissive victim—is quite remarkable. While one can only speculate as to why such a quick conversion took place,[14] it is quite obvious that the culture's strong emphasis on humility would tend to impede the development of autobiography by generally discouraging any literary act of self-description as inappropriately "boastful." Even once written, the autobiographical texts may later have run a much higher than usual risk of being not copied (and thus not preserved) by pious clerics who might consider them blasphemous attempts to question God's will rather than submit to it. Taking all that into consideration, one should actually be amazed not at the meager quantity of medieval Russian autobiography but at the fact that such works exist at all.

Miraculously enough, we have several autobiographical digressions from the turn of the twelfth century in the Kievan *Primary Chronicle*, and, inserted into the same manuscript, a brief, mostly factual, description of the life and deeds of Prince Vladimir Monomakh in his "Admonitions to His Children." Around the same time someone who called himself Daniil Zatochnik (Daniil the Exile) composed a remarkable *Supplication* which contains rare colloquial language and details of everyday life as well as passages that are as emotional as they are misogynist. Several centuries later (c. 1470), a Russian merchant named Afanasy Nikitin wrote, with an apparent intention to make it available for other travelers, a rather personal journal of his travels in India. In a letter to a political enemy in 1564, Ivan IV ("Ivan the Terrible") became the first Russian writer we know to explore a possible connection between his behavior as a grown-up and the traumas of his childhood.[15] Finally, at the very end of the medieval period—the last quarter of the seventeenth century—Russia produced its first full-length autobiography, *Zhitie protopopa Avvakuma im samim napisannoe* (*The Life of Archpriest Avvakum Written by Himself*) (c. 1680), in which the arch conservative religious leader defied the very system of the old beliefs he was so fanatically fighting for by presumptuously writing his own vita. But as much as this work could have influenced the development of early Russian autobiography, it did not reach a wide reading audience until 1861, when autobiographies had suddenly become so popular that Russian publishers began to unearth and publish older specimens.

That late wave of enthusiasm (which seems to have been at least partially occasioned by the interests of Russian Slavophiles and their sympathizers who wanted to enrich the culture's awareness of its past) also brought about the publication of a score of other autobiographical writings, mostly from the eighteenth century. Some of those autobiographies appear to have been previously unpublished not only for cultural but also for political reasons. Thus the memoirs of Princess Ekaterina Dashkova (1743–1810), an ambitious and capable woman who became the first and only female director of the Russian Academy of Sciences, had to be actually smuggled to England to avoid the wrath of Paul I, who did not appreciate Dashkova's role in helping Catherine II to usurp the throne. The memoirs, although published in England in 1840 and translated into Russian in 1859, were not published in Russia itself until 1881, more than seventy years after Dashkova's death. The same political sensitivity affected the fate of the memoirs of Catherine II herself (1729–1796), which were also published in London in 1859, and of Gavriil Derzhavin (1743–

1816), Catherine's court poet and a statesman. Ironically, Derzhavin's work, first published in 1861 and called *Zapiska* (*Note*), devotes very little attention to either his inner life or his literary pursuits, although many consider him the greatest poet of his era.[16]

To say, as Andrew Wachtel does in his recent book, that "Before 1852 [that is, before Tolstoy's *Childhood*] there were practically no first-person accounts of childhood in Russia"[17] is to overstate the case. Yet it is quite true that among all autobiographies written in the eighteenth century only a few stand out as analytical or philosophical attempts to analyze the life of an individual rather than that of the whole country. Such is, for example, the unfinished *Open-Hearted Confession of My Deeds and Thoughts* (*Chistoserdechnoe priznanie v delakh moikh i pomyshleniiakh*) by Denis Fonvizin (1745–1792), a major playwright of the period. The work was written in the years immediately preceding his death and was modeled after Rousseau's and St. Augustine's *Confessions*. Also interesting in this connection are the works of Princess Natal'ia Dolgorukaia (1714–1771), whose memoirs describe her painful experiences connected with her trip to Siberia to follow her husband into exile, and of A. E. Labzina (1758–1828), whose reminiscences about her first marriage read like a Russian version of Richardson's *Clarissa*, by which her account was, no doubt, strongly affected. Other examples of a developing subjective impulse include the autobiographies of Andrei Bolotov (1738–1793) and G. S. Vinsky (1752–c. 1820), both refreshingly complete with extensive descriptions of childhood and numerous trivial details of everyday life.[18]

Of all these works, Goncharov could have read none in full and only a few in extracts prior to writing *A Common Story*. He could conceivably have read some parts of Dolgorukaia's account, published in fragments in 1810 in a rather minor periodical (*Drug iunoshestva* [*A Friend of Youth*]), and he may have also read the brief selections from Dashkova's memoirs published in 1845 by the same *Sovremennik* which would publish his first novel two years later. In addition, Goncharov was most likely familiar with the memoirs of Nadezhda Durova (1783–1866), published in 1836 also by *Sovremennik*. In it Durova described her truly dual existence as a young woman who always wanted to be a soldier and her later experience as a soldier in the Russian army who pretended for several years to be a man. But even if he read all those reminiscences and autobiographies, the experience was not likely to allay his apprehensions about the culture's censure of self-exposure: needless to say, another long-standing cultural tradition held it that women, unlike men, were more entitled to dwell upon their private lives since, not being public figures (Dashkova was a rare exception here), they had nothing loftier to focus on. The *Zapiska* of Russian general Vasily Nashchokin typified the male autobiography published at the time of Goncharov's work on his first novel. Written in the 1750s and not published until 1842, it dealt mostly with such a public topic as Russia's past military glory.[19]

Soon after Nashchokin wrote those memoirs, Russian literature started experiencing the significant influence of more "subjective" European sentimentalism and later romanticism. Particularly influential in this respect were the works of Nikolai Karamzin, Goncharov's fellow Simbirsk native, whose writing was strongly affected by Sterne's *Sentimental Journey through France and Italy* and Rousseau's *Confessions*. Though Andrew Wachtel is convinced that Tolstoy's *Childhood* was a "threshold work" that started the myth of "happy childhood" in Russian literature,[20] this is not exactly so. Boris Eikhenbaum, who saw Tolstoy's first novel as but *one* of the works that set the trend, was much more accurate in his assessment when he cited Karamzin's *The Knight of Our Time* (*Rytsar' nashego vremeni*) as an earlier example of the same tradition.[21] By fictionalizing his own childhood in the novel, which, though unfinished, was published in *Vestnik Evropy* in 1803, Karamzin truly anticipated later works—not only Tolstoy's *Childhood* (1852) but also Aksakov's *The Childhood Years of Bagrov's Grandson* (1859) and Goncharov's own "Oblomov's Dream" (1849).[22]

As a boy, Goncharov was fascinated by Karamzin: "[Y]outhful heart [was] seeking affinities with writers, it . . . gave itself totally to Karamzin . . . as the most humanist of all writers," he wrote in 1858.[23] He also called Karamzin his "first direct teacher . . . in a moral sphere."[24] But the popularity of Karamzin and his followers, already declining in the early twenties, started to fade rapidly after his death in 1826, so that by the 1840s, when Goncharov was ready to write his own "subjective" novel, sentimentalism—as well as romanticism—was totally out of vogue. Still, Goncharov remained loyal to Karamzin and bravely defended him from the increasing attacks of the new school of critics, who, the writer complained, were all too ready "to define the nature of the Karamzin era only with one word, for example as 'sentimental,' as if Karamzin has given nothing else to Russian civilization besides sentimentality!"[25] But this bravery came after Goncharov's first novel had already been published and his reputation established. By then Goncharov was so sure of himself that he even dared to publish "Oblomov's Dream," a poignant and more transparently autobiographical piece, which was later incorporated into his famous *Oblomov* (1859). The extent to which "Oblomov's Dream" was nostalgically autobiographical (despite its equally visible ridicule of a small-town pace and mentality) can be judged, for example, by a letter that Goncharov wrote to the Maikovs the same year that the piece was published in *Sovremennik*. He was at the time in his native Simbirsk, visiting his mother. In the letter, he talks about the bliss of being at home, surrounded by those who love him, and quotes directly from "Oblomov's Dream" to describe the idyllic quality of the place of his childhood.[26]

Yet back in the years preceding the success of *A Common Story* Goncharov still lacked enough confidence to follow the example of Karamzin or, for that matter, Pushkin, his one and only literary "idol,"[27] who had consistently challenged the cultural taboo against self-revelations. In addition to the extremely personal nature of Pushkin's poetry, the "subjective" authorial voice in *Eugene Onegin* (1833), and the use of family history in the unfinished *The Moor of Peter the Great* (1829), Pushkin actually made several attempts to write an autobiography but had to destroy most of his notes in 1825 because he feared that they might further implicate him and his friends as Decembrist sympathizers. Like Karamzin's, Pushkin's posthumous reputation was detrimentally affected by the Belinsky-inspired militant retreat from that brief period of relative subjectivism in Russian literature.[28]

It would be an oversimplification, however, to suggest that confidence was all that Goncharov lacked in the 1840s in order to challenge Belinsky and the long-standing cultural taboos. He also lacked conviction, for he had his own misgivings to battle with. Still an unknown writer, bitterly disappointed about his earlier literary attempts and his creative potential in general, Goncharov considered it highly presumptuous to assume that the public would be interested in his insignificant life and personality. He was also apprehensive lest the conspicuous act of self-indulgence make him appear too much of "an egotist"—a term he had feared ever since his childhood when his mother used it "to reveal the full depth of her anger."[29] But most importantly, Ivan Goncharov, despite his desire to fictionalize his own life, had always been an extremely private person. The occasional candor with which he would talk about his novels at the end of his life was mostly a testimony to the popularity of autobiographical writings then—they were so popular, in fact, that even Goncharov could own to the autobiographical nature of his works. For the truth was that Ivan Goncharov had a fear of self-exposure which often bordered on paranoia.

When, for example, as a famous writer he was asked by magazines and publishing houses for brief autobiographies to preface his works, Goncharov granted their requests ever so grudgingly, complaining that he had serious misgivings about "exposing myself."[30] In the 1870s and 1880s, when autobiographical writings became so common, he criticized "petty, empty, even personal, intimate [reminiscences] which do not have any significance for the society in general"[31] and constantly apologized for writing his own, rather modest, memoirs. He also worried about the possibility that other people might publish his personal letters, and on several occasions responded angrily to friends who asked to go public with their less-than-intimate correspondence with him.[32] Moreover, several years before his death he even launched a strong campaign demanding that his publishers should respect his last will and destroy his personal letters immediately upon the decease of their addressees.

"In England, if I am not mistaken," he lectured them in 1889, "there is a law which forbids to mention in print any details of personal, family life of a private citizen without his consent. All this is done even if that life does not contain anything unworthy of publicizing. An Englishman's domestic life, his *home,* are sanctuaries protected from the curiosity of the public. It would have served us well too, especially since we like so much to borrow things from abroad, to borrow this good rule from them!"[33] One of his closest friends, A. F. Koni, perhaps best summarized Goncharov's distaste for revealing himself: "He knew that one should be very careful in letting visitors into the temple of his soul out of fear that they, having entered with cold curiosity, would fill it with dirty footprints and dumped cigarette butts."[34]

It is hard to say how much of Goncharov's humility and fear of self-exposure were peculiar to himself and how much they could be traced back to his culture. It is obvious, however, that young Goncharov, contemplating using his own personality and life as materials for the novel, faced a very difficult decision. The difficulty, as has been mentioned earlier, was further compounded by the strong reaction that the contemporary intelligentsia felt against the sentimentalists and the romantics. Goncharov, therefore, would have felt not only "naked" and "boastful" but also unduly romantic if his fictionalized autobiographical experiences were easily recognizable, and if they failed to transcend the boundaries of the "petty, empty, even personal" presentation to reach a "significance for the society in general"—in short, if they did not become an "obyknovennaia istoriia" or a "common story" of a whole generation.

2

"Heart" vs. "Mind" in *A Common Story*

The amount of autobiographical material that Goncharov intended to put into the novel was truly immense. There would be, in fact, very little in the finished work that did not come directly from the writer's life—a fact that he himself finally acknowledged in 1879, deciding that it was "Better Late Than Never" ("Luchshe pozdno, chem nikogda," the actual title of his article) to set the record straight: "When I was writing *Obyknovennaia istoriia*, I naturally had in mind both myself and many others like myself who got educated at home or university, lived in quiet sleepy towns under the protective wings of kind mothers and later tore themselves away from the domestic bliss and comforts . . . to appear at the main arena of activity—Petersburg."[1] While André Mazon's and Evgeny Liatsky's biographies of the writer are most helpful for anyone who is interested in the similarities between Goncharov's life and his novels, by simply reading whatever is available of Goncharov's letters, memoirs, and the reminiscences of his friends and relatives one can clearly establish most of the numerous parallels that exist between the writer's personal experiences and his first work.

There is only one aspect of Aleksandr Aduev's early life that is hard to verify as having come from the writer's own life—the protagonist's experience with women. Mazon sometimes speculates about the young writer's amorous connections but he has virtually no proof; and even Liatsky, who usually has a ready autobiographical parallel in Goncharov's life to almost every incident in Aleksandr Aduev's life, is quite at a loss here: "'Oh, there was a time when I, too, had a her,' wrote Goncharov, 'it was when I was young.' . . . Who that 'she' was for Aleksandr, we know—Nadezhda Aleksandrovna Liubetskaia. Who was that 'she' for Goncharov?

We do not know and, perhaps, will never know."[2] The critic's statement may be overly dramatic, but his pessimism is quite well grounded. Nowhere did Goncharov's passion for privacy reveal itself as powerfully as in his secretiveness about the matters of his heart. It would only be natural to suspect that, like Piotr Aduev, who gleefully burns his early love letters to Aleksandr's aunt, Goncharov had somehow obtained from the addressees the "embarrassing" epistles and subsequently destroyed them.

But hard as it is to establish the close parallels between the author's and his protagonist's love experiences, such a connection seems a strong likelihood since young Aduev clearly inherited all the other circumstances of his early life directly from his creator. Like Goncharov, Aleksandr Aduev was born in the vicinity of a "sleepy" provincial town that remarkably resembles the writer's own descriptions of Simbirsk, where "one's only desire, when looking at its desolation, at sleepy windows with curtains and shutters drawn, at sleepy faces of people in their houses or occasionally on the street, is himself to fall asleep."[3] "How pleasant everything looks there!" Aleksandr remembers in a brief moment of nostalgia for home when first confronted with the imperial coldness of the huge Russian capital. "One house has a peaked roof and a garden filled with acacias. Here is a little pent-house on the roof—a shelter for pigeons. . . . And the quiet, the stillness, the monotony! In the streets, in the faces of people, the same stillness" (55–56).

Likewise Aleksandr's mother bears an unmistakable likeness to Avdot'ia Matveevna Goncharova, also a deeply religious widow who ran a large and bountiful household. Indeed, even Aduev Jr.'s servants Evsei and the lovingly spiteful Agrafena appear to have had their real-life prototypes in "the loyal servants of the Goncharov family, Nikita and Sof'ia."[4] With a further autobiographical touch, Goncharov made Aleksandr suffer from a chaotic and largely inadequate early education that results in the same lack of the "[right] sort of upbringing and correct views of life" (215) about which Goncharov so bitterly complained once in a letter to a friend: "I had with enormous efforts to create in myself, with my own hands, that which in other people is placed there by nature or those surrounding them—while I did not even have any natural resources from which I could build anything—that's how they had been damaged by the lack of early and careful education."[5] Aduev also shares with the author three years at Moscow University. While there, Aleksandr is said to have worshipped the eloquence of "our great, unforgettable Ivan Semionych" (66), whose rhetorical style closely resembles that of Nikolai Ivanovich Nadezhdin, young Goncharov's own beloved professor of esthetics.[6]

There is the same irresistible longing for Petersburg and the same tearful departure from home—Avdot'ia Matveevna Goncharova apparently cried so hard whenever her son was leaving Simbirsk that she often collapsed.[7] Aleksandr Aduev follows in the footsteps of young Goncharov once again when he arrives in the capital with a head full of dreams about a speedy and glorious career and a bag full of verses meant for instant success. Aduev's poems were the same poems that had appeared only a few years earlier under Goncharov's name in the Maikovs' magazine. In a further act of literary self-parody, the writer even made Aleksandr quote from the same few chapters of *Atar-Gull* that he had translated back in 1832 (222). The department where Aleksandr, to his great disappointment, starts at a low-level job, could not have been very different from Goncharov's own department. And Aduev's job as a translator is directly fashioned after the writer's own past: according to the archives of the Ministry of Finances, on May 18, 1835, the same month that he arrived in Petersburg, Ivan Goncharov was given a position as a translator in the Ministry's Department of Foreign Trade.[8]

Beyond the larger autobiographical parallels listed here, a wealth of smaller details of Goncharov's early home and city existence also found their way into the life of young Aduev. Thus the old songs of Goncharov's nurse Annushka, to whom he was particularly attached, are echoed in the book by a fictional nurse singing to Aleksandr "that he would always be rich and never know sorrow" (21). In the protagonist's behavior in Petersburg and his newly acquired habits (not attending the church, frequently dining out, spending free summer mornings fishing in the country) we can easily detect a trace of Goncharov's own city life.[9]

But Goncharov's use of autobiography in the novel does not end with the character of the young poet. Many years after the publication of his work, Goncharov used to mock his critics, who were just starting to probe the autobiographical elements in his novels, about how they were often "at a loss as to where to place me within a certain novel, for example, whether I was the uncle or the nephew in *Obyknovennaia istoriia.*"[10] The truth was, of course, that he was both. It was by this unusual splitting of his autobiographical self into two that the writer had found a powerful way to express the inner duality that he considered so essential in himself.

When Milton Ehre, the author of *Oblomov and His Creator,* objects to the "neat divisions into the two Goncharovs . . . [that] can be as simplistic as earlier searches for the single character of a fiction who embodies the creator," he misses the point by attributing those simplistic tendencies to Goncharov's critics rather than to Goncharov himself. While it is true, as Ehre points out, that "[a]rt is not mere projection" and that "[i]f Goncharov started out with projections of differing aspects of his personality, in the process of creation he turned his private dilemma into an intellectual problem,"[11] the final result should not diminish the stark "neat" nature of the contrasts that were laid at the foundation of the novel. For it was Ivan Goncharov, not his critics, who tended to view the world, and consequently himself, in terms of rather unsubtle and simplistic dichotomies.

"Is it good or bad to be alive?" he characteristically wrote around 1838 in a rather verbose essay. "Both yes and no. Life consists of the two different halves: one *practical,* another *ideal.* In the first we are slaves of toil and anxieties: like a bee, everyone has to bring a daily drop of his honey for *the public good.* In that life the absolute ruler is *the mind* [and] one offers many sacrifices to this despot. . . . The other part is different . . . there you stop living for the good of everybody and live only for *yourself.* . . . That is the esthetical half—in it there is plenty of room for *the heart.* . . . In that life there rules certain lightness, *freedom,* and one does not bend his head under the weight of constant thoughts about *duty,* work, and obligations" (my emphasis).[12] Goncharov's letters, too, often contain such juxtapositions: "*Youth* is egotistical and *emotional,*" he wrote in a letter to Grand Duke Konstantin Romanov in 1887, "it loves to share its overflowing feelings with everyone. Yet approaching *maturity* one already learns to control himself, not to spread himself too thin, to be *practical* and reserved in sentiment" (my emphasis).[13] "*Severe duty* pulls me to one side, *indulged-in imagination* to the other," he complained to a friend in 1866 (my emphasis).[14]

Youth versus *maturity, practical* versus *ideal, heart* versus *mind, public good* versus *individual happiness, duty* versus *freedom*—readers of *A Common Story* will immediately recognize these as the stark contrasts that are embodied in the characters of the nephew and the uncle. Perhaps Goncharov's most remarkable statement on his self-perceived duality, insofar as it illuminates with so much clarity how the writer's assessment of himself affected his novel, can be found in his letter to A. F. Koni, where Goncharov describes how he had survived painful experiences of love: "While twisting in the agony of passion I could simultaneously see how everything I was going through was silly and comic . . . [w]hile suffering *subjectively*, I also analyzed the whole drama objectively" (my emphasis).[15] Goncharov's inner interplay between a *subjective* participant and an *objective* spectator is closely paralleled in the novel by the numerous confrontations of the Aduevs whenever Aleksandr finds himself in the grips of love and Piotr gets his chance to view "the whole drama objectively," if somewhat mercilessly.

To many of Goncharov's contemporaries, the Aduevs closely resembled the writer's departmental boss, Vladimir Solonitsyn, an intelligent and practical man, and Solonitsyn's nephew, "Solik," a passionate and idealistic youth, who was a striking opposite to his uncle.[16] The Solonitsyns' differences were often the focal point of the Maikovs' gatherings, and it was most likely there that Goncharov, realizing how much their conflicts were similar to his own, first conceived the plan of using a fictional pairing of uncle and nephew as his split autobiographical self. That the two Aduevs neatly stood for "two Goncharovs" in Goncharov's mind becomes increasingly clear as soon as one pieces together both the obvious and the well-hidden parts of the book's puzzle, starting with the most vital biographical statistics—names and ages.

The choice of names for the characters was, most likely, a playful trick—obscured enough to have remained, as far as I know, totally unnoticed, yet too neat not to have been deliberate. The Aduevs are *Aleksandr* Fiodorovich and Piotr *Ivanovich* and therefore between them, although in reverse order, they share the first name and the patronymic of their creator—*Ivan Aleksandrovich* Goncharov. It is significant that while Goncharov adopted the name Aduev from the protagonist of his earlier story, "Schastlivaiia oshibka" ("A Fortunate Error"),[17] the other character's first name and patronymic, Egor Petrovich, were dropped. While we shall never know for sure why Goncharov borrowed only his earlier protagonist's last name, it is tempting to assume that this decision was indeed dictated by his desire to split his own name between the Aduevs.

The ages of the characters are equally revealing: the uncle, who, as we have seen earlier, had inherited from the author a propensity to be vague about his age, is in his mid-thirties (thirty-seven, to be exact) which was approximately Goncharov's age as he was finishing *A Common Story* in 1846. The nephew is twenty when he arrives in the capital, which makes him as old as his uncle had been upon his move to Petersburg, and nearly as old as Goncharov himself when he came to the city. In the epilogue, when Aleksandr finally "matures" sufficiently to become a replica of Piotr Aduev, he is thirty-five and thus approximately as old as the uncle at the beginning of the story and almost the exact age of Goncharov himself.

Furthermore, they were both born in "Grachi" (Rooks); not being brothers, they could not share the same biological parents, and yet Goncharov makes the uncle lose his parents early enough for his older brother and sister-in-law to replace them: ". . . he could not but remember how his deceased brother and that same Anna Pavlovna had seen him off, seventeen years previously . . . he remembered her tears on parting with him, how she had blessed him *like a mother,* her caresses, her pies . . ." (49, my emphasis).

There is even ample proof that most of Aleksandr Aduev's experiences are nothing more than the repetition of what Piotr had gone through before him—which goes a long way toward explaining the uncle's remarkable "omniscience" when it comes to divining not only what is going on in his nephew's life at the moment but also how it will all end. Thus they both had their first loves back in "Grachi," picked for the ladies of their respective hearts the same "yellow flowers," and cherished the young maidens' ribbons and locks of hair as the same "tangible signs of intangible relations" (67). There was the same tearful departure for the capital and, once there, immediate disillusionment with the provincial "baryshni" (damsels), followed by new attachments. They started their careers in the same department, and in the first days on the job the nephew is tricked into lending a hundred rubles to the same person who has been owing an equal sum to Aleksandr's uncle ever since Piotr's own beginnings seventeen years ago. At the end of the novel Aleksandr even gets the same reward for being a good bureaucrat—frequent pains in his back.

The fact that the Aduevs largely represent different developmental stages of the same individual is crucial for explaining not only their near-identity at the end of the book but also their profound initial contrast. The closest parallel to Piotr Aduev's extreme reaction towards his younger relative's idealistic tendencies is how he feels about his own youth, which, as he reluctantly admits, was almost as "foolish" (104). Hence the uncle's intolerance of his nephew's immaturity is merely the natural impatience of a person who has been there himself and does not want to be reminded of the ambitious grandeur of his own unfulfilled dreams. Knowing from first-hand experience the futility of the nephew's romantic pursuits, he constantly attacks Aleksandr's values and opposes them with his own, trying hard to hasten what he knows is otherwise a very slow and devastating process of "growing up."

While one can clearly perceive Goncharov's tendency to dichotomize the world and himself throughout his whole life and in all three of his novels (in his characters Oblomov and Shtolz, for example), nowhere in the writer's works is the contrast between any two characters quite as stark as it is in his first novel. The reader is bombarded by endless manifestations of the incompatibility of the protagonists' values: Aleksandr is a poet and Piotr a bureaucrat; one is emotional, the other exhibits self-control; the nephew is idealistic and the practical uncle is firmly grounded in reality; Aleksandr is still "provincial," his uncle is already a sophisticated city-dweller.[18] "What a difference there was between them," writes Goncharov two-thirds of the way through his book, when even the thickest reader has had enough opportunity to appreciate the difference,

> one a head higher than the other, well-built, stout . . . with assurance in his glance and manners. The thoughts and character of Pyotr Ivanich were not to be guessed at from his glance, his movements, or his words—so skillfully was everything in him concealed by his manners and self-control. . . . His pale, imperturbable countenance showed that in this man the play of the passions was held in

> strict subservience by the mind, that his heart beat high or subsided according to the dictates of his mind.
>
> In Alexander, on the contrary, everything betrayed a weak and delicate constitution—the changing expressions flitting over his face, a kind of languor, slowness and uncertainty in his movements, the limpid glance which showed every sensation of his heart, every thought stirring in his mind. (259–60)

This propensity to contrasts that are extremely obvious and simplistic is rather puzzling even if we take into consideration Piotr's well-motivated intolerance and the fact that Goncharov, as a beginning writer, could have lacked a certain professional sophistication. The relatively inexperienced Goncharov may also be paying an excessive tribute to the modish philosophical preoccupation of his day. As Irina Paperno points out in *Chernyshevsky and the Age of Realism,* by the 1840s the opposition involving reason and emotion (which can be traced all the way back to Plato and St. Augustine, among others) had evolved in Russia "into a cultural cliché separated from its original literary and metaphysical contexts."[19] For Belinsky, as for many of his followers, the choice between the "heart" and the "mind" often amounted to the choice between "vulgar idealism" and "reality."[20] Consequently, the juxtaposition also became—just as it reveals itself in Goncharov's novel—virtually synonymous with the confrontation between sentimentalism and romanticism on the one hand and realism on the other.

And yet, despite the familiarity of Goncharov's culture with the dichotomy that he chose as the foundation of his first novel, it is only when we realize that his obsessive use of it points back to his own life, as does almost everything else in the novel, that things become clearer. For this was an extremely difficult period in the writer's career, a period filled with so many forced readjustments and uncertainties that it could not fail to heighten Goncharov's tendency to polarize different elements in himself and his surroundings. And it was there, in what the writer perceived as the severe tensions between the old and newly emerging selves as they were splitting his own personality, that the fictional Aduevs' conflicts had originated and taken shape. It had been ten years since Goncharov had come to Petersburg, yet he was no closer to his artistic goal than when he first arrived. Ironically, the very act of writing *A Common Story* could have only compounded Goncharov's frustration since it appeared to have prolonged his indecision as to whether he was content with the reality of being just a useful bureaucrat or still wanted to pursue his unrealistic dreams.

It did not help any that the popular sentiment had it that being a bureaucrat was not just an occupation but "a state of mind" and, as such, incompatible with creativity. Thus the independently wealthy Ivan Turgenev was said to have been appalled in 1847 that "the apathetic bureaucrat Ivan Aleksandrovich Goncharov . . . a bureaucrat at heart . . . [who is] afraid to talk about [social problems] lest he lose his bureaucratic loyalty" was encouraged to be a writer.[21] Extremely insecure as he was, Goncharov must have found it highly unlikely that his novel would ever be published, much less liked. "I was always extremely distrustful of myself," he reminisced in 1875 about his work on *A Common Story*. "I constantly tortured myself with questions like 'Am I writing total nonsense? . . . is what I write any good? . . . what if it's all rubbish?'"[22] What he most likely envisioned instead of success was a perfect case of life imitating art, where the creator of Aleksandr Aduev would follow his character's suit by using yet another work for wallpaper and finally settling for a more ordinary career.

He was also approaching thirty-five, an age that he seems to have regarded as the time by which one is expected to leave behind the shaky idealism of youth for the safe practicality of maturity: Aleksandr's metamorphosis is complete by that age, for example. In a later novel, *Obryv* (*The Precipice*, 1869), Goncharov would characterize Raisky's age, which was also "about thirty-five," as "the time of one's life when the confrontation between youth and maturity has already taken place, when one has crossed into the second half of life, where each experience, feeling, illness leave their traces."[23] His own confrontation was still taking place and far from being resolved. On the one hand, he was indeed finding it increasingly hard to remain idealistic about the world, but, on the other, he felt very bitter about having to part with his youthful naiveté. How ambivalent his feelings were about the change that was supposed to take place by the age of thirty-five can be well seen in a half-serious observation he made to a friend once: "Byron was right," he wrote to Iunia Efremova in

1849, "when he said that a decent person should not live longer than 35. Beyond 35 only bureaucrats live well if they have stolen enough to buy themselves houses, carriages, and other good things."[24]

He never let go of his innocence quite as finally as Piotr Aduev does in the novel; in fact, for the rest of his life Goncharov strongly and somewhat secretly identified himself with the unhappy breed of disillusioned idealists: "I will tell you, finally, that which I have never told anyone," he confessed once in a letter to a friend. "From the very first minute, when I started writing for publication (I was already past thirty and had some experience) I had one artistic ideal: it was the depiction of an honest, kind, compassionate person, an idealist in the highest degree, who throughout his whole life tries not to give up searching for truth. Instead, he only finds lies everywhere and is always deceived until, finally, he gets totally disillusioned and is seized by apathy . . ."[25]

Simultaneously embarrassed by this "youthful" side of his maturing personality and apprehensive lest it make him more and more vulnerable to the cruelties of other people, Goncharov appears to have begun to seek protection in his ability to be a cool observer and to distance himself from his own emotions and from other people. This was largely Ivan Goncharov's public self—a somber, unemotional, and practical bureaucrat whom not only Turgenev but almost everyone else thought to be "apathetic," "cold," and, alas, "egotistical." It took just a year after the publication of the novel for this reputation to establish itself firmly: thus D. V. Grigorovich complained that his fellow-writer had "a cold temperament" and a talent for "controlling his feelings well enough to hide . . . the unhealthy vanity."[26] *Sovremennik*'s Nekrasov and Belinsky were so put off by Goncharov's manners and his practical sense—which revealed itself in the writer's contemplation of selling his first novel to a rival literary magazine for more money—that they called him "a brute" ("skot")[27] and "a petty and repulsive individual" ("chelovek poshlyi i gaden'kii").[28]

Iuly Aikhenval'd, one of the more perceptive Goncharov critics, was definitely right to describe Goncharov as "a poet [who was] only too successful and skillful at pretending to be prosaic."[29] Yet as often a victim of his success as its beneficiary, Goncharov frequently resented people for not noticing his "softer," more "poetic" side. "You are scared by . . . the coldness of my analysis," he wrote to a young poet in 1853 after treating the man's poems with a total lack of charity worthy of Piotr Aduev. "But you imagine more of it in me than there really is: there are things which are so tender, pure, and also sincere that I am moved in their presence, like Pushkin's devil who saw an angel at the paradise gate."[30] Goncharov's confession here is very interesting, for it not only underscores once again Goncharov's well-formed sense of his inner duality but also leads us back to a rare instance in *A Common Story* when this duality was couched in symbolic terms. Like Milton's Satan, Pushkin's devil is only a fallen angel, and as such he makes his appearance in the novel in the shape of Piotr Aduev—"Sometimes I seem to see Pushkin's Demon in him," writes the nephew about his uncle (66)—who is sadly watching and at the same time actively aiding the inevitable process of Aleksandr's own fall.[31]

The fact that the book offers no reconciliation between the protagonists until the nephew finally loses his wings tells us a great deal about Goncharov's severe frustration with the conflicting forces tearing him apart; the end of the book, however, makes it equally clear that he did not believe that he could possibly settle the conflict by always ignoring his idealistic and emotional "half." The book's finale would be as neat and simplistic as most of Goncharov's juxtapositions were it not for a certain irony in Aleksandr's transformation. For as the nephew finally masters his emotions and begins to emulate his uncle, Piotr, whose pragmatic approach is slowly killing his young wife, resigns his government post and astonishes everyone by declaring that he does "not want to go on living by the head alone" (417). Piotr Aduev's present is most likely Aleksandr Aduev's future. At the age of thirty-five Aleksandr becomes a clone of his uncle as the latter appeared to us at the beginning of the book; at the age of fifty he will probably find out for himself that the conflict between the practical and the emotional approaches to life does not really have a neat resolution and that forsaking one for the other may lead to tragic results.

Given the weight of autobiographical material that went into the creation of Goncharov's novel, one is at times tempted to agree with Evgeny Liatsky that the novelist was, indeed, one of "the most subjective" of all Russian writers.[32] And yet, Liatsky's statement distorts the true flavor of the novel, which, like almost everything else in Goncharov's life, was so peculiarly dual. If Goncharov's impulse to use autobiography in *A Common Story* appears to have been truly irrepressible, so were his desire for a "universal" novel and his fear of self-exposure. Most likely it was in order to protect his privacy that he incorporated several "nonautobiographical" elements into the lives of his characters. Thus, assuming perhaps that due to the similarity of ages and his own "cold" public image, he would be more recognizable in the character of Piotr Aduev, Goncharov, himself a bachelor, made Piotr marry soon after Aleksandr's arrival. This marriage, and later Aleksandr's imminent wedding to his boss's daughter, also helped to make them more typical since men in their late thirties were much more likely to have a wife. Goncharov further attempted to distinguish himself from the uncle by making him not only a bureaucrat but also a part owner in a china factory.

Piotr's ownership of the china factory is also quite interesting for an additional reason—it actually hints at yet another important outside source for the Aduevs which, unlike the case with the Solonitsyns, has so far been overlooked. In his introduction to *Ocherki russkoi litteratury* (*Essays on Russian Literature,* 1839), which we know Goncharov read,[33] the Russian critic, novelist, and historian Nikolai Polevoi describes fierce confrontations that took place between himself and his pragmatic father in terms very similar to those that Goncharov would use several years later when portraying the conflict between the Aduevs. Polevoi's father was a merchant who, like Piotr Aduev, combined business sense with substantial erudition and love for reading. Among the enterprises that he was involved in during his lengthy commercial career was ownership of a china factory in Irkutsk. Similarly to Piotr Aduev in his dealings with Aleksandr, Aleksei Polevoi strongly opposed his son's preoccupation with writing at the expense of business, calling it "bezdel'e," a waste of time.[34]

There is, in fact, a passage in Polevoi's description of his arguments with his father that appears to have been virtually copied by Goncharov for the scene where Aleksandr Aduev is persuaded by his uncle to burn his writings and turn his attention to business. "My father," writes Nikolai Polevoi, "and the whole family went to Moscow [where Nikolai had gone before them] in June of 1812. 'How much money do you have left?' and 'what did you do in Moscow?' were his first questions. I pointed to a heap of books I had bought and a pile of paper I have written on. 'And what about business? ['A dela?'].' I was silent. The pile of paper was immediately subjected to burning, I was forbidden to read books and we occupied ourselves with *business* ('prinialis' za *dela*')" (his emphasis).[35] Copying the scene was hardly a simple act of plagiarism on Goncharov's part. Not wanting to restrict his novel to a mere depiction of his own experience, Goncharov must have felt that including the plight of a fellow writer, with whom he shared both the merchant background and the lack of "proper" intellectual upbringing,[36] could only help to turn the book into a more universal story.

But it was in his preoccupation with the idea of authorial detachment that Goncharov's desire for a universal and impersonal novel revealed itself most vividly. There are several indications in the novel itself that Goncharov believed that a writer could succeed in creating a worthwhile work only by maintaining an emotional distance from his narrative. Thus even Aleksandr soon realizes that being in love is not a good time for writing prose, and postpones his work until "some other time, when his heart should beat less wildly, his thoughts should be ranged systematically" (145). However, the most vivid testimony to Goncharov's belief in a novelist's detachment comes later in the book when, almost a century before Joyce's famous Flaubert-inspired equation of an artist with "the God of the creation . . . [who] remains within or behind or beyond or above his handiwork, invisible, refined out of existence, indifferent, paring his fingernails,"[37] Ivan Goncharov formulates his own concept of artistic impersonality, which strikingly foreshadows Joyce's notion: "[A] writer only writes to the purpose," says the editor who rejects Aleksandr Aduev's immature writings, "when not carried away by self-absorption and prejudice. He must cast a calm, radiant glance at life and humanity, otherwise he will express nothing but his own *ego*, which nobody cares a rap about" (248, Goncharov's emphasis).[38]

Goncharov must have known that the personal nature of his materials made his task of maintaining authorial distance so much more formidable, and that he needed some especially clever strategies to minimize his own risk of "being carried away by self-absorption and prejudice." In his real life the writer was, of course, a frequent practitioner of self-detachment, relying on his dualistic ability of being simultaneously an actor in a drama and its spectator. Remarkably enough, he managed to transfer into his fictional life not only this general capacity for distancing himself from his emotions but also its very mechanism. For while we will never know for sure whether he first hit on the idea of splitting his alter ego into two independent characters primarily as a means for expressing his inner duality or as a skillful strategy to keep "the cigarette butts" out of his soul and express much more than "his own ego," it is nevertheless clear that the device fit perfectly all these purposes. Thus Goncharov's risk of self-exposure could be greatly minimized by distributing the weight of autobiographical material evenly between the two characters, as a result of which each character alone would be less recognizable as the writer's self-portrait. The dynamics of the novel's confrontation between an emotional participant and a cool observer were also immensely helpful in his attempt to control distance inasmuch as the fictional conflict injected a note of self-irony so familiar to him in his "nonfictional" existence. Furthermore, the phenomenon of physical duality and the interaction of the two selves, possible only in one's creative imagination, could serve as a constant reminder of the artificial nature of the writer's work, in which, like a good puppeteer, Goncharov could maintain the illusion of his characters' independence by skillfully obscuring the strings that connected them to himself.

As an additional benefit, the same technique could also offer a certain therapeutic effect: the fictional pair enabled Goncharov to manipulate his "different halves" and orchestrate their responses to each other, whereas in real life he often felt manipulated and orchestrated by them. Needless to say, the comforting power of this reversal could only further Goncharov's success in keeping his emotions at bay and his writer's sanity intact. He needed all his detachment and composure if he wanted to offset the strong subjective element in the novel by choosing his emphases carefully and systematically, and by bringing to the forefront those dimensions of the book that could be easily recognized as "common experiences." Being able to stay detached from his autobiographical characters, he could try to avoid the ego-centered temptation of stressing their uniqueness at the expense of their "representativeness"; distancing himself from his own life, he could turn Aleksandr Aduev's story into a typical journey to maturity, and give the theme such a universal dimension that his creation would draw most of the attention onto itself and away from all the particular autobiographical ingredients that went into its formation.

Judging by the reaction of the critics to *A Common Story,* Goncharov's attempt to "objectify" his first novel succeeded only too well. Upon the book's publication in 1847, some reviewers found its author to be, in fact, too impersonal, and the work itself "as cold as ice and as lifeless as marble."[39] Vissarion Belinsky, who was generally very enthusiastic about the novel and instrumental in its publication, lamented, in words that would sound like a great compliment only half a century later, that the young author was "a poet, an artist and nothing else . . . [who] has neither love nor hostility for the characters he creates."[40] Whether because it sounded so convincing or because Belinsky was so influential among his contemporaries, his judgment was upheld by several generations of Russian critics. Dmitry Pisarev, for example, echoing his literary and ideological mentor fifteen years later, would also reproach Goncharov for indifference towards his characters: "Constantly calm and uninvolved our novelist . . . dispassionately and objectively observes the situation. . . . Having read *Obyknovennaia istoriia* a reader cannot say that the author sympathizes with Aduev Sr. and cannot say that he finds him wrong either. Likewise, no sympathy can be detected towards Aduev Jr. . . . As a result of that a reader, finishing the last page of the novel, feels dissatisfied."[41] Around the same time, another critic, A. M. Skabichevsky, would go even further by describing Goncharov not as "an artist" but a mere "draftsman": "Belinsky was totally right when he defined Goncharov's talent as that of nothing else but a talented draftsman who draws his figures, characters, and scenes primarily in order to enjoy his ability to draw."[42]

Not everyone was critical of Goncharov's authorial detachment. He got praise from those critics who saw in his work a welcome and refreshing change from the moralizing tendencies of other authors. A reviewer for the highly influential *Otechestvennye zapiski* (*Notes of the Fatherland*), A. A. Galakhov, particularly commended "the character of the novel [which] sharply distinguishes itself by its objective, sculptured depiction of reality which is so rare nowadays given the prevalent desire [of writers] to always sound their own voices . . ."[43] Another critic must have especially pleased the young author when he emphasized Goncharov's difference from other writers by stating that "the talent of Mr. Goncharov is a talent which is original: he goes his own way, imitating no one, not even Gogol—and that is no small deed nowadays."[44] But whether they praised his objectivity or criticized his coldness, the fact remains that his contemporaries did not appear to be at all aware of the other, "subjective" side of Goncharov's novel.

Evgeny Liatsky once tried to explain this critical oversight as a result of the novelist's "unconscious and unwilling act of misleading his contemporary critics."[45] There may be a small grain of truth in this, for it is quite likely that even if Goncharov had not intended to mislead them, the critics would have overlooked the book's personal dimension because of the new writer's obscurity and the generally underdeveloped sense of fictional and nonfictional autobiographies in Russian culture. An example of the lack of sophistication about autobiographies can be found in an incident that happened four years after the publication of Goncharov's novel. Another as yet unknown author, Lev Tolstoy, submitted to the same *Sovremennik* his first novel. The title of his work was *Detstvo* (*Childhood*), but, due to the book's transparency, Nikolai Nekrasov knew right away that it had to be autobiographical and changed the title (and, consequently, the book's very genre) to *Istoriia moego detstva* (*The Story of My Childhood*), thus totally disregarding the fact that Tolstoy had deliberately made the protagonist's name different from his own.

But Liatsky never explains why, having unwillingly misled his critics, Goncharov was equally unwilling to put them on the right path. The answer is, of course, that there was nothing unconscious in Goncharov's actions, and the reaction of Belinsky and other critics to his novel was a sure sign to the author that he had hidden his "strings" skillfully enough to allow the outsiders to see only his novel's public side. He would not have been Ivan Goncharov had not a part of him now and then resented the critics' ineptitude in not seeing the devil's "umilen'e" (tender emotion) at the sight of an angel, and not realizing, despite all the obstacles he had created, how much of his own personality was woven into this "cold" and "objective" novel. "In vain did I wait," he exclaimed at the end of his life, "for someone besides me to read between the lines and, having taken my images to heart, make a whole out of it and realize what this whole says. But that did not happen."[46] It did not happen, of course, because he did not really want it to happen. That he was generally pleased with the critical response to his novel is quite clear from the fact that for many years he felt content not to challenge his critics even though at times he may have been tempted to do so.

Thus, for example, while the end of the book must have appeared to Goncharov almost inevitable, having originated as it did from his profound sense of inner duality, the critics who were oblivious to the autobiographical foundation of *A Common Story* often found the last pages of the novel particularly illogical. Here, too, Vissarion Belinsky set the tone when he strongly protested that it would have been much more likely for the nephew to end up as "a mystic, a fanatic, a sectarian, better yet . . . a slavophile," and declared that the book's finale "spoils the whole impression from this wonderful novel because it is unnatural and untrue."[47] It is not known whether Goncharov ever objected to this and similar pronouncements in his private conversations with the critic, but, except for a half-hearted attempt to defend his epilogue on the grounds that "Aduev ended up as most people then did,"[48] he never challenged Belinsky's views publicly. Furthermore, he even went so far as to agree fully with the Russian critic's often simplistic interpretation of the novel, thus letting into his already complicated life yet another contradiction, the essence of which is so well captured by Iuly Aikhenval'd's statement that in Goncharov "the commentator slanders the artist."[49]

He maintained this public silence on the issue of autobiographical elements in his novels until 1879, the year he wrote "Better Late Than Never." But even there, except for the general admission that "I have written only . . . what I have seen and known intimately"[50] and subtle hints about "images" that form "a whole," he was not forthcoming enough to start shaking the foundation of the overwhelming reputation of his works as merely objective epics. Thus, while he freely admitted to the overall autobiographical nature of Aleksandr's early years, he did not link himself to Piotr, and throughout the whole article still mostly echoed Belinsky, talking of both the nephew and the uncle as primarily social types, whose struggle "reflects . . . the break . . . with old conceptions and morals, with sentimentality, the absurd exaggeration of the feelings of love and friendship, the poetry of idleness . . ."[51] How much of this break was his own, and how the old parts refused to die and found it hard to coexist with the new ones, he did not say.

3

Autobiography, Duality, and Co-Consciousness

In order to analyze further the particular quality of Goncharov's presentation of duality, it is important to place his "double" in the context of the extensive literature of the doppelgänger. A traditional literary double is either a mirror image or a projection of the protagonist, and as such can be found in many classic works of nineteenth-century literature. Just to give a few examples, in Fiodor Dostoevsky's *Dvoinik* (*Double,* 1846) Goliadkin's alter ego is his twin image; so is the portrait of Oscar Wilde's protagonist in *The Picture of Dorian Gray* (1890) and the counterpart of Edgar Allan Poe's William Wilson ("William Wilson," 1839). Hans Christian Andersen's "The Shadow" (1847) and Adelbert von Chamisso's *Peter Schlemihl* (1814), where the protagonist sells his shadow to the devil and it becomes his opposing self, provide, on the other hand, good examples of the double-as-a-projection.

It has often been noted that several creators of mirror doubles were themselves subject to split-personality visions and hallucinations. Thus E. T. A. Hoffmann apparently "often thought he saw before him his living mirror-image, his double, and other spectral figures in disguise,"[1] and Guy de Maupassant, who, like many of the fictional characters discussed here, ended his life in madness, was reported to have had several visions of "*his own self entering,* who sits down opposite him and rests his head on his hand" (biographer's emphasis).[2] However, while it is quite plausible that in several cases the phenomenon of a mirrored self can itself mirror the writer's own visual experience of duality, one suspects that as a rule cases of literary duality were the outgrowths of an established and constantly self-perpetuating literary tradition rather than a mental disorder. After all, most of the classical examples usually appear to follow the same line of development that Otto Rank once attributed to the evolution of the concept of a double in general: "Originally, the double was an identical self (shadow, reflection), promising personal survival in the *future*; later, the double retained together with the individual's life his personal *past*; ultimately, he became an opposing self, appearing in the form of evil which represents the perishable and mortal part of the personality repudiated by the social self" (his emphasis).[3]

As in Rank's description of a "cultural" double, the likeness of the literary double to the "primary" self usually coexists with the double's opposition and, frequently, hostility to the protagonist—a phenomenon that helps to underscore the tragic irony of two selves being so similar on the surface yet so vastly different under it. It is mostly this irony and the dramatic possibilities it creates for cases of "mistaken identity"—in Hoffmann's *Die Elixiere des Teufels* (1815), for example, a double even runs the risk of being executed for the primary self's crimes—that separate the classical representations of the theme of a double from their less traditional counterparts, where, as in Goncharov, protagonists' alter egos are no longer their identical images.[4]

The fashion in which the two parts split—whether they do so by duplication or by division, the distinction suggested by Ralph Tymms in 1949—seems of relatively minor importance. Tymms's theory distinguishes between an internal division ("within") and an external duplication ("outside"). Thus when a double splits off the primary self in such a way that both parts appear to be interdependent, alternating selves, or, in Tymms's words, "separate but allied persons"[5] (as, for example, in Robert Louis Stevenson's *The Strange Case of Dr. Jekyll and Mr. Hyde,* 1886), we have a case of "doubles-by-division." But when the alter egos appear as independent entities seemingly outside of the primary self (as in Dostoevsky's *Double* and Poe's "William Wilson"), they constitute the "doubles-by-duplication."

Tymms's formula tends to be rather vague. In the case of Goncharov's Aduevs, for instance, the distinction fails altogether: insofar as the characters can be seen as embodying alternating (public/private, common sense/emotional, etc.) sides of one personality, Piotr and Aleksandr could be classified as the "doubles-by-division"; yet, insofar as they are physically independent of each other and in that very much unlike Jekyll and Hyde, they would appear to belong to Tymms's category of the "doubles-by-duplication." And even if we accept Tymms's classification as a valid one for most of the other cases, the distinction still appears largely a technicality for, as Masao Miyoshi rightfully pointed out, the differences between the "doubles-by-division" and the "doubles-by-duplication" are only secondary "to what is essential to both, the disintegration of the person."[6]

A much more meaningful distinction, wherever appropriate, is drawn based upon the essential nature of the double: whether it represents the protagonist's "better"—that is, morally or socially more acceptable—self (as in "William Wilson" or, to a certain extent, in Dostoevsky's *Double*) or his "worse," more selfish, and often even criminal self (as in *Dr. Jekyll and Mr. Hyde,* for example). Freudian critics habitually seize on this distinction when they talk about doubles in terms of the "super-ego" or "ego-ideal" in the first case and the "id" in the second, and even a non-Freudian critic will find it hard not to refer to these phenomena in Freud's familiar and evocative terms.

At first glance it may seem that Goncharov's conflict between the socially minded and pragmatic uncle and the selfish and emotional nephew could also neatly fit Freud's juxtaposition of the "ego," which "represents what may be called reason and common sense," and the "id," "which contains passions."[7] Likewise, Goncharov's general discussion of the "practical" and "ideal" halves of one's existence, cited earlier, could be easily recouched in Freudian terms as a confrontation between the "reality principle" (which the ego "endeavours" to impose on the id) and the "pleasure principle" ("which reigns unrestrictedly in the id"[15]). It may seem, in fact, largely an exercise in paraphrasing: what Freud called the ego, or "the mental agency which supervises all its own constituent processes" (7), Goncharov and many before and after him had simply called the "mind." What to the Viennese psychoanalyst constituted the id, or the entity driven by "instinct" (15), the Petersburg writer, again following a long-standing tradition, had viewed simply as the "heart." Freud himself appears to be saying as much when he links the ego to reason and common sense, and identifies the id with "the passions" (15). But the Freudian ego and id, of course, go beyond the mere distinction between what is rational and what is passional into the murky waters of what is conscious and unconscious. It is at this point that Freudian symbols, as applied to Goncharov's manifestation of his duality, stop being a mere paraphrase and become much more problematic than the older, organic, terms.

In *The Ego and the Id* (1923), Freud describes the relationship between the two as "the antithesis between the coherent ego and the repressed which is split off from it" (7). While other parts of the ego can be "conscious" (that is, sensed and perceived by the "ego"), "preconscious" ("latent but capable of becoming conscious" [5], or, as Freud later tended to believe more and more, "unconscious" [that is, unsensed by the "ego"]), the "id," being "repressed," is by definition "unconscious" since, according to Freud, "we obtain our concept of the unconscious from the theory of repression . . . all that is repressed is unconscious" (5, 8). In addition to the id, the ego has another counterpart in what Freud calls the "super-ego," or the "ego-ideal," the essence of which seems to lie in what the ego likes (or is trained) to identify itself with. Similarly to the id, the super-ego represents the internal world and hence stands in contrast to the ego which "is essentially the representative of the external world" (26) and, again not unlike the id, the super-ego "can to a great extent remain unconscious and inaccessible to the ego" (29). This antithesis between the ego, the super-ego, and the id (and less often, a Jungian variation on the same tripartite structure—the "ego," the "self," and the "shadow") has been for years a primary formula for many critics who deal with the problem of a split personality in literature.

Often the formula proves to be quite effective, as when it is applied to works where a writer deliberately explores the "dark," "instinctual," and often clinically "pathological" elements of one's psyche, the elements that a rational self cannot control. These works may include, for example, Stevenson's *Dr. Jekyll and Mr. Hyde,* which one psychopathologist found "so true a picture of what is actually observed in cases of double personality that it can be used almost as well as an actual case from life."[8] In the novel, Henry Jekyll's light-hearted experiment with a new identity soon turns to tragedy, as the rational scientist gradually loses all control over his *alter idem,* the murderous Edward Hyde. Similarly, in

Maupassant's "Le Horla" (1887), the narrator finds himself incapable of controlling an invisible but willful phantom, and in Andersen's "Shadow," the artful double becomes in fact so independent of its rational counterpart that it manages to annihilate him and yet stay alive. Of Dostoevsky's *Double* Marc Slonim writes in *The Epic of Russian Literature* that "in Freudian terms, the tragedy of Golyadkin, this new incarnation of the 'subliminal man,' is the result of the conflict between his Ego and his Super-Ego, his double symbolizing all that Golyadkin wished to be."[9]

Some psychologists, however, believe that even in those instances the Freudian notion of the unconscious is too broad and vague. They give preference to the notion of "subconscious" which was first introduced by Pierre Janet as early as the 1880s specifically for cases of multiple personalities. Ironically, in introducing the term "subconscious," the French psychologist was trying to avoid the excesses of the term "unconscious" which, in fact, had been widely circulating for most of the nineteenth century, much before Freud.[10] Pierre Janet's terminology and his general theory of "désagrégation," or "dissociation" of personality, was at the time accepted by some of the most influential of Freud's contemporaries in Europe and the United States, such as Alfred Binet, William James, and, most importantly, Morton Prince and Boris Sidis. Sidis's *Multiple Personality* (1904)[11] and Prince's *Dissociation of a Personality* (1905)[12] became classic analyses of divided consciousness. Although in later years the overwhelming attraction to psychoanalysis and Freudian emphasis on "repression" rather than "dissociation" largely obscured the earlier theory, Gardner Murphy returned to it in 1947 in *Personality: A Biosocial Approach to Origins and Structure,* and the last two decades have witnessed its further revival with several books—among them Ernest R. Hilgard's *Divided Consciousness: Multiple Control in Human Thought and Action* (1977)—having been written on the subject. The theory is enjoying some popularity in literary studies as well. Thus Jeremy Hawthorn discusses Prince's works in *Multiple Personality and the Disintegration of Literary Character: From Oliver Goldsmith to Sylvia Plath* (1983) and Karl Miller devotes a chapter to Janet, Prince, William James, and Murphy in his *Doubles: Studies in Literary History* (1985).

Janet's term "subconscious," as it applies to the studies of split personality, also stresses the existence of a "secondary consciousness," a subordinate personality (or personalities) that splits off the "primary" personality and becomes autonomous in cases of derangement or "hysteria." Once the split occurs, there is "commonly some amnesic barrier that prevents integration of the dissociated systems at least during the time that dissociation persists."[13] Janet's notions of "subconsciousness" and "dissociation" of personality appear to describe quite aptly, and in a more specific way than Freud's more general terminology, the doppelgänger phenomenon that had interested such writers as Hoffmann, Poe, Maupassant, and, of course, Dostoevsky, whose *Double* exploits the very conflict created by the "amnesic barrier" between different levels of consciousness that provided the foundation for early dissociation theories.[14]

And yet, given the choice, a literary critic will, most likely, still lean toward Freud in analyzing a doppelgänger, even though other psychologists appear more precise when they discuss the same subject. A critic's affinity with Freud is quite understandable: there is something so irresistibly poetic in the Freudian notion of the somewhat devilish id (is it because "a true Poet" is, indeed, always "of the Devil's party?") that, when applied to literature, the very vagueness of the term can be its main richness. When, for example, used to illuminate the morbid allegories of Poe or Maupassant, Freudian notions can be suggestive whereas Janet's and Prince's seem too clinical and dry. It is in those works where examples of literary duality are much more tame than Poe's or Maupassant's that Freudian dichotomies tend to fall apart. Interestingly enough, Freud himself had on occasion an "uncanny" foreboding that many writers concerned with less extreme cases of inner duality would disagree with what he proposed as a mechanism for the *Ichspaltung.* "I cannot help thinking," he writes in one of the footnotes to "The 'Uncanny'" (1919), "that when poets complain that two souls dwell within the human breast, and when popular psychologists talk of the splitting of the ego in an individual, they have some notion of th[e] division . . . between the critical faculty and the rest of the ego, and *not the antithesis discovered by psycho-analysis between the ego and what is unconscious and repressed*" (my emphasis).[15]

In Goncharov's treatment of split personality this dissociation between "the critical faculty," or the "head," and "the rest of the ego," or the "heart," is much more likely as a mechanism for ego-splitting than the "antithesis . . . between the ego and what is unconscious and repressed." Simply put, Goncharov's fictional re-creation of a man's disintegration into two conflicting halves lacks the irrational, devilish id of traditional doppelgänger works. It also does not present the total mental and/or physical disintegration of a character that is associated with the stories of that kind. Thus Dostoevsky's Goliadkin, suffering from unresolvable dualism, quite predictably ends up in a mental asylum; Wilde's Dorian Gray, Poe's William Wilson, Stevenson's Dr. Jekyll, and the protagonist in Maupassant's "Le Horla," among many others, all try to destroy their doubles but can only succeed at the price of killing themselves. Even in some of the less traditional treatments of the theme of duality, as in Emily Brontë's *Wuthering Heights* (1847), the formula of insanity (Heathcliff) and death (Cathy, Heathcliff) often prevails. The message in all these works is quite clear: whether it is the conflict between the rational and the passional as in the *Wuthering Heights* or youth and age as in *The Picture of Dorian Gray*, there is no possibility for reconciliation of the discordant parts. Once a personality splits, the dream of wholeness is but a dream while any attempt to restore harmony by suppressing the second self back into oblivion only leads to self-destruction.

Goncharov's conflicts were very similar to those of other writers of duality. Like Wilde, he was interested in dilemmas of "innocence" and "experience"; like Dostoevsky he concerned himself with the problem of private and public behavior; like Brontë, he pondered the confrontation of emotions and common sense. Furthermore, as we have seen earlier, Goncharov did not appear to believe in the possibility of reconciliation either. At the end of the novel, the nephew may have fooled himself that he has succeeded in becoming a rational and pragmatic being, but the writer himself is not fooled. The nephew's transformation into a replica of his uncle at the same moment that the uncle himself is losing his balance and striving to regain his "emotional" self is, of course, far from an ideal resolution. Goncharov may have been, in fact, quite as adamant as any other writer of the double in his belief that destroying a troublesome self did not necessarily lead to desired harmony and wholesomeness.

What he seems to have doubted, though, is that, in his case, this troublesome self was ever in the state of oblivion and that his own consciousness was so mysterious and his instincts so "dark" that the inevitable duality or multiplicity could trigger an extreme reaction. Unlike Maupassant or Hoffmann, Goncharov does not appear to have been subject to hallucinations or visions; neither did he share Dostoevsky's obsession with psychological abnormalities. Most likely, there was nothing in Goncharov's dualistic existence that ever went too far beyond the most common experience: being split and torn apart may have been inconvenient, unsettling, and even, figuratively speaking, maddening, but it never was really a threat to either his private sense of sanity or his morally and socially acceptable public image. Being suspicious by nature, he may have seen "murderous" instincts in others[16] and thus have striven to make himself less vulnerable to "cruelty," but in himself, at least from what we know of him and his writings, he saw none. In that he may have been a rather typical representative of the intelligentsia of his time, which scorned the "inexplicable" and "mysterious" as unnecessarily "romantic." He was also a man who, simply by virtue of his temperament, would be likely to prefer the safety of "the known" at any age. Be that as it may, Ivan Goncharov did not believe in overmystifying his inner conflicts, and seeing Aleksandr in terms of Goncharov's intentional presentation of what is "repressed," "hidden," and thus "unconscious" would be largely erroneous.

A Freudian critic may say that Goncharov's intentions are quite irrelevant here since a writer often reveals more than he either wishes or is aware of. The same critic may also point out that Goncharov skillfully hid and therefore "repressed" his "emotional" half when in public. Yet it is not the public Goncharov but the private one who is of primary concern to us here, for it is only in the response of the individual to himself that he or we can discern what he denies in his personality and what he acknowledges. As the evidence in chapters 1 and 2 suggests, it is highly doubtful that the private Goncharov ever seriously attempted to repress the idealistic, emotional component within himself. For one thing, he may have been embarrassed by his idealism but never ashamed of it; in fact, he rather cherished it as the remnant of his younger and, in many ways, *better* self. (There may be, after all, an element of Freud's "ego-ideal" in Aleksandr.)

As a result, whereas many dual characters are either so appalled or shamed by their other side that they instinctively turn to self-deception—

Goliadkin, for the most part, vehemently denies his connection with the "impostor"; Dorian Gray hides his portrait in the attic; William Wilson attempts to persuade himself that his double's name and physical resemblance are pure coincidence—Goncharov's Piotr Aduev freely, if somewhat regretfully, accepts Aleksandr as a truthful portrait of his own younger, idealistic self. And while Dostoevsky, Poe, and Maupassant seem to be intentionally exploiting the conflict between the two vastly different strata of consciousness, of which one can be called "subconscious" or "unconscious," depending on whose terminology we want to use, Goncharov does not appear to plunge into a psychological abyss of any sort. Instead, he seems to think of his characters as equally conscious or co-conscious aspects of his personality.

The term "co-consciousness" (or "concomitant consciousness") has been widely used in a different mode. It was suggested at the turn of the century by Morton Prince, who was searching for ways to further modify Janet's "subconscious" by emphasizing the idea of "coexistence." And while the idea of coexistence makes the term very attractive for our purposes, it is necessary to point out that by using Prince's terminology for Goncharov's literary presentation of duality, we are taking certain liberties. Prince's "co-consciousness" is largely "subconscious," for it presupposes a coexistence of the primary "conscious" mind with an "extra, co-acting mind of which the primary self is not aware."[17]

One may argue, though, that it is the idea of coexistence, not the lack of awareness, that is central in Prince's term. Being a psychopathologist, Prince was naturally concerned with the clinical cases of dissociation, where, as in the celebrated case of "Miss Beauchamp," there was often a definite "amnesic barrier" present between different layers of consciousness. Yet by the turn of the century many of Prince's contemporaries were postulating that a tendency toward splitting one's personality is a common trait in many healthy psyches. Thus Max Dessoir treated the dual personality as a normal phenomenon in *Das Doppel-Ich* (1896), and Boris Sidis stated in 1904 that "multiple consciousness is not the exception, but the law."[18] "Even in the normal individual, character-splitting is by no means impossible," C. G. Jung, one of Pierre Janet's more famous students, echoed the earlier views. "We are, therefore, perfectly justified in treating the question of dissociation of personality also as a problem of normal psychology."[19] Furthermore, by 1924 Prince himself came to believe that one did not have to be clinically ill to "have as many selves as we have moods, or contrasting traits, or sides to our personalities," and that so-called abnormal cases merely took those rather benign *Ichspaltung* tendencies to pathological extremes.[20]

If we accept this commonly held view that "ego splitting" is quite universal, and that the degree of awareness serves as "the primary mark that distinguishes between alternating normal roles and alternating personalities as found in psychopathology,"[21] we may be quite justified in using the term "co-conscious" differently in those two situations. We will still be able to use it in the traditional sense of "subconscious" in the case of a Miss Beauchamp, whose primary self is not aware of "an extra, coacting mind" due to a certain malfunction of memory, and, perhaps, as "simultaneously conscious" in cases where there is no amnesia present between the different streams of consciousness. That such parallel consciousness is, in fact, a psychological possibility and not just a layman's invention has been for many years a strong opinion of a number of psychologists. Their different approaches to this phenomenon, while by themselves not enough to illuminate fully Goncharov's duality, may nevertheless help to highlight some of its more important aspects.

Thus, insofar as Goncharov's duality often reveals the common tensions between his public and private images, it can be reasonably well described in terms of the Jungian "persona" and "soul" (or "anima"), where "the persona" is one's public "mask, which he knows corresponds with his conscious intentions, while it also meets the requirements and opinions of his environment."[22] "Persona," wrote Jung elsewhere, "is a compromise between individual and society as to what a man should appear to be. He takes a name, earns a title, represents an office, he is this or that. In a certain sense all this is real, yet in relation to the essential individuality of the person concerned it is only a secondary reality, a product of compromise, in making which others often have a greater share than he."[23] As we have seen earlier, there are, indeed, many aspects of Piotr Aduev that could be attributed to Goncharov's compromise with society and his public "mask." Aleksandr, on the other hand, with his idealism and reliance on the "heart," may fit quite nicely Jung's notion of the "soul" or the "private" self.[24]

Another aspect of the Piotr/Aleksandr interaction in the novel could be, perhaps, best understood by interpreting the Aduevs through Boris Sidis's distinction between the "conscious" and "self-conscious" parts of a "waking" personality. "[M]ind is synthesis of many systems, of many moments' consciousness," Sidis wrote in *Multiple Personality.* "One great principle must be at the foundation of psychology, and that is the synthesis of multiple consciousness in normal, and its disintegration in abnormal mental life."[25] What Sidis understands by "the synthesis" in "normal" mental life is best explained in *The Psychology of Suggestion* (1898), where he states: "The two selves in normal man are so coordinated that they blend into one. For all practical purposes a unity, the conscious individual is still a duality. The self-conscious personality, although apparently blended with the sub-waking self, is still not of the latter."[26]

Sidis may have been, in fact, one of the people on Freud's mind when, in the footnote from "The 'Uncanny'" cited earlier, he referred to the "popular psychologists" who "have some notion of th[e] division . . . between the critical faculty and the rest of the ego," as the schema for the *Ichspaltung.* Freud's "critical faculty" appears to be quite synonymous with Sidis's "self-consciousness," and in the statement from "The Relation of the Poet to Day-Dreaming" which I quoted in the introduction, Freud appears to go along with that view when he designates "self-observation" as the mechanism through which "modern writers . . . split up their ego . . . into many component parts." Sidis's "self-consciousness" and Freud's "critical function" or "self-observation" seem to describe perfectly a crucial aspect of the "ego splitting" in Ivan Goncharov, who, as we have seen in the previous chapter, was such an ardent practitioner of the art of self-detachment. It is, of course, Piotr Aduev who often functions in the novel as the spectator, "observing and criticizing the self and exercising a censorship within the mind,"[27] and it is Aleksandr who largely represents this "self" or "the rest of the ego."

Yet another potentially helpful insight into the nature of "co-consciousness" in general and Goncharov's duality in particular may be found in recent studies of "the stream of consciousness" as a bilateral phenomenon. In a 1968 summary of his investigation of split-brain patients, Dr. R. A. Sperry wrote that "instead of the normally unified single stream of consciousness, these patients behave in many ways as if they had two independent streams of conscious awareness, one in each hemisphere . . ."[28] According to several psychologists, there is sufficient evidence that the brain can produce not one but two streams of consciousness, each coming from a different part of the brain. There have also been studies to suggest that the two streams of consciousness are qualitatively different and that the left hemisphere of a human brain appears to be superior in "analysis [and] logic," while the "right brain" functions best, among other things, in "tasks involving imagery."[29]

"The two modes are antagonistic and complementary, suggesting that a unity and struggle of opposites is characteristic of mental functioning,"[30] writes Paul Bakan in his 1978 review of the research on bilateral streams of consciousness. This statement with its "antagonistic and complementary" modes of "unity and struggle of opposites" reads like an ideal description of many literary manifestations of the split personality. It will take a brave critic to undertake a thorough investigation of psychobiological research into the human brain, yet the implications of such research for the study of the doppelgänger in literature could be quite significant. I hope that we are much more than the mere summation of detectable mental processes; yet the possibility that the conflict between the analytical and logical Piotr and the imaginative and emotional Aleksandr may at least partially reflect the inner confrontation of the left and the right hemispheres of their creator's brain is quite intriguing.

But fascinating as all these theories are, the exact psychological nature of Goncharov's ego-splits will, by definition, always remain enigmatic. Goncharov's remarkable artistic use of this co-consciousness, however, as an "extrapersonal" literary device for writing an autobiographical novel that strives to avoid the dangers of self-centered and self-expository presentation is more palpable and, due to its direct relevance to a literary work, perhaps even more deserving of our attention.

When I describe *A Common Story* as an autobiographical novel I inevitably step on theoretical grounds that are shaky at best. "[T]he term 'autobiography,'" wrote John Pilling recently, "tends to be rather liberally applied to any kind of personal writing which has to do with the facts of the author's life. . . . There is also another shadowy area obtaining between autobiography (however defined) and the novel which is known, for one reason or another, to take its life from the facts of its author's life. . . . [Thus] I feel bound to acknowledge that I am concerned with what I take to be observable species existing within the bounds of a more or less ill-defined genre."[31] Anyone who ever pondered the theoretical issues concerning autobiography will find it impossible not to sympathize with Pilling's predicament.

To give just one concrete example of the kind of questions that arise when one tries to define the "bounds of a more or less ill-defined genre," let us consider for a moment three works by Vladimir Nabokov: *Speak, Memory,* which is his "nonfictional" autobiography, and his novels *Mary* and *The Gift,* which are generally described as "autobiographical." In all three works the traditional distinctions between fact and fiction are deliberately blurred by the writer himself. The novels are in certain ways more revealing of the author's "real" life than Nabokov's autobiography (Nabokov himself admitted that, in *Mary,* there exists "a headier extract of personal reality" than in *Speak, Memory*[32]), which, in its turn, is no less artistically structured and patterned than the best of Nabokov's fiction. But if *Speak, Memory* is no less "fictional" than *The Gift* and *Mary,* and *The Gift* and *Mary* are no less "factual" than *Speak, Memory,* is there really any difference between the two works in terms of the writer's "autobiography"? Many critics do in fact point out that it is virtually impossible—and therefore unnecessary—"to distinguish between the autobiography invaded by fiction and . . . fiction involving the autobiography of the author."[33] "Most autobiographies," writes Northrop Frye in *Anatomy of Criticism,* "are inspired by a creative, and therefore fictional impulse. . . . We may call this very important form of prose fiction the confession form."[34]

But even if we agree that clear-cut distinctions between fact and fiction in autobiography do not really exist, we still face a larger problem of definition. Were one to use even the most general description of autobiography—the one that simply defines it as "an account of a man's life by himself"[35]—he or she will soon realize that this definition actually excludes many of the present-day autobiographies that are often written not totally by their subjects themselves but with the help of hired professionals. Yet hard as it may be to define autobiographies, attempts at definitions do persist and run all the way from impossibly restrictive to meaninglessly loose. "Autobiography as we know it," states Elizabeth Bruss, "is dependent on distinctions between fiction and nonfiction, between rhetorical and empirical first-person narration."[36] Nothing of the sort, suggests William C. Spengemann, according to whom it is not even the inclusion of autobiographical material that shapes fictional autobiographies "but their efforts to discover, through a fictive action, some ground upon which conflicting aspects of the writer's own nature might be reconciled in complete being."[37] Consequently, Spengemann considers *David Copperfield* an autobiographical novel not because it often parallels Dickens's own life but because "it expresses through the deployment of conventional narrative personae and through the allegorical tenor of its language Dickens's over-riding concern with the realization of his self, the achievement of true being."[38] It is easy to see problems with both concepts. If we accept Bruss's definition of autobiography, we will have to struggle with the difficult distinction between fact and fiction. We will also have to place Nabokov's allegedly factual *Speak, Memory* not next to his fictional *Mary* and *Gift* but in a different category where it is doomed to coexist with the allegedly nonfictional lives of Hollywood stars, famous athletes, and self-made billionaires. If, on the other hand, we follow Spengemann and do not draw *any* distinction between *Speak, Memory* and *Mary* and *The Gift,* we will have to regard not only these two novels but most works of fiction as essentially autobiographical since there is virtually no writer who fails to exhibit, in one form or another, this "over-riding concern with the realization of his self."

There are, to be sure, definitions of autobiography that are less restrictive than Bruss's and more limited than Spengemann's. But even they often raise more questions than they answer. Thus in *The Turning Key: Autobiography and the Subjective Impulse since 1800,* Jerome H. Buckley gives the following definition of what he calls the "ideal" autobiography:

> The ideal autobiography presents a retrospect of some length on the writer's life and character, in which the actual events matter far less

> than the truth and depth of his experience. It describes a voyage of self-discovery, a life-journey confused by frequent misdirections and even crises of identity but reaching at last a sense of perspective and integration. It traces through the alert awakened memory a continuity from early childhood to maturity or even to old age.[39]

Buckley is clearly describing an autobiography as a bildungsroman here. In his definition, the distinction between fact and fiction does not really matter as long as there is a triumphant progression from ignorance to knowledge, from childhood to maturity. Thus if we apply Buckley's definition to Nabokov's works, *The Gift,* with its more definite bildungsroman progression, will actually be closer to an "ideal autobiography" than *Speak, Memory*, which deliberately thwarts similar expectations of an upward character development. And yet who says that only the life that develops in a Hegelian spiral, with "self-discovery" inevitably leading to "sense of perspective and integration," can serve as material for an "ideal" autobiography? What if, as in *A Common Story,* the spiral is replaced by a vicious circle and self-discovery often results not in "integration" but in its opposite? What if, as in *Ulysses,* the novel is compressed to twenty-four hours and thus mocks the very precept of a bildungsroman? Does a circular structure, a disintegrated self, or a short time span automatically negate the presence of a "true" autobiography?

It is hard not to agree with Avrom Fleishman when he complains in *Figures of Autobiography: The Language of Self-Writing in Victorian and Modern England* that too many scholars of autobiography "fall into a well-known trap of generic criticism: the codification of norms" and that "a wide audience of modern readers has reached a higher sophistication in regard to autobiography than some members of the critical fraternity."[40] Trying to fit autobiography within clearly defined bounds, modes, structures, or themes is as futile as attempting to impose strict parameters on the varieties of human experiences on which autobiographies are based. Autobiography as a concept is, in fact, so laden with problems of definition that perhaps it should be taken out of critical circulation altogether. Northrop Frye, for one, came very close to doing just that when he categorically declared that there is really "no such thing as self-expression in literature."[41] And yet, common sense tells us that there should be some middle ground somewhere between Spengemann's belief that most of literature is a form of self-expression and Frye's conviction that self-expression in literature does not exist. Fleishman finds that middle ground by redefining the issue of "what is autobiography" as the question of "how the age-old activity of writing life stories has organized itself at various periods of literary history."[42] Many may find such a solution unsatisfactory—how can one even start discussing that which one cannot define? And yet trying to set some manageable working parameters of an admittedly vague concept is, in my opinion, a healthier critical instinct than trying to define the undefinable. It is obvious to me that Goncharov, Woolf, and Joyce were indeed engaged in "the age-old activity of writing life stories" and what interests me most, as their reader, is how they chose to organize these stories and why.

By calling *A Common Story* an autobiographical novel I do not wish to imply that the presence of easily discernible autobiographical material is a sine qua non for *all* autobiographies. Far from it: I believe that Poe's or Hoffmann's fictional presentations of their inner dualities, while lacking similar "factual" material, are hardly any less "true" as autobiographies than Goncharov's novel. If by "genuineness" of an autobiography we understand the degree to which the author is willing to penetrate and reveal the deepest layers of his or her consciousness, then the profoundly confessional nature of many of the classic works of the doppelgänger may make them even "truer" autobiographies than *A Common Story.* Were one to choose between the "inner" and the "outer" life of a writer as the most crucial element in autobiography, very few would be likely to disagree with Buckley who describes an "ideal" autobiography as the one that "concentrates on the inner life, hidden from all others and accessible only in part even to the author."[43] Yet the inclusion of the circumstances of one's "outer" life *is* one way of bringing a strong autobiographical dimension to a work of fiction, and, what is even more important for our present discussion, such an inclusion leads to certain consequences that writers of "inner" autobiographies do not necessarily have to face. For whereas Hoffmann or Poe could feel relatively safe that the inner conflicts they fictionalized would not be easily recognizable as their own since on the surface the characters did not resemble their creators, Goncharov had to look elsewhere to protect his privacy and ensure against expressing "nothing but his own ego, which nobody cares a rap about."

It should be noted, however, that in his obsessive desire to mask and neutralize his "outer" autobiography, Goncharov also stands apart from many authors of other "outer" autobiographies that similarly incorporate huge amounts of autobiographical material. Such novels—whether Samuel Butler's *The Way of All Flesh* or André Gide's *La Porte étroite*—are often simplistically defined as "autobiographies in the guise of fiction" or "thinly concealed autobiographies."[44] Such definitions may be ill-conceived but they largely stem from one's sense that the authors of such transparently autobiographical novels frequently choose to sacrifice both their privacy and a large degree of their artistic detachment in order to achieve what they consider more important—the therapeutic benefits of a public confession, a desire to recapture and relive past experiences, or, simply, the easy availability of the material. While choosing to use the materials of his life for very similar therapeutic and pragmatic reasons, Goncharov, as we have seen earlier, was horrified at the very idea of an egotistic presentation and the slightest possibility of public exposure. As a result, his work strove to be not a "thinly concealed autobiography," but a thickly concealed one, masterfully disguised as an impersonal novel, and as seemingly objective as fiction ever gets. And it was precisely Goncharov's use of two coactive protagonists, not only as a means of expressing duality but also as a conscious literary device, that made this task possible.

A further comparison with other fictional autobiographies may help to illuminate this point. While we rarely associate first-person autobiographical novels with *Ichspaltung,* there is a natural, built-in dualism in those works, where an older and more mature narrator presents his younger and less experienced self as the protagonist of the book. Thus in *David Copperfield,* for example, there are from the very beginning not one but two Davids—the David who is merely "born" in chapter one, and the quite seasoned David, wondering whether "upon reflection," he will turn out to be "the hero of my life."[45] This split, maintained by the temporal distance between David's selves throughout most of the novel, closes only at the very end of the book when the protagonist becomes old enough to be the narrator, and David's two personalities thus happily merge into one. But though present through most of the book, David's two selves are never quite equal. While the voice of the narrator is heard quite clearly through numerous interjections of "I recollect," "I am grateful to remember," "when I look back," his presence is largely immaterial and static. He is not an actor in his own play: he can reflect on his younger self and comment on his actions yet he can never directly interact with the character.

David Copperfield had not yet been written when Goncharov was working on his first novel, but he was obviously familiar with this tandem of narrator and character from earlier first-person "simulated" fictional autobiographies, especially Defoe's *Robinson Crusoe* and Sterne's *Tristram Shandy,* which were immensely popular in Russia. Yet using the same formula for a novel where he contemplated using large chunks of his real life could have hardly satisfied Goncharov. His "egophobia" and fear of self-exposure, pronounced most strongly in those early years of relative obscurity, could not mix well with the thin disguise of the first-person narrative. And even if Goncharov had not been so preoccupied with a desire to hide the personal nature of his novel, it is highly doubtful that the built-in dualism of first-person pseudo-autobiographies would have been enough to satisfy him as means for expressing his own duality. The conflict between Goncharov's selves was probably too powerful and went too far beyond mere age-related differences (maturity, wisdom, experience) to be adequately embodied by the main protagonist and the largely passive persona of the narrator.[46]

What Goncharov needed instead was a modified third-person novel that could serve as an ideal vehicle for both his "shy" autobiography and his duality. It was probably largely with those ends in mind that Goncharov conceived the idea of using two rather equal, co-conscious fictional alter egos, allowing the older self of the protagonist not only to reflect on his younger counterpart, but also to interact with him directly. As an additional benefit, this strategy also enabled Goncharov to split his ego not just two, but three, ways, and thus remove himself even further from his autobiographical protagonists by publicly claiming the only part he was really comfortable with—that of the detached author and uninterested observer. This luxury of impersonality is rarely afforded to writers of first-person autobiographical novels, who are frequently confused in the public eye with their books' "implied authors."

There were still more levels on which Goncharov's literary co-consciousness worked as a skillful artistic device. Thus, as has been already noted, Goncharov's use of two autobiographical characters allowed the writer to parody the then-fashionable bildungsroman, where a young hero's development from youth to maturity constitutes the main suspense of a novel. In Goncharov's bildungsroman there is no suspense, since the final product coexists with the developing character almost from the very onset of the book. With the endpoint of the nephew's journey through life thus anticipated from the start in the personality and circumstances of the uncle, the bildungsroman's traditional open-ended progression is here replaced by its antithesis—a closed and vicious circle.

Mikhail Bakhtin distinguishes between two kinds of "education" novels as directly opposed to each other: one showing "a typically repeating path of man's emergence from youthful idealism and fantasies to mature sobriety and practicality," the other, largely "biographical (and autobiographical) type," depicting a process of emergence that "takes place in biographical time and . . . passes through unrepeatable, individual stages."[47] But Goncharov's novel defies Bakhtin's categorization by fitting both definitions at once. A writer who apparently did not believe that an individual passes "through unrepeatable . . . stages," Goncharov reduced his own experience to a predictable and well-trodden path in his autobiographical bildungsroman. By doing so he simultaneously gave his work the appearance of "a common story" and expressed his deep skepticism about the validity of accepted myths of human development. Goncharov would express this skepticism even more strongly in *Oblomov* by creating a novel that is virtually a perfect antithesis to a bildungsroman: despite everyone else's expectations, its otherwise intelligent and likable protagonist simply refuses to "develop" as the book patiently portrays the perfect and almost uninterrupted circularity of Oblomov's dormant existence.

Goncharov's use of a split autobiographical self to do both—depict his inner divisions and experiment with the artistic possibilities such a doubling creates—was not totally unusual for the period. In certain ways, Goncharov's artistic manipulation of the fictionalized split personality has its parallels in similar techniques employed in many classic works of the double. Thus while the other stories of the doppelgänger may focus primarily on the dramatization of the inner conflicts, they rarely overlook the largely playful "comedy of errors" possibilities that the physical presence of two identical likenesses can create. In Hoffmann's *Die Elixiere des Teufels,* as we have already seen, the double comes suspensefully close to being executed instead of the protagonist, and in Andersen's story, the shadow, masquerading as a man, woos and weds an unsuspecting princess. Finally, the most ironic and poignant instances of mistaken identity occur when the protagonists also mistake their twin images for independent entities and destroy themselves while attempting merely to destroy their doubles. In that respect, Andersen's tale may be also seen as a parody of the whole genre of the double: it is actually the shadow, not the primary self, who attempts to destroy its counterpart and, unlike the humans, it even succeeds in annihilating the troublesome "other" without annihilating itself.

What is remarkable in Goncharov's strategy, though, is how skillfully he employs a fictionalized split self to satisfy several crucial needs, both personal and artistic. He uses the technique (1) to highlight the "inner" autobiography, which only he can recognize; (2) to obscure the "outer" autobiography, which he does not want anyone to see; (3) to secure a stronger degree of detachment between himself and his life experiences; and (4) to mock the belief that a bildungsroman progression has anything to do with human development. In all that, Goncharov strikingly anticipated, as we will see in the following chapters, similar efforts and results of two of the most influential novelists in the century to come—Virginia Woolf and James Joyce.

I don't know if I'm like Mrs Ramsay: as my mother died when I was 13 probably it is a child's view of her: but I have some sentimental delight in thinking that you like her. She has haunted me: but then so did that old wretch my father.

Virginia Woolf

4

"Sense and Sensibility" in *To the Lighthouse*

It is highly doubtful that Virginia Woolf ever read Goncharov's first novel, even though Garnett's English translation of *A Common Story* had been available as early as 1894, three years after the Russian writer's death. When, in her article "The Russian Point of View," Woolf summarized that point of view as "the . . . call upon us to understand our fellow-sufferers, 'and not with the mind—for it is easy with the mind—but with the heart,'"[1] she was also most likely unaware how much of this traditional heart/mind conflict was at the core of Goncharov's fiction. In fact, were she even to have read *A Common Story* in Russian and thus not "stripped of its style" (*CR,* 178)—she and her husband undertook to learn Russian with the help of their Russian friend S. S. Koteliansky in 1921 but soon gave up—she might have found very little to admire in the functional, rather unsophisticated quality of the Russian writer's prose. And yet, despite their extremely different cultural and literary sensibilities, inevitably reflected in their novels, Woolf and Goncharov are firmly bound together by a fundamental similarity of techniques in the fictional transformation of their autobiographical materials.

Unlike the case of *A Common Story,* the largely autobiographical nature of Woolf's *To the Lighthouse,* published in 1927, is well established. "*To the Lighthouse* is going to be fairly short," wrote Woolf in her diary in 1925, "to have father's character done complete in it; and mother's; and St Ives; and childhood . . ." (*D,* III, 18). Some of her motivations for writing an autobiographical novel are also better known than Goncharov's. "Autobiography," writes J. H. Buckley in his 1984 study, "frequently represents the writer's effort to come to terms belatedly with his father or mother, to understand, as only the adult can, the vitality of his parents' being and the meaning of the relationship out of which he was born."[2] That is exactly what Virginia Woolf was trying to do. "I used to think of him [Leslie Stephen, Woolf's father] and mother daily," she wrote in 1928, "but writing *The Lighthouse* laid them in my mind. . . . I was obsessed by them both, unhealthily; and writing of them was a necessary act." Ten years later, in "A Sketch of the Past," Woolf reaffirmed the long-lasting therapeutic effect of her novel: "I wrote the book very quickly; and when it was written, I ceased to be obsessed by my mother. I no longer hear her voice; I do not see her" (*MB,* 81).

Woolf's initial plan was in fact so focused on the personalities of her deceased parents that almost no other single character was to be given any prominence. The eight children of the Ramsays (corresponding to the eight children of the Stephens) were to be mostly "undifferentiated."[3] Only the youngest child of the family, Mrs. Ramsay's favorite (as in real life the Stephens' youngest, Adrian, was, Woolf thought, the recipient of most of Julia Stephen's tenderness), was to be distinguished from his siblings through his intimacy with Mrs. Ramsay and his childish and Oedipal hatred for his father as the rival for her affections. The numerous guests in the Ramsays' summer house (with its strong resemblance to the Stephens' Talland House in St. Ives) were also supposed to be largely "undifferentiated" and merely symbolic of Mrs. Ramsay's human and womanly appeal. Among them, in an early draft of *To the Lighthouse,* there appears a certain "Miss Sophie Briscoe," an old maid of fifty-five, "a rosy lady who spent much of her life sketching" and fearing Mr. Ramsay's possible attempts to communicate with her "so low as she was in the scale of intelligence."[4] Yet already at the initial stages of writing the novel, which was indeed progressing very fast—"22 pages straight off in less than a fortnight," she records in her diary in September of 1925 (*D,* III, 39)—Woolf began to hesitate about her plan. At one point she worried that she had thought out her novel "perhaps too clearly" (*D,* III, 29), and within a month noted: "The thing is I vacillate between a single and intense character of father and a far wider slower book." "I think I might do something in *To the Lighthouse* to split up emotions more completely," she writes on July 30, 1925. "I think I'm working in that direction" (*D,* III, 38).

What she meant by splitting up emotions "more completely" may become clearer if we ponder the subsequent changes in the novel. One of them was the transformation of Miss Briscoe—now Lily, not Sophie—from a silly old lady to a character much closer to Virginia Woolf herself: an intelligent and serious professional, some twenty years younger than her predecessor, and "puckered"[5] rather than "rosy." In that new form the painter emerged from the original mass of rather episodic characters to become the strongest voice in the novel: according to Mitchell A. Leaska's stylistic and statistical study of *To the Lighthouse,* it is not Mrs. Ramsay but Lily who, in fact, dominates the book's multivoiced narration.[6]

How close Virginia Woolf felt to her fictional character can be seen (along with other much more fundamental things to be discussed later) in a revealing blunder she made in Lily's age. When the book was begun in 1925 and the two final sections just projected, Virginia Woolf made her character thirty-three years old (81), figuring that at the end of the book, ten Septembers later, Lily would be forty-three, and thus the actual age of her creator. But in the final section of the novel, which takes place, as Woolf originally intended, exactly ten years after the first, a careful reader will notice that Lily instead of turning forty-three has turned forty-four (224). The final section was, of course, written in 1926, when Woolf herself was already forty-four years old, and adding a year to Lily's age was but a natural slip for the writer whose identification with the character was so strong.

The eight "undifferentiated" children of the Ramsays had also undergone rather extensive personalization, in which most of them obtained individual features or voices of their own. In one of them, Cam, Mrs. Ramsay's wild and unpredictable daughter, we can find numerous traces of young Virginia Stephen; together with Lily Briscoe she becomes the most prominent presence in the final section of the book. Her poignant reflections on the past, the present, and on her parents became as important as Lily's in giving final shape to the central theme of the novel.

Simply put, what was first intended as merely a portrait of the writer's parents had become, in the process of writing, also a self-portrait. Not unlike the Aduevs in *A Common Story,* Cam Ramsay and Lily Briscoe can be seen as complementary autobiographical characters who reflect Woolf's attempt to come to terms with her past and her contradictory feelings about herself and her family. Yet Woolf's novel is, of course, anything but simple. The relationship of the fictionalized selves in *To the Lighthouse* is more subtle and intricate than that in *A Common Story*, and one needs to proceed with greater care in order to give Woolf's presentation full justice.

The centrality of Mrs. Ramsay/Julia Stephen rather than her husband is yet another change from the original plan that is worth pondering. After all it was her father's character that was supposed to be "done complete" in the novel, not her mother's. Yet as the book was being written, Mr. Ramsay's point of view became largely subsidiary to his wife's. Jean Guiguet attributes this change in plans to "certain deep affinities which became fixed and idealized at the same time through [Julia Stephen's] premature death"[7] in 1895. Although he prefers, partially due to the unavailability of most of Woolf's autobiographical materials in 1962, not to speculate on the nature of those "deep affinities," his statement is crucial for our understanding of Woolf's bond with her mother. When Phyllis Rose quotes Vanessa Bell's story about how Virginia at the age of six "on the whole, preferred father" and concludes that "the intellectual, analytic spirit in itself [was] strong proof of her identification with her father,"[8] an eminent Victorian man of letters, Rose may be substituting the rational for the real.

For reason would certainly dictate that Virginia Stephen, herself an aspiring writer, would have more affinities with her father than with her less intellectual mother. And yet that does not appear to have been the case. Leslie Stephen not only prided himself on his analytical powers but also considered them as virtually incompatible with the "artistic" ones—"I have always been shy with artistic people, who inhabit a world very unfamiliar to me," he confessed in *The Mausoleum Book*.[9] That may explain why his writings, while full of solid common sense and encyclopedic knowledge, are so wanting in artistry and refinement. He was also not a very good psychologist or judge of character, as becomes apparent when one reads the oversimplified, one-dimensional portraits of people he knew—whether his friends at Cambridge (*Some Early Impressions*), his brother (*Life of Sir James Fitzjames Stephen*), or his wife (*The Mausoleum Book*). Woolf could never quite relate to those qualities of her father's personality, to this "disparity, so obvious in his books, between the critical and the imaginative power," to his characters, who are "so crude, so elementary, so conventional, that a child with a box of chalks could make a more subtle portrait" (*MB*, 146).

It is, interestingly enough, her mother whom she often associates with writing. "Here I am experimenting with the parent of all pens—the black J.," she writes in her diary in 1918, "*the* pen, as I used to think it, along with other objects, as a child, because mother used it; and therefore all other pens were varieties and eccentricities" (*D*, I, 208; her emphasis). Needless to say, a pen is not just a pen for Woolf, but the most immediate professional tool, and the status of *the* pen being given to one of her mother's, rather than her father's, is quite revealing. "I see her writing at her table in London," wrote Woolf in "A Sketch of the Past," describing one of her haunting visions of her mother, "and the silver candlesticks, and high carved chair with the claws and the pink seat; and the three-cornered brass ink pot" (*MB*, 84). What she was writing were not just the staples of every Victorian lady's routine communications: polite thank you notes, letters of condolences, and invitations. She also wrote stories for children and well-thought-through essays on nursing, domestic arrangements, and agnostic women.

"The children had all gone to the seaside for the summer," starts one of Julia's stories. "They used to paddle and bathe and find shells. Sometimes they were able to dig such deep holes in the sand with their spades that they could stand up to their knees in the hole, and little Ginia, the youngest, was almost buried in the sand."[10] When "little Ginia" grew up she wrote her own story about the seaside, and the summer, and the children looking for shells, and while Virginia Woolf's talent as a writer dwarfs her mother's, now and then the simple yet artistically smooth style of Julia Stephen's stories sounds almost familiar: "The next day her mama said she would go into the little fishing town near which they lived, to get a new pair of shoes. Ginia wanted to go too, but her mama said as she had been so mischievous she must stay at home, and Annie and Harry went."[11] Virginia may have thought her mother's stories too moralistic and the essays rather conventional in their glorification of a woman's role as the "angel in the house." At the same time, however, Julia Stephen's verbal skills and her special "feel" for people—a term that recurs in *A Room of One's Own*—gained Woolf's unconditional respect.

"It has often occurred to me," she wrote in *Moments of Being*, "to regret that no one ever wrote down her sayings and vivid ways of speech since she had the gift of turning words in a manner peculiar to her . . . I can see her, standing by the open door of a railway carriage which was taking Stella and some others to Cambridge, and striking out in phrase or two pictures of all the people who came past her along the platform, and so she kept them laughing till the train went" (*MB*, 36).

Her mother also had a gift of imagination. Her stories are inhabited by talking animals, and even her essays, which mostly deal with the impossibly mundane matters of taking care of the sick and handling the servants, sometimes take one aback by a burst of unexpected playfulness. "Among the number of small evils which haunt illness," she writes in "Notes from Sick Rooms," her only published work, "the greatest, in the misery which it can cause, though the smallest in size, is crumbs. The origin of most things has been decided on, but the origin of crumbs in bed has never excited sufficient attention among the scientific world . . . I will forbear to give my own explanation, which would be neither scientific nor orthodox, and will merely beg that their evil existence may be recognized and, as far as human nature allows, guarded against."[12]

This may explain why young Virginia sought the approval of her mother, not her father, when she penned her first fiction for the family's publication of the "Hyde Park Gate News." "How excited I used to be," she remembered later, "when the 'Hyde Park Gate News' was laid on her plate on Monday morning, and she liked something I had written! Never shall I forget my extremity of pleasure . . . when I found that she had sent a story of mine to Madge Symonds; it was so imaginative, she said; it was about souls flying round and choosing bodies to be born into" (*MB*, 95). Even back then the aspiring young writer must have already felt that when it came to fancy her mother was a much more appreciative judge than her mostly analytical father.

Julia's imaginative flair is dutifully recorded in *To the Lighthouse*. Mrs. Ramsay is often accused by her husband of exaggerating and "teaching your daughters to exaggerate" (102). Exaggeration is, obviously, against the principles of the man who so strongly believes in the omnipotence of factual truths, but it is an essential component of the creative impulse. The Ramsays' sensibilities are contrasted throughout the book. Mrs.

Ramsay, while never at ease in intellectual discussions of literature, has a natural instinct for beauty and poetry. Her husband's reaction to literature is much more critical and intellectual; he is mostly immune to the often unanalyzable beauties of flowers, poetry, or music: it is this quality of being "congenitally unaware of music, of art" (*MB,* 146) that Sir Leslie's daughter blamed for most of her father's shortcomings as a writer. Lily Briscoe, who associates Ramsay's metaphysics with a "kitchen table" because those were the terms in which Andrew tried to explain his father's theories to her (38)[13] is similarly struck by how different Mr. Ramsay's preoccupation is from hers: "The kitchen table was something visionary, austere; something bare, hard, not ornamental. There was no colour to it; it was all edges and angles; it was uncompromisingly plain" (232).

In a characteristic scene from the novel, the Ramsays come out from their experience of reading literature with very different emotions: "Her mind was still going up and down, up and down with the poetry; he was still feeling very vigorous, very forthright, after reading about Steenie's funeral" (183). Reading poetry gives Mrs. Ramsay a profound shock that unbalances her whole being; reading Scott's *The Antiquary,* with the scene of the death of a fisherman in it, invigorates her husband's physical and intellectual powers and fills him with a sense of purpose. Mrs. Ramsay may feel more fit to arrange marriages for her friends than to appreciate the value of poetry—yet, ironically, at the end of the book she is proven to have been a much better judge of the power of poetry than of her friends' compatibility: the Rayleys' marriage falls apart, but poetry triumphs: "The war, people said, had revived their interest in poetry" (202).

In Virginia Woolf one can see a wonderful synthesis of her parents' qualities. No reader of Woolf's numerous literary essays will ever accuse her of lacking analytical and critical powers. And it is true, as Avrom Fleishman points out, that "Woolf herself felt the same way" about Scott's work and the scene of the fisherman's death.[14] Yet it was her feeling for poetry—whether in verse or in prose—and her power of imagination (and, as many of her friends testified, her consequently strong tendency to exaggerate) that she most valued in her literary abilities. Essays were merely passing journalism that, she felt, would not give her any lasting fame; her books were her only hope to subdue the troubling question that haunted her father and haunts Mr. Ramsay in the novel: "How long would they endure?" (191). She may have exaggerated the creative impulse in her mother by seeing so little of it in Leslie Stephen and assuming that she must have inherited it all from Julia—but the fact remains it was her mother, not her father, whom she was inclined to see as the precursor of her literary sensibility.

When in her original plans she intended to concentrate primarily on the character of her father, she must have been moved by the fact that her experience with him was more recent (Sir Leslie died in 1904, almost ten years after his wife) and her memories of him fresher and more mature than those of Julia Stephen. Yet her deeper bond with her mother must have become more and more obvious to her as she was writing the novel, and it is Mrs. Ramsay who was to emerge as "the lighthouse" of the book, the central character around whom everything revolves, the visible yet distant presence who casts her light on every character in the novel.

While it was more important for the daughter to analyze her feelings for her mother and what she represented, it was also more difficult, for she perceived her mother's nature as more enigmatic than her father's. Lily Briscoe in the novel feels she needs "fifty pairs of eyes" (294) to grasp the true Mrs. Ramsay and that is, most likely, how Woolf herself felt about the portrayal of Mrs. Stephen. She did not have a hundred eyes, yet she had more than two: the eyes of the child through which most of the image of her mother had been formed, and the eyes of a mature woman, within five years of the age of her mother at the time of her death, capable of reshaping and reevaluating the pictures from her childhood. And this is where Lily Briscoe comes in.

The strength of Lily Briscoe's feelings for Mrs. Ramsay may appear at times almost excessive. We could, as Jean Guiguet suggests, try to interpret Lily's feelings for another woman as a projection of the author's lesbianism and cite the fact that the time of writing the novel coincided with the most intense period in Woolf's relationship with Vita Sackville-West.[15] But this explanation, though quite legitimate, cannot be complete unless we specify that it was the motherly qualities in Mrs. Ramsay that made her so attractive to the motherless thirty-three-year-old painter longing for a surrogate mother. It is, in fact, this need for maternal protection in both Lily, Mrs. Ramsay's "little Brisk" (78), and in her creator that makes their real-life and fictionalized experiences most comparable. "[Vita] lavishes on me the maternal protection which, for some reason, is what I have always most wished from everyone," Woolf wrote in her diary in December of 1925 (*D,* III, 52), reflecting on the fact that her desire for motherly love made itself manifest in most of her important relationships with other women: her older sister Vanessa, Violet Dickinson, and, later in life, Ethel Smyth. The paradoxical fact that Vita Sackville-West, unlike the other three, was not an "older" woman but ten years younger than her friend goes a long way to show how truly pervasive Woolf's need for "maternal protection" was.[16]

Lily's mixed feelings about Mr. Ramsay and her frequent hostility to this "petty, vain, egotistical . . . tyrant" (40), while they may, indeed, have certain overtones of sexual jealousy, can also best be understood as the strong reaction of a daughter. Lily's sentiments are, in fact, strikingly similar to little James's Oedipal hatred for the same man, his father, who he thinks deserves to be killed with an ax or a poker for "casting ridicule upon his wife, who was ten thousand times better in every way than he was" (10). How much those reactions were Virginia Woolf's own becomes abundantly clear when one reads her diaries and autobiographical writings. She had, she admitted in "Old Bloomsbury" (1922), "passionate affection for my father alternating with passionate hatred of him" (*MB,* 183). Her husband, Leonard Woolf, once noted that Virginia's tendency to exaggerate the shortcomings of Leslie Stephen was an outgrowth of "a complicated variety of the Oedipus complex," very much present in most of Sir Leslie's children.[17]

Thus, in a peculiar twist, made possible by what she herself called the "elastic" quality of a novel[18] where past and present can coexist on the same plane, Lily Briscoe appears to have inherited both her creator's longing for a surrogate mother and Woolf's real mother, the way Woolf remembered her from childhood and felt about her in her adult years. But Woolf makes Lily a painter, not a writer like herself, and her choice may seem somewhat puzzling. After all, she only had second-hand experience of painting; a large contingent of Bloomsbury, including her sister, were painters, and after the novel was completed she dreaded their professional judgment of the painting scenes. "God! how you'll laugh at the painting bits in *The Lighthouse!*" she wrote to Vanessa in May of 1927 (*D,* III, 372). At the same time, Woolf often mocked her sister and Vanessa's lover, Duncan Grant, for having "smooth broad spaces in their minds" (*D,* I, 69), and, as Quentin Bell tells us, "affected, not quite seriously, to consider the painters as little better than cretins and quite desperately ignorant."[19]

Her decision to make Lily a painter may have had something to do with protecting her privacy: like many other writers before and after her (to name just a few, Henry James in *The Real Thing*, D. H. Lawrence in *Sons and Lovers,* and Joyce Cary in *The Horse's Mouth*), she imagined she would be less recognizable in an autobiographical character who, while an artist, is yet not a writer. But that must have been a minor consideration. The truth is that her mockery was indeed mostly affected, and, as Diane F. Gillespie points out in *The Sisters' Arts,* artistically Virginia felt close enough to her sister to want to "raid . . . Vanessa's [medium], in search of appropriate ways to embody her perceptions."[20] Woolf often enjoyed thinking of the closeness that could exist between writing and painting. "[P]ainting and writing have much to tell each other," she wrote in her essay on Walter Sickert. "The novelist after all wants to make us see" (*CDB,* 198). Allusions to painting are quite frequent in her autobiographical writings: "If I were a painter, I should paint [my] first impressions in pale, yellow, silver, and green . . . I should make a picture that was globular; semi-transparent" (*MB, 66*); "If I were painting myself I should have to find some—rod, shall I say—something that would stand for conception" (*MB,* 72–73). When she was working on *Mrs. Dalloway* in 1924, she vividly described the process of retyping the novel in terms of finishing a painting: "I am now galloping over *Mrs. Dalloway*, retyping it entirely from the start . . . a good method, I believe, as thus one works with a wet brush over the whole and joins parts separately composed and gone dry" (*D,* II, 323).

She obviously had reasons to feel that she was more akin to such innovative artists as Vanessa, Duncan Grant, and Roger Fry than to her literary father, or, for that matter, to most writers of her own generation. Most important in her decision to make Lily a painter appears to have been a belief that a visual artist could get closer to the essence of her mother's enigmatic nature than a writer could: "[I]f one could give a sense of my mother's personality one would have to be an artist. It would be as difficult to do that, as it should be done, as to paint a Cezanne" (*MB*, 85). Lily Briscoe thus became Woolf's choice for the artist to "paint a Cezanne," and that she is shown to have succeeded at the end is an incredible achievement both for her and for her creator. Yet while Lily's main preoccupation is with painting, writing is never far behind—like Woolf, Woolf's character always keeps the two teamed together in her mind: "women can't paint, women can't write" (75); "she couldn't paint . . . she couldn't create" (237); "Phrases came. Visions came. Beautiful pictures. Beautiful phrases" (287). At one point Lily even appears to forget for a moment that she is not a writer but a painter: "('Alone' she heard [Mr. Ramsay] say, 'Perished' she heard him say) and like everything else this strange morning the words became symbols, wrote themselves all over the grey-green walls. If only she could put them together, she felt, write them out in some sentence, then she would have got at the truth of things" (219). Woolf did not really have to dread the reaction of Bloomsbury painters: the artistic impulse she recorded in Lily Briscoe is universal and transcends the boundaries of any specific medium. As Roger Fry kindly informed her in a letter after reading the novel, Woolf came through her portrayal of a painter "unscathed and triumphant though a little breathless and anxious perhaps."[21]

The deep and not easily explicable bond that Virginia Woolf felt with her mother also unites Lily Briscoe and the subject of her painting. Throughout the novel there are subtle but persistent hints about the affinity between the two women, who on the surface appear so different. Phyllis Rose is right when she notes that Woolf "conceptualiz[ed] Mrs. Ramsay as an artist"[22] but there is more to her artistry than being a perfect Victorian "angel in the house" (*DM*, 237). As Alex Zwerdling astutely points out, describing Mrs. Ramsay's housewifely qualities as "art" is "a very modern bit of legerdemain" anyway: "The traditional praise for Mrs. Ramsay's domestic gifts, whether it stressed spirituality like Coventry Patmore or practical efficiency like Mrs. Beeton, did not generally use the language of art. In the scornful words of the classical archaeologist Jane Harrison, 'Some people speak of a cook as an "artist," and a pudding as a "perfect poem," but a healthy instinct rebels.'"[23]

No, Mrs. Ramsay is an artist for a reason other than her French culinary skills, although they are good enough to satisfy even the pedantic tastes of a William Bankes. Her husband, who is deeply moved by the sight of a hen on a Westmoreland road spreading her wings to protect her chicks (34–35), may like to perceive her largely as a glorified "mother hen," but even he cannot help noticing and being disturbed by a side of her that to him is out of reach. It is her moody artistic sensibility—whether in admiring the beauty of the flowers, getting lost in thought, allowing the poetry to penetrate the deepest layers of her consciousness, or letting her eyes feast on every line and curve in Rose's picture-perfect fruit arrangement and wishing that it should not be disturbed—that brings her close to Lily Briscoe. She even attempts to conceal her private moments from the eyes of others for the same reason that Lily hides her paintings (and that their creator agonized over the reaction of strangers to her books)—they make her feel exposed and vulnerable: "Had she known that he [Mr. Ramsay] was looking at her, she thought, she would not have let herself sit there, thinking. She disliked anything that reminded her that she had been seen sitting thinking" (104). The artistic affinity between the two women reaches its climax when, several years after Mrs. Ramsay's death, Lily feels the need to conjure up her image in order to complete her picture:

> . . . Mrs Ramsay saying, 'Life stand still here'; Mrs Ramsay making of the moment something permanent (as in another sphere Lily herself tried to make of the moment something permanent)—this was of the nature of a revelation. In the midst of chaos there was shape; this eternal passing and flowing (she looked at the clouds going and the leaves shaking) was struck into stability. Life stand still here, Mrs Ramsay said. 'Mrs Ramsay! Mrs Ramsay!' she repeated. She owed it all to her. (241)

There is, of course, deep irony in the fact that despite such fundamental similarities in their temperaments, Mrs. Ramsay "could not take [Lily's] painting very seriously" (29). Her discouragement of Lily's professional ambitions, if they are to replace marriage and family in her life, hurts Lily so much more than Charles Tansley's "women can't paint, women can't write" precisely because she feels that Mrs. Ramsay, of all people, should be able to understand the impulse that is driving Lily to art. It was her own inevitable conflict with her mother, had her mother lived long enough to see the adult Virginia, that Woolf appears to have put into the center of Lily and Mrs. Ramsay's relationship. There were some differences between the real-life pair and their fictional representatives, but they were not essential. While it is true that, unlike Mrs. Ramsay, Julia Stephen had a more profound interest in nursing, it is also true that she refused to practice it as a paid "professional" and considered it a part of her womanly duties, together with the two most important ones: being a good wife and a mother. Unlike Lily Briscoe, Virginia Woolf did not remain single, but, like Lily, she did not possess the main ingredient that constituted Mrs. Ramsay and Julia Stephen's notion of family—children.

Mrs. Ramsay's attitude in the novel makes Lily even more miserable because she often fears that the older woman may be right. The painter is quite divided on the subject of children and often has "much ado to control her impulse to fling herself . . . at Mrs Ramsay's knee and say to her . . . 'I'm in love with this all,' waving her hand at the hedge, at the house, at children" (32). Woolf herself was not just divided, she was often mercilessly torn. It was the decision of her doctors and Leonard Woolf early in 1913 after three earlier (and, as it turned out, one impending) bouts with insanity that Virginia should not have children. She told a friend later that she was "always angry with myself for not having forced Leonard to take the risk in spite of doctors" (*L,* III, 329).[24] As a result, she frequently envied her sister for "the feeling that she gives of a whole nature in use" (*D,* I, 69), "her overflowing household" (*D,* I, 298), and "that astonishing brightness in the heart of darkness" (*D,* II, 73) that was created by Vanessa's three children. In one characteristic entry in her diary in the years preceding *To the Lighthouse* she wrote: "We came back from Rodmell yesterday, and I am in one of my moods. . . . And what is it and why? A desire for children, I suppose, for Nessa's life; for the sense of flowers breaking all around me involuntarily. . . . Years and years ago . . . I said to myself . . . never pretend that the things you haven't got are not worth having . . . Never pretend that children, for instance, can be replaced by other things" (*D,* II, 221).

Being childless gave Woolf a sense of incompleteness (she did not have her "whole nature in use"), and driven by this feeling of inadequacy, she tended to divide all women into two categories: "real" women—those who had; and women like herself—those who had not. In conversations with Vanessa she often maintained that "being childless I was less normal than she" (*D,* II, 159); while describing Vita Sackville-West in her diary in 1925, she stated: "There is her maturity and full breastedness . . . her motherhood . . . her being in short (what I have never been) a real woman" (*D,* III, 52). "I love the distracted busy ways of these mothers," she wrote about her friend Molly MacCarthy after the birth of Molly's child in 1924, "no parsimony of life, as there is with the childless—always something that must be decided, or done" (*D,* II, 286). Upon meeting Mrs. Thomas Hardy in July of 1926, Woolf seems to have instinctively projected her own feelings onto the other woman—Mrs. Hardy, Woolf thought, had the "large sad lack lustre eyes of a childless woman" (*D,* III, 96).

In September of 1926, while still working on *To the Lighthouse,* she attempted to describe her state of mind when seized by this powerful anxiety over her childlessness: "Let me watch the wave rise. I watch. Vanessa. Children. Failure. Yes; I detect that. Failure failure . . . I wish I were dead! I've only a few years to live I hope. I can't face this horror any more . . ." (*D,* III, 110). In *To the Lighthouse* Lily goes through a similar state of mind when, having thought she had solved her problems by getting a better grasp of her art, she immediately experiences a strong sense of anxiety: "Some wave of white went over the window pane. . . . Her heart leapt at her and seized her and tortured her. 'Mrs Ramsay! Mrs Ramsay!' she cried, feeling the old horror come back—to want and want and not to have" (300). "Horror" was a frequent word that Woolf associated with having no children. "I was going to have written to Jacques [Raverat] about his children, and about my having none—I mean, these efforts of mine to communicate with people are partly childlessness, and the horror that sometimes overcomes me," she wrote to Gwen Raverat in 1925 (*L,* III, 172).

The "horror" of being childless was further heightened by the fact that Woolf felt she always had to prove her worth by other means. Her demands on herself were merciless and unrealistic. In her bouts with anxiety, as in the description quoted above, her thoughts of childlessness and her sense of failure are always interlocked; yet it is not the failure of having produced no children she is talking about—it is the failure to be as good a writer as she felt she should have been to compensate for her childlessness. Whereas her father could justify his professional deficiencies, as does Mr. Ramsay in the novel, by saying "But the father of eight children has no choice" (69)—and Mrs. Ramsay uses the same justification for not thinking seriously about setting up "a model dairy and a hospital up here" (89)—Woolf thought she had no excuses. "Indeed, I am amazed, a little alarmed (for as you have the children, the fame by rights belongs to me) by your combination of pure artistic vision and brilliance of imagination," she wrote to Vanessa in 1926 (*L,* III, 271). She *was* alarmed. It would have been more comforting for her to always know that by having herself "exiled from this profound natural happiness" (*D,* III, 73), as she once put it, she had at least made it more possible that she would eventually achieve true professional success, the sense of going all the way from A to Z, without getting stuck, as Mr. Ramsay does, two-thirds of the way through. Seeing Vanessa display her artistic "brilliance" despite her three children made Woolf wonder whether that was really the case.

She was also jealous of the bond that she perceived Vanessa, as a mother, must have felt with Julia Stephen. "Vanessa both in nature and in person [is] something like a reflection of her mother," she wrote in 1908, and her strange use of "her" where one might expect "our" strongly hints that Vanessa's bond with their late parent had been somehow achieved by deliberately excluding Virginia (*MB,* 46). Woolf's sibling rivalry with Vanessa in regards to their mother shows itself also in a letter she wrote to her sister after the publication of *To the Lighthouse:* "Probably there is a great deal of you in Mrs Ramsay; though, in fact, I think you and mother are very different in my mind" (*L,* III, 383). She most likely kept them "very different" in her mind because she liked to think that in most other ways she was the one closer in nature to Julia Stephen. Similarly, in the novel, while Lily Briscoe envies the special bond between Mrs. Ramsay and Minta Doyle, who, though not yet a mother, is well on her way to becoming one through her marriage to Paul Rayley (and Lily, Mrs. Ramsay thought, "faded, under Minta's glow; became more inconspicuous than ever" [156]), Woolf makes sure that there is never a question as to whom Mrs. Ramsay really prefers: "Yet, thought Mrs Ramsay, comparing her with Minta . . . of the two, Lily at forty will be better. There was in Lily a thread of something; a flair of something; something of her own which Mrs Ramsay liked very much indeed . . ." (156–57).[25]

It was important for Woolf to think that, had her mother been alive, she would have liked Virginia "very much indeed" despite her daughter's unconventional choices in life. A lot has been written about the deep antagonism between the values of Mrs. Ramsay and Lily Briscoe concerning family, professional interests, and women's roles. To highlight this point, many critics like to quote Woolf's speech to professional women in 1931, when she described to a "younger and happier generation" how she killed the Victorian "angel in the house": "I turned upon her and caught her by the throat. I did my best to kill her. . . . Had I not killed her, she would have killed me. She would have plucked the heart out of my writing" (*DM*, 237–38). But what is good for oratory is not necessarily good for writing. Woolf's novel is, fortunately, much subtler than her speech. Despite their differences, Lily does not kill the angel in the house in order to become a real artist; on the contrary, she revives her. It is the homage to Mrs. Ramsay that allows the forty-four-year-old painter to attain her vision. It is the realization of life's complexity, rather than its stark contrasts—a revelation that she thought she owed entirely to Mrs. Ramsay—that becomes Lily's highest personal as well as artistic achievement. Consequently, it becomes Woolf's greatest personal triumph, too, for through Lily and her understandably mixed but essentially loving feelings for Mrs. Ramsay, Woolf manages to avoid doing in her novel what she had promised herself never to do "years and years ago"—to pretend that the things she did not have were not worth having.

Hers was not a dogmatic mind. She had strong opinions but she also had strong doubts. She was all for a new order in life, where both sexes could pursue their professional careers and enjoy full equality, and yet sometimes she wished "that old laws of life held good: a husband, a house, servants, establishments" (*D*, I, 308). She was all for a "new" woman, who could disregard the moral and ideological inheritance of the past, yet she also confessed that "[l]ike my father, I am attracted by the simple and affectionate and womanly" (*D*, II, 162). In most of Virginia Woolf's writings one can always feel, to use Zwerdling's words, this "powerful longing for the whole system of family life that Woolf's generation had worked so hard to discredit."[26]

One can also easily perceive that, as Lyndall Gordon puts it, "[h]owever much Virginia criticized the Victorians for their attitudes, she was nostalgic for their manners."[27] While she shared with her socialist husband the belief in democracy, she could also remark: "I'm critical, intellectually, of the aristocrats but sensually they charm" (*D,* I, 309). In "A Sketch from the Past" there is an interesting description of Woolf's experience of going to society balls with her half-brother George Duckworth, which goes to the heart of her mixed feelings about the old order:

> Perhaps I was too young. Perhaps I was wrongly adjusted. At any rate I never met a man or a woman with whom I struck up any real relationship. All the same there was the excitement of clothes, of lights, of society, in short; and the queerness, the strangeness of being alone, on my own, for a moment, with some complete stranger: he in white waistcoat and gloves, I in white satin and gloves. (*1MB,* 134)

The well-dressed crowd may have bored her intellectually, yet her senses refused to follow her mind.

Even her notions of love were, much as she was embarrassed to admit it, permeated by the Victorian myth. At first she did not take her brother Thoby's Cambridge friends seriously as suitors (although she eventually married one of them) because she felt that marriage, while "a very low down affair," had to be reserved for "young men who had been in the Eton Eleven and dressed for dinner" (*MB,* 191). The romantic and utterly traditional engagement of her half-sister Stella Duckworth to Jack Hills in 1896 (no doubt idealized even more because of Stella's death the following year) left such a deep imprint on Woolf, that, as she wrote later, it had given her "a standard of love; a sense that nothing in the whole world is so lyrical, so musical, as a young man and a young woman in their first love for each other. I connect it with respectable engagements; unofficial love never gives me the same feeling" (*MB,* 105). This is, indeed, a surprising confession coming from someone who was in the center of Bloomsbury where love, as practiced by most, was anything but "official": in her circle of friends there may have been more triangles than couples and more homosexuals than heterosexuals; Woolf herself had lesbian relationships, and her sister Vanessa and Clive Bell, while never officially divorced, lived mostly apart and freely pursued other love interests.

Woolf's being of two minds on most of the issues concerning the old and the new orders found its reflection in the character of Lily Briscoe and thus brought her even closer to Mrs. Ramsay, the representative of this older generation of women, which the young painter wants to be able to reject outright but cannot. "Intellectually," she knows all that is wrong with Mrs. Ramsay and what she stands for; "sensually," she cannot help admiring her way of life and even envying it. Her response to Paul and Minta's engagement, helped along and sanctioned by Mrs. Ramsay, is a good example of Lily's complex reaction. Like Mrs. Ramsay, Lily sees Paul and Minta for what they are—two rather ordinary and conventional individuals; unlike Mrs. Ramsay, Lily knows better than to think that marriage will magically turn them into happy and fulfilled beings. Yet, very much despite herself, Lily is as affected by the young couple's engagement as the older woman: "It came over her too now—the emotion, the vibration, of love. How inconspicuous she felt herself by Paul's side!" (153). She even reacts to the proposed expedition to the beach to look for Minta's lost brooch with the same emotion as does Mrs. Ramsay ("'How I wish I could come with you!' [Mrs. Ramsay] cried" [175]): "[Lily] . . . said with an emotion that she seldom let appear—'Let me come with you'" (153–54). Ten years later Lily still remembers the feeling that "intoxicated her" that night, and thinking back on their engagement and already knowing for a fact what a fiasco this marriage proved to be, she nevertheless feels the same powerful, "headlong desire to throw herself off the cliff and be drowned looking for a pearl brooch on a beach" (261).[28]

It was because of her ambiguity about her cultural inheritance and the Victorian institutions of tradition, morality, and domesticity, as applied to women, that Woolf felt the necessity to "split up emotions more completely," and develop fully fleshed fictional characters not merely for Leslie Stephen, as she originally had planned, but also for Julia Stephen and her own "present" self. In the fictionalized interaction of Lily Briscoe and Mrs. Ramsay, Woolf hoped to rediscover for herself the dear but conflicting image of her late mother, to re-establish their relationship on a new, more mature, footing, and to analyze and work through her own divided feelings.

But although the character of her father had lost most of its preeminence in the novel to the fictional portrayal of those two women, it nevertheless remained vitally important. And so did the other component of her original plan: the portrayal of her childhood. Several years before her suicide, while working on autobiographical sketches that she had always wanted to write down, Woolf mused that "[i]t would be interesting to make the two people, I now, I then, come out in contrast" (*MB*, 75). The juxtaposition of her present and past selves always fascinated her, and more than ten years prior to her autobiography, Woolf made a similar attempt at contrasting "I now, I then" in *To the Lighthouse* through the characters of Lily Briscoe and Cam Ramsay.

5

Woolf's Fictionalizing of Her Younger Self

We catch hardly a glimpse of Cam Ramsay in the first and longest section of the book, and the information we get about her is minimal. We know that she, like Virginia Stephen, was the second-youngest child in the family, and that a "tenpenny tea set made Cam happy for days" (90). We also learn that she is "wild and fierce" (36), "a wild villain," as Mr. Bankes, whose special favorite she is, lovingly calls her (83). Thus she is not unlike her creator who, according to Quentin Bell, "was felt to be incalculable, eccentric, and prone to accidents" as a child.[1] Like young Woolf, Cam is also a visionary, constantly driven by enigmatic forces not quite clear even to her mother: "She was off like a bird, bullet, or arrow, impelled by what desire, shot by whom, at what directed, who could say? What, what? Mrs Ramsay pondered, watching her. It might be a vision—of a shell, of a wheelbarrow, of a fairy kingdom on the far side of the hedge; or it might be the glory of speed; no one knew" (84). Virginia Woolf described the same qualities of speed and vision in her younger self as "eagerness to grasp the whole universe" (*D,* II, 23). But Cam's visions also keep her awake at night, and Mrs. Ramsay has to comfort her daughter by laying her head next to hers on the pillow and telling her about "flowers and bells and birds singing and little goats and antelopes" (172). Similarly, Julia Stephen used to make little Virginia go to sleep by telling her about "rainbows and bells" (*MB,* 82). Her visionary nature makes Cam likely to become a writer, and so does her attention to detail: Mrs. Ramsay has to listen patiently to Cam's description of "an old woman with very red cheeks, drinking soup out of a basin" (84–85) before she gets the answer to her question of whether Paul and Minta have come back.

Cam also likes flowers, and, when we first meet her, she is picking "Sweet Alice on the bank" (36). Little Virginia's most profound revelation, Woolf recalled later, was when, looking at the flower bed at St. Ives, she suddenly realized: "That is the whole." She saw very clearly, she wrote, "that the flower itself was a part of the earth; that a ring enclosed what was the flower; and that was the real flower; part earth; part flower" (*MB,* 71). There may be a similar discovery going through Cam's mind when, much to her annoyance, her nursemaid and William Bankes attempt to take her flower away from her. Her reaction is definitely "fierce": "She would not 'give a flower to the gentleman' as the nursemaid told her. No! no! no! she would not! She clenched her fist. She stamped" (36). Cam's special feeling for flowers is the strongest link between her and her mother; in everything else it is James who, of the eight children, is closest to Mrs. Ramsay. In one scene Mrs. Ramsay is actually "relieved" when Cam leaves the room, thus letting her and James continue to read in perfect unity, "for she and James shared the same tastes and were comfortable together" (86). In another, while reflecting on how she never has time for anything while some of her children are still small, Mrs. Ramsay exclaims to herself "Oh, but she never wanted James to grow a day older!" and then adds, but only as a guilty afterthought, "or Cam either" (89).

In her later autobiographical "Sketch of the Past," Woolf tried to understand why she always felt like such an outcast as a child and why her mother, despite her physical closeness, seemed so distant to her:

> [O]f course she was central. I suspect the word 'central' gets closest to the general feeling I had of living so completely in her atmosphere that one never got far away from her to see her as a person. . . . I see now . . . why it was that it was impossible for her to leave a very private and particular impression upon a child. She was keeping what I call in my shorthand the panoply of life—that which we all lived in common—in being. I see now that she was living on such an extended surface that she had not time, nor strength, to concentrate, except for a moment if one were ill or in some child's crisis, upon me, or upon anyone—unless it were Adrian. Him she cherished separately; she called him 'My Joy.' (*MB,* 83)

It must have been hard for a young sensitive girl to be just one of eight children who seemed to her mostly "undifferentiated." And it was back then perhaps, when Julia Stephen was still alive, that Woolf started to develop the fierce need for maternal protection, which only became more acute with her mother's death. Given this semidistant childhood relationship with her mother, Woolf most likely felt that making Cam a major figure in the section where Mrs. Ramsay was so "central" would have been both unreasonably egotistical (as we will see later, Woolf was as afraid of being an egotist as was Goncharov) and false. She did reevaluate their closeness already as a grown-up, and she did realize that in nature she was perhaps even closer to her late mother than were her brothers and sisters—and it was comforting for her to do so and thus to overcome the impersonality of their early relationship—but as a child she had had no such claim.

Yet though she could not give much prominence to Cam in the section where Mrs. Ramsay was still alive, she could nevertheless fill the pages of her novel with the sights, sounds, and smells of her childhood. "Why am I so incredibly and incurably romantic about Cornwall?" she asked herself in 1921. "One's past, I suppose: I see children running in the garden. A spring day. Life so new. People so enchanting. The sound of the sea at night . . ." (*D*, II, 103). Just as for Nabokov childhood was forever associated with his family's summer estate at Vyra, so for Woolf the time her family spent at their summer residence in a small Cornish town became the symbol of her happy early years. Consequently, the setting of *To the Lighthouse* is very reminiscent of the Stephens' Talland House in the bay of St. Ives, which is located near the southwesternmost point of England. The Godrevy Lighthouse stands several miles off St. Ives Bay, and Woolf chose this lighthouse as the model for the one in her novel.

The geography of St. Ives is different from the fictional bay in the novel, though. The Ramsays' summer retreat is said to be on the Isle of Skye (14), in the Scottish Hebrides, also off the west coast but far north. Woolf had never been to the Hebrides prior to the publication of *To the Lighthouse*; for her it was a highly fictional place, akin to paradise ("I should like to be with you in the Hebrides at this moment," she wrote in March of 1926 to Vita [*L*, III, 244]) and thus to Cornwall. After the book came out, several people wrote to tell her "that my horticulture and natural history is in every instance wrong: there are no rooks, elms, or dahlias in the Hebrides; my sparrows are wrong; so are my carnations" (*L,* III, 379). People who knew her had no doubt she was describing Cornwall.[2]

Among the deepest impressions of her childhood was that of the sea. "If life has a base that it stands upon," she wrote in her memoirs, "if it is a bowl that one fills and fills—then my bowl without a doubt stands upon this memory. It is of lying half asleep, half awake, in bed in the nursery of St Ives. It is of hearing the waves breaking, one, two, one, two, and sending a splash of water over the beach, and then breaking, one, two, one, two. . . . It is of lying and hearing this splash and seeing this light, and feeling it is almost impossible that I should be here, of feeling the purest ecstasy I can conceive" (*MB,* 64–65).

The sounds of the waves "breaking one, two, one, two," on the beaches of St. Ives Bay became the book's symbolic image and its musical accompaniment. The waves make their first appearance on the very first pages of the novel in a rather menacing form. Mrs. Ramsay, trying to produce empathy in her children, asks them to imagine the life of the lighthouse keeper and his little boy: "For how would you like . . . to see the same dreary waves breaking week after week, and then a dreadful storm coming" (11–12). From then on the waves always have a dual connotation for Mrs. Ramsay. They can bring comfort, when they "beat a measured and soothing tattoo to her thoughts and . . . consolingly . . . repeat the words of some cradle song. . . , 'I am guarding you—I am your support,'" and they can bring anxiety when they "remorselessly beat the measure of life" and make one aware "of the destruction of the island and its engulfment in the sea and . . . that it was all ephemeral as a rainbow" (27–28). But it is not the state of the waves that affects Mrs. Ramsay's perception; it is her own state of mind that attributes to the waves those two antagonistic characteristics: a destroyer and a guardian. For the waves *are* Mrs. Ramsay's state of mind; they are the extension of her mental life and of her own fears and hopes. Lily Briscoe has a similar deeply personal concept of the waves: to her, too, waves are a metaphor for the ups and downs of one's life—"curled and whole like a wave which bore one up with it and threw one down with it, there, with a dash on the beach" (73). Anyone reading Woolf's later novel *The Waves* and her descriptions of her state of mind when seized by anxiety (like the one quoted earlier—"Let me watch the wave rise. I watch. . . . Failure") will immediately recognize this image as one of the most pervasive and dominant images in her writings.

But the full realization of the dual nature of the waves must have come later in life. When she was young, Woolf's reaction to the waves was, as she tells us, "purest ecstasy." This supremely loving, even worshipful, attitude toward the sea found its way into the novel through a child of the Ramsays. Curiously enough, however, it found its way not through Cam, who may be too young to fully verbalize her sensations, but through her older sister Nancy.[3] Watching the waves break on the shore while on her walk with Paul and Minta, Nancy is "hypnotized" by the sea and "bound hand and foot and unable to move by the intensity of feelings which reduced her own body, her own life, and the lives of all the people in the world, for ever, to nothingness" (115).

Woolf's other strong memory from childhood was that of the smells of Cornwall. "It still makes me feel warm," she wrote in 1939, "as if everything were ripe; humming; sunny; smelling so many smells at once; and all making a whole that even now makes me stop. . . . The gardens gave off a murmur of bees; the apples were red and gold; there were also pink flowers; and grey and silver leaves. The buzz, the croon, the smell, all seemed to press voluptuously against some membrane; not to burst it; but to hum round one such a complete rapture of pleasure that I stopped, smelt, looked" (*MB,* 66). *To the Lighthouse* is so permeated by warm, ripe smells of flowers and fruits that even people most immune to the sensual beauties of the external world cannot help noticing them. Thus, at the end of his expedition to town with Mrs. Ramsay, Charles Tansley, usually "odious" in his lack of any refined feelings (12), finds himself inhaling "the wind and the cyclamen and the violets" (25). Surrounding the Ramsays and their guests are enough bright and sweet smelling flora to fill even the Garden of Eden: "purple passion flowers" (33), Cam's favorite, Sweet Alice, "roses and pinks" (52), "red geraniums" (66), "the flowering hedge" (68), "dahlias" (101), "red-hot pokers" (102), "Evening Primroses" (108). James, who adores his mother, likens her to "a rosy-flowered fruit tree laid with leaves and dancing boughs" (60), and Mrs. Ramsay herself decides that the best way to think of people and their "otherness" is in the familiar terms of smells and bees: "How then, she had asked herself, did one know one thing or another thing about people, sealed as they were? Only like a bee, drawn by some sweetness or sharpness in the air intangible to touch or taste . . ." (79–80).

The scenes, smells, and sounds of childhood come to an abrupt end with Mrs. Ramsay's death and the beginning of World War I. In the ten years that the Ramsays' house stands abandoned and nearly perishes, Nature, once so motherly, soothing and tame, rebels and throws the Garden of Eden into complete chaos: "Poppies sowed themselves among dahlias; the lawn waved with long grass; giant artichokes towered among roses; a fringed carnation flowered among the cabbages," long weeds "tapp[ed] . . . at the window" (207). The musical sound of the waves is overpowered by the sharp sounds of "wind and destruction" (193), "as if a giant voice had shrieked so loud in its agony that tumblers stood inside a cupboard vibrated too" (200). The sea itself, once "the great plateful of blue water" that made Mrs. Ramsay exclaim, despite Tansley's presence, "'Oh, how beautiful!'" (23) turns into a pool of blood: the islanders say they saw "a purplish stain upon the bland surface of the sea as if something had boiled and bled, invisibly, beneath" (201).

Ten years later, when the much thinned family (Prue, like Stella Duckworth, died in childbirth two years after her mother; Andrew, like Thoby Stephen, was the next to go) comes back to the Hebrides, the sea has regained its "voice of beauty" (213), the weeds have been pulled out, the grass scythed and mowed, the house scrubbed and fixed—yet, as Mrs. Bast, the cleaning lady, predicted, it is not the same. The Ramsays and their old friends find the house and the world around it much changed. The change is particularly painful for the seventeen-year-old Cam Ramsay, and her poignant nostalgia and reflections on the complex relationship of one's past to one's present become the focal point of this part of the novel.

Cam is no longer "wild" or driven by "the glory of speed." On the contrary, Lily Briscoe, who is again staying with the Ramsays, finds Cam's "spirits subdued" (222). Lily also notices that Cam and her brother James now form "a serious, melancholy couple" (230), with "a pallor in their eyes which made [Lily] feel that they suffered something beyond their years in silence" (231). Cam does not run anymore: she stumbles (222), lags (230), falters, and flags (231). But she is still a visionary and she is one step closer to being a writer: Cam is, in fact, already a storyteller. Sitting in the boat that is finally, with a delay of ten years, taking her, James, and their father to the lighthouse, Cam fights the tedium of their mostly silent voyage by telling herself "a story of adventure about escaping from a sinking ship" (280). When she slips into reflecting about her childhood, Cam's diction is unmistakably poetic: it masterfully evokes a haunting mood of nostalgia and beautifully presents a poignant, truly Woolfian vision of the past as a "distant and peaceful and strange . . . something . . . in which one has no longer any part" (247).[4]

Cam is obviously drawn to literature, and, angry as she is with her father and determined "to resist [his] tyranny to the death" (243), she cannot help recalling the appealing picture of him sitting in his study writing, "so equally, so neatly from one side of the page to another." She also remembers the feeling that struck her, as she stood there watching Mr. Ramsay, about the wonderful elasticity of writing, how "one could let whatever one thought expand here like a leaf in water" (282).

"Virginia Woolf," writes Lyndall Gordon in her 1984 biography of the writer, "discovered herself to be the sum of two parts; in the process of fusion a new being emerged. . . . [In *To the Lighthouse*] she intended . . . to break the self down into separate components, derived from father and mother, as though she were cracking a genetic code."[5] Gordon's statement may sound overly simplistic, yet it is important to realize that viewing herself as a person split down the middle was very much Woolf's own idea.

Thus, like Goncharov, she often felt the common division between one's "public" and "private" selves, and when several years after *To the Lighthouse* she started working on *The Waves,* she commented in the novel's draft on "a certain inevitable disparity" between those two selves, "the outer and the inner."[6] In her published essay on Montaigne she likewise maintained that it was almost impossible to remain always true to our inner sense of who we are: "[B]eyond the difficulty of communicating oneself, there is a supreme difficulty of being oneself. This soul, or life within us, by no means agrees with the life outside us. If one has the courage to ask her what she thinks, she is always saying the very opposite to what other people say" (*CR,* 61).

And yet, mostly due to the different circumstances of their lives, Woolf's conflict between the outer and the inner selves was never as pronounced as that of the Russian writer. She rarely had to wear a public mask in order either to succeed in her job or be accepted by a strict society. Unlike Goncharov, she was a professional writer, and soon after the Woolfs' establishment of their own Hogarth Press in 1917, she did not even have to depend on pleasing other publishers in order to see her works in print. (That fact satisfied her immensely since it also meant the end of dependence on her half-brother, Gerald Duckworth, who owned the firm that published Woolf's first two novels.) Her immediate society was anything but "strict" and, except for Bloomsbury sympathizers among the aristocracy, she rarely ventured into the more conventional world where she had to be unlike herself.

There was a curious exchange between Woolf and one of her aristocratic friends, Lady Ottoline Morrell, in 1917, which can shed some light on how Woolf really felt about the interplay of her private and public selves. "When we were talking about keeping a journal," wrote Lady Ottoline in her diary, "I said mine was filled with thoughts and struggles of my inner life. She opened her eyes wide in astonishment."[7] "Ottoline keeps [a diary] . . . ," Woolf recorded in hers, "devoted however to her 'inner life'; which made me reflect that I haven't an inner life" (*D*, I, 79). What Woolf meant, most likely, was that she did not have an "inner life" that was much of a secret from others. Although a very private person, Woolf was yet quite generous (though often repentant after the fact) about sharing her innermost secrets with her sister, husband, and close friends: such was, in fact, the accepted mode of her circle.

Woolf appears to have felt much more acutely another division—that between her intellect and her senses, and it is the very same struggle of "mind" versus "heart" that obsessed Goncharov at the time of writing *A Common Story*. "No intelligence bridles the old hag—nature, to wit" (*D*, II, 183), Woolf once quipped, imitating Shakespeare. The sentiment may be old and rather trivial—yet, Woolf felt, it was still quite capable of capturing the essence of her inner conflicts. It all started, she thought, from the peculiar mix of people in their house as she was growing up: there was her father, one of the more prominent Victorian thinkers, and there were her half-brothers, who, though intellectual midgets in her opinion, represented the empty but attractive splendor of society. "The division in our life was curious," she reminisced later. "Downstairs there was pure convention: upstairs pure intellect. But there was no connection between them" (*MB*, 157).

The other duality that seems to have interested Woolf immensely as she was writing her novel was a direct outgrowth of this larger confrontation of intelligence and nature, but it had more of a "professional," rather than "personal," significance. It was, as Gordon points out, the coexistence in the daughter of two parental ingredients, which, though often conflicting within her, together constituted a sine qua non for a good writer: her mother's artistic sensibility and her father's critical and rational power. As I have noted, Woolf treasured the gift of sensibility above the gift of analytical powers ("when I write I am merely a sensibility," she said once[8]); yet it would be wrong to minimize Woolf's opinion of her father's contribution to her "genetic code." In the novel, while the writer's strong affinity with her artistic mother is reflected in the relationship of Lily Briscoe and Mrs. Ramsay, Woolf's deeply felt sympathy with her analytical father also plays a vital role and is shown in the fictional triangle of Lily, Cam, and Mr. Ramsay.

Though it was Julia Stephen's pen that in Woolf's mind achieved the status of "the parent of all pens," she had nothing but admiration for Leslie Stephen's pens, too. Among Woolf's autobiographical sketches there is a vivid description of her father's writing tools: "[T]here was his fine steel pen and the curious china inkpot, with a well, lidded, out at the side. All his books were dipped out of that well on the point of Joseph Gillott's long shanked steel pens. And I remember the little flat shield that his pen had rubbed smooth and hard on the joint of his forefinger" (*MB*, 119). Like Cam, young Woolf frequently pretended to be looking for a book in her father's study while, in fact, watching him write.

In "'Cam the Wicked': Woolf's Portrait of the Artist as Her Father's Daughter," Elizabeth Abel argues that by being a silent observer of her father's intellectual pursuits or a gratified listener to his philosophical discussions with other men, "Cam's education in the study prepares her to inherit her mother's position rather than her father's." Being but a daughter herself, Woolf, according to Abel, "was well aware that being wed to a tradition was not being its heir."[9] Abel's conclusion is, it seems to me, unduly pessimistic. It is true that, like her mother, Cam is still susceptible to being intimidated by the "admirable fabric of the masculine intelligence" (159). In "Agnostic Women," Woolf's own mother exclaimed that "women are said to be complex creatures, but what can be said of men . . . ?"[10] But while Mrs. Ramsay's mind wanders off in the midst of men's conversations, refusing to follow all the implications of "the influence of somebody upon somebody," Cam lets her mind take it all in and "expand . . . like a leaf in water." It is Mrs. Ramsay who is "wed" to a tradition (as represented by her husband) without even attempting to become its "heir"—but her daughter already appears to be on her way to contending with the men in her family for the rights of inheritance. Whether, in the eyes of the society or her father, Cam could succeed as a legitimate heir is a different question: Virginia Woolf herself never felt she was allowed to join what she thought was the exclusively male club of supreme intellectuals no matter how intelligent, educated, or talented she proved to be. Yet Woolf did feel that being able to watch her father silently in the study, though still a largely traditionally feminine posture, definitely helped her to realize her own dreams for the future. By his mere existence and the nature of his occupation her father was showing her the way, and that filled Woolf with such "passionate affection" for him that she was ready to forgive Leslie Stephen most of his wrongdoing.

And there was a lot to forgive, especially, as is well known by now, after Julia Stephen's death in 1895. His grief took the form of extreme self-pity and, like a spoiled child, often forgetting that the others in the family also suffered an immeasurable loss and may have needed as much sympathy, Leslie Stephen demanded from his daughters not only their full attention and unqualified compassion, but also the same domestic perfection that he came to identify with his late wife. After the marriage and then death of Julia's oldest daughter, Stella Duckworth, the task of filling their late mother's shoes fell on Vanessa, who was neither as skillful as Stella in saving money and running the house nor as humble. The next several years until Leslie Stephen's death of cancer in 1904 witnessed horrible domestic scenes so vividly described by Virginia in her autobiographical writings.

At such moments Virginia Stephen would feel nothing but "passionate hatred." She resented her father because she felt he showed unreasonable outbursts of rage and paranoia only in the company of women. With men he was always much more guarded and emotionally balanced. "His creed," Woolf thought, "made him ashamed to confess this need of sympathy to men" (*1MB*, 125), and in that he may well have been a typical Victorian. "He was a man," writes Quentin Bell in his introduction to Woolf's diaries, "who was ready to lead a revolution against God, who would not have been afraid of political innovations, but who so completely accepted the conventions and prohibitions of his age and class that he was ready to regard them almost as laws of nature."[11]

And yet, at the same time, Leslie Stephen, who was aware of some of his shortcomings, as *The Mausoleum Book* shows, proved to be in many ways a remarkable father for his unconventional daughters. Unlike Mr. Ramsay, who habitually comments on the "folly" (50) and "vagueness" (249) of women's minds, Leslie Stephen appears to have respected the intelligence of his wife and his daughters. Not always pleased with his wife's frequent staying away from the house, he nevertheless took Julia Stephen's devotion to nursing quite seriously, and, as Woolf testifies in her article "Leslie Stephen," he also did nothing to discourage his daughters from becoming professionals:

> If at one moment he rebuked a daughter sharply for smoking a cigarette—smoking was not in his opinion a nice habit in the other sex—she had only to ask him if she might become a painter and he assured her that as long as she took her work seriously he would give her all the help he could. . . . It was the same with the perhaps more difficult problem of literature. Even today there may be parents who would doubt the wisdom of allowing a girl of fifteen the free run of a large and quite unexpurgated library. But my father allowed it. (*CDB*, 74)

Virginia seems to have been Leslie Stephen's favorite child, and he recognized her talents quite early: "She takes in a great deal and will really be an author in time," he wrote in 1893.[12] Sir Leslie's statement is curiously revealing not only of the interest that he took in his child's gifts, but also, through his choice of words, of the fundamental difference between himself and his daughter. Woolf did not want to be "an author," a word much too general and all-encompassing for her taste. Her father was an author. He "authored" the *History of English Thought in the*

Eighteenth Century, several books on ethics, biographies, memoirs, and several entries to *The Dictionary of National Biography* (the initial volumes of which he also edited). But his daughter wanted to be a writer, which to her was synonymous with being a creative artist.

When later she was to complain about his lack of interest in music or painting (all his friends knew that "music, good music . . . [was] thrown away upon Stephen" and he himself confessed to being "hopelessly unmusical"[13]) and his crude characterizations, she was really complaining about his not being a creative writer but merely "an author." Yet she admired his professionalism, his ability to support himself and his family by the work of his intellect, and also the strong, solid quality of this intellect. Like Mr. Ramsay in *To the Lighthouse,* Leslie Stephen believed in the "supremacy of thought" (292), and the daughter inherited both her father's veneration for intellectualism and his clear logical mind. In the wide range of essays that feature not only other writers but also historians and philosophers, Woolf, in fact, created her own "History of English Thought" and found out, while writing it, that though her appreciation of literature had more angles and dimensions, her taste in authors was often very similar to her late father's.

Thus Woolf's attitude toward Leslie Stephen was, in many ways, a study in even sharper contrasts than her attitude toward her mother. She admired his "critical powers" but pitied his lack of "creative" ones; she liked him for letting his daughters be somewhat unconventional but resented him for having such a comfortably Victorian view on the place of women in general. She was proud of him for encouraging her to be a writer, but felt that, had he lived longer, she would have had to abandon her ambitions. "His life would have entirely ended mine," she wrote in her diary in 1928. "What would have happened? No writing, no books;—inconceivable" (*D,* III, 208). This latter sentiment finds a strong echo in Lily's inability to paint when Mr. Ramsay is around: she feels she cannot "achieve that razor edge of balance between two opposite forces; Mr Ramsay and the picture; which was necessary" (287).

Lily's responses to Mr. Ramsay are in general every bit as mixed as her creator's responses to her father. She resents his selfish tyranny over his wife, his extreme reliance on women for sympathy, his singling women out as witnesses of his emotional outbursts—yet at the same time Lily feels that Mr. Ramsay is in many ways "the most sincere of men, the truest. . . , the best" (72). Like Woolf, Lily is also struck by the lack of artistry in the man's pursuits—"no colour to it; . . . all edges and angles"—but, again like Woolf, she is nevertheless awed by his professional devotion and the stern, purely intellectual beauty of his subject: "Mr. Ramsay kept always his eyes fixed upon it, never allowed himself to be distracted or deluded, until his face became worn too and ascetic and partook of this unornamented beauty which so deeply impressed her" (232). Lily also knows that, while she cannot always share his interests or opinions, there is at least one thing that deeply bonds them: their unsettling anxiety over failing. For they are equally beset by "the demons" (32) who whisper in their ears that their work "will not endure" as, in real life, both Leslie Stephen and his daughter were mercilessly haunted by the same dark specter of professional failure.

Lily's reaction to Mr. Ramsay is also very similar to Cam's. They even use the same words to define the negative traits of his personality: Ramsay's daughter thinks of her father as tyrannical (243) and resents the "exquisite pleasure" he takes in "women's sympathy" (248). But, like Lily, Cam is also deeply convinced that, despite his maddening shortcomings, Mr. Ramsay is still "the truest" and "the best" of all men: he is "so brave, . . . so adventurous" (246), that, like Scott's Steenie, he would not hesitate to risk his life in the turbulent sea.

At one point Cam's passionate declaration of love for her father even revives for us the "wild and fierce" little girl whom we met in the first section of the novel: "For no one attracted her more; his hands were beautiful, and his feet, and his voice, and his words, and his haste, and his temper, and his oddity, and his passion, and his saying straight out before every one, we perish, each alone, and his remoteness" (253). And even in that, both in this childish outburst of emotion and this newfound ability to control herself (for she remains silent despite her emotional upheavals through most of the trip), Cam is remarkably similar to Lily Briscoe. For Lily, too, has her "wild" and passionate moments, which she finds necessary to keep in check—like her desire to fling herself down on her knees in front of Mrs. Ramsay, professing her love for "it all," or her impulse to dive off the cliff in search of Minta's brooch.

Cam's and Lily's similarities are, of course, no coincidence, for, as becomes more and more obvious in the third section of the book, the characters are deeply interconnected. There is a place in Woolf's text where she so obviously specifies their link that it should leave very little doubt that Cam and Lily were meant to be complementary characters. After the boat left on its voyage to the lighthouse, Lily, Woolf tells us, "felt curiously divided as if one part of her were drawn out there. . . ; the other had fixed itself doggedly, solidly here on the lawn" (233–34). From then on the narration unfailingly (with only one exception, on page 301, when it shifts to James) goes back and forth between Lily and Cam in what Woolf described as a chance to give one "the sense of reading the two things at once" (*D,* III, 106). Ruth Z. Temple appropriately defines the effect as "the 'ironical antiphony' of Cam and Lily, both masks for Leslie Stephen's daughter."[14] The back-and-forth shifts in narration (there are eight of them in all) are also somewhat reminiscent of the game Prue and Jasper play in the first part of the book (110–11) where the two play catch and try to keep the ball up in the air.

But Cam and Lily do not merely echo each other; they also influence each other's actions. This becomes obvious when one realizes that Lily's guilt at having rejected Mr. Ramsay's plea for her feminine sympathy miraculously disappears at the exact moment that Cam extends her sympathy to her father at the end of their journey to the lighthouse. For while most of the afternoon Lily has been anxious because "[t]he sympathy she had not given him weighed her down . . . made it difficult for her to paint" (254), at the time of Cam's acceptance of her father ("Ask us anything and we will give it you," Cam and James beg silently of their father [307–8]), Lily suddenly feels "relieved" because "[w]hatever she had wanted to give him, when he left that morning, she had given him at last" (308–9). But, as we know, there has been no further contact between her and Mr. Ramsay since he left in the morning. Furthermore, with Lily's mind preoccupied with Mrs. Ramsay for most of the afternoon, she has hardly had any time to work through her conflicting feelings toward Mr. Ramsay. It is obviously through Cam, who in this section of the book acts not only for herself but also for Lily, that the painter comes to terms with Cam's father. And it is only after Cam's decision to forgive her father's "tyranny" and selfishness that Lily can paint with ease and successfully complete her artistic "vision" (310).

It is fascinating to watch Woolf skillfully use Cam and Lily as her fictional agents in working through her own contradictory feelings about her parents. Cam is made to focus on Mr. Ramsay and reach the lighthouse having come to terms with her divided feelings about him; Lily, on the other hand, is made to concentrate on Mrs. Ramsay and finish her painting, having found wholeness and complexity where she once saw merely fragments and contradictions. Between the two of them, Woolf's protagonists manage to achieve for Woolf what made her write this autobiographical novel in the first place: the resolution of obsession and the feeling of reconciliation to the two people who she thought were largely responsible for both her tribulations and her triumphs as an artist.

6

Woolf's Artistic Uses of Co-Consciousness

In the light of the larger problem posed by this work—modes of fictional expression of autobiography and duality—comparing Woolf's use of a split fictionalized self to Goncharov's is revealing in both differences and similarities. As we have seen, in both *A Common Story* and *To the Lighthouse* the two characters represent the different life stages of their authors, their younger and their more mature selves. But whereas both Aduevs are "complete" characters insofar as they fully embody those different chronological phases of the writer's life, in *To the Lighthouse* only Lily can be seen as a fully developed character, while Cam appears rather infrequently in the first and by far the longest section of the book. Instead, Woolf chooses to portray her earlier years through the "collective" experiences of several young children—Cam, Nancy, and, to a certain extent, James—and through Cornwall's sights, smells, and sounds.

As we have seen in the chapter on Goncharov, by the end of *A Common Story* the younger self becomes an almost exact copy of the more mature self as it appeared at the beginning of the book. By the end, Aleksandr is the same age as Piotr when we first met him; he also shares with his uncle his profession, his standing in society, his interests and beliefs. In *To the Lighthouse,* on the other hand, there is no such clear-cut, complete circle: at the end of the novel Cam is still much younger than Lily at the beginning of the book; and we simply do not know enough about her interests and beliefs to be certain that she is, in fact, becoming a replica of the older woman. Yet, as we have seen, there are some important resemblances between the two; and, most importantly, like the Aduevs, they can also be seen as belonging or aspiring to the same profession despite the fact that Cam is much more likely to become a writer than a painter. For, as we have seen in her statements on writing and painting, Woolf often thought of those two arts as directly related, and Lily herself unfailingly unites them whenever she thinks about herself as an artist. Insofar as Lily can be associated with the visual side of art and Cam with the verbal, the two characters can actually be viewed as two aspects of the same artistic sensibility (Woolf's)—its "sensual" (Julia Stephen) side and its "intellectual" (Leslie Stephen) side. Furthermore, there are other significant ways in which Cam, like Aleksandr, ends up being very similar to the older protagonist: at the end of the novel Cam, like Lily at the book's beginning, is motherless and has an aging father to take care of.

Another interesting similarity between the two works lies in the function of the mature self as an "observer." Like Goncharov, Woolf seems to have founded her fictional split on the same self-perceived ability of being simultaneously a subjective participant and an objective, detached observer. Woolf's and Goncharov's descriptions of the inner interplay between the two are, in fact, so remarkably similar that it is worth quoting Goncharov's again to appreciate the resemblance. "While twisting in the agony of passion," wrote the Russian writer in 1888, "I could simultaneously see how everything I was going through was silly and comic . . . [w]hile suffering subjectively, I also analyzed the whole drama objectively."[1] "There was a spectator in me," wrote Woolf in 1939 about her relationship with George Duckworth, "who, even while I squirmed and obeyed, remained observant, note taking for some future revision" (*MB*, 154).

Being a painter, Lily is, by definition, an observer. Looking through the window at Mrs. Ramsay and James, who are inside the house, she positions herself exactly the way she feels she should if she wants to become a good artist: as a detached outsider.[2] Likewise, in her relationship with Cam, Lily does all the observing: she observes Cam's "wildness" as a child, her changed spirits as a teenager, her voyage to the lighthouse with her father. Cam, on the other hand, is peculiarly unaware of Lily's presence through the whole novel. At one point little Cam "grazed [Lily's] easel by an inch [and] would not stop for Mr. Bankes and Lily Briscoe" (83)—but that is about as close as they ever come to physical contact of any sort, which makes their preternaturally close connection at the end of the book so much more striking. Their relationship is, in fact, not unlike that of a narrator and protagonist in a more typical autobiographical novel where, while a close connection obviously exists, there is no physical interaction between the two autobiographical selves. In that *To the Lighthouse* is, of course, very different from *A Common Story,* where such interaction is at the core of the book.

Since there is hardly any physical contact between the two characters, there is also no antagonism between them of the sort that exists between the Aduevs. This lack of conflict between two autobiographical selves cannot be attributed, however, to lesser tensions between the inner divisions; rather it is actually a consequence of how Woolf chooses to cast those divisions. For unlike Aleksandr and Piotr, Cam and Lily are from the very beginning strongly divided against themselves; in contrast to the Aduevs, they are never set in one particular state of mind for any significant length of time. Thus staying with the Ramsays makes Lily constantly "feel violently two opposite things at the same time" (154) and the older Cam often finds herself "exposed to . . . pressure and division of feeling" (252). Furthermore, whereas in Goncharov the nephew and the uncle shoulder all the burden of their creator's mental and emotional contradictions, *To the Lighthouse* has not two but four characters who help Woolf fictionalize her personal conflicts. It is through the strong identification of Lily and Cam to Mrs. and Mr. Ramsay that most of the novel's major juxtapositions are set up and the contradictions explored.

What all these differences amount to, finally, is the indisputable fact that Woolf's novel is in many ways subtler and more intricate than Goncharov's: there is no obvious split in the middle and no stark, easily predictable contrast. And yet, in essence, Goncharov's and Woolf's approaches to fictionalizing a split self are remarkably alike inasmuch as they both use their fictional selves not only as a means of depicting their inner divisions but also as a vehicle for their larger and very similar artistic goals.

Woolf's use in the final section of the book of two characters to represent one personality accurately reflects not only her sense of inner duality but also her belief in the possibility of multiple states of consciousness. Thus in April of 1925, at the time she was conceptualizing *To the Lighthouse,* Woolf noted in her diary: "[M]y present reflection is that people have any number of states of consciousness: and I should like to investigate the party consciousness, the frock consciousness etc." Later, upon rereading her entry, she added in the margins, "second selves is what I mean" (*D,* III, 12). States of consciousness and their minute expressions in one's thoughts and actions were among her main preoccupations as a writer. Feeling handicapped that she could not read Dostoevsky in Russian and complaining that she "c[ould]n't bear [his] style . . . very often," Woolf was nevertheless fascinated by the man's interest in the depths of human psychology and his ability to "create . . . wonders, with very subtle brains, & fearful sufferings" (*D,* I, 23).

She was also curious about Freud and, although she did not read him carefully till the last year of her life, Woolf was, of course, quite familiar with most of Freud's theories prior to that experience. Freud was very much in the air of Bloomsbury: Woolf's friends James and Alix Strachey had already become Freud's English editors and translators in the early twenties and the Woolfs' own Hogarth Press started publishing his collected works and papers in 1924. At least one critic, Elizabeth Abel, even believes that Woolf's prose could have been directly informed by the psychoanalytical theories of both Freud and Melanie Klein.[3] But whether the affinity with Freud or his direct impact was truly there or not—and I do believe that both were much less powerful than Abel suggests—it should be quite clear that to someone such as Woolf the idea that people can have "second selves," as Dostoevsky's Goliadkin does in *The Double,* would have been hardly a profound "reflection" in 1925 unless she perceived this phenomenon in terms different from either Dostoevsky's or Freud's. And most likely she did: neither the "party consciousness" nor the "frock consciousness" sound particularly "repressed" or "unconscious"—they are, in fact, just different venues of one's everyday mental life which could, at least in a layman's estimate, easily coexist on equally conscious levels.

That is how different states of mind often coexist in Woolf's writings prior to *Between the Acts.* In *To the Lighthouse,* what Rosamond Lehmann called Woolf's "sense of the duality in human consciousness—the I forever watching the I"[4] is hardly "disturbing": instead of hopeless fragmentation, the novel suggests a possibility of "fragmented" balance, a balance that could be achieved by carefully saving all the fragments, putting them side by side, and being patient if they do not amount to a perfect design. For that is what Virginia Woolf managed to do for most of her mature life: her intellectual and her emotional selves did, overall, coexist side by side, despite the occasional and quite severe conflicts (as when she had her breakdowns).

And so did her past and her present. Thus, in a beautifully worded passage from her 1905 diary which immediately reminds one of Cam's elegiac reflections, Woolf writes: "[W]e should find our past preserved, as though through all this time it had been guarded and treasured for us to come to one day . . . to see once more the silent but palpable forms which for more than ten years we had seen only in dreams, or in the visions of waking hours."[5] And many years later, in "A Sketch of the Past," Woolf made past and present interlink even more closely: "The present when backed by the past is a thousand times deeper than the present when it presses so close that you can feel nothing else . . ." (*MB*, 98). Woolf's youthful experience contained an inordinate share of premature deaths in the family as well as the torment of the incestuous caresses of her half-brothers[6]—yet Woolf appears to have cherished her past. Characteristically, in the novel, Lily's triumphs as an artist and a human being occur exactly at the moment when she realizes that only by using both her intellect (reconciling herself with Mr. Ramsay) *and* her senses (making peace with Mrs. Ramsay), her awareness of the present *and* her memories, can she ever hope to grasp all the richness and complexity of life and art.

There appears to be nothing of the Freudian ego/id/superego relationship in Woolf's portrayal of her past and present selves in Cam Ramsay and Lily Briscoe. The "psychology" of their relationship is, in fact, hardly important at all; like Goncharov, Woolf (at least in this novel) does not appear to be interested in penetrating the surface in order to explore the mysteries of the hidden layers of one's consciousness. As in *A Common Story,* the two autobiographical alter egos in *To the Lighthouse* can be largely seen as co-conscious characters and as a useful artistic tool in writing an impersonal work of art as well as an alternative to a traditional autobiographical bildungsroman.

Woolf shared with Goncharov the same strong distaste for narcissism and the same fear of "the great egotism, the magnification of self" (*D,* III,

86), as she herself called it. One's ego, Woolf thought, was simultaneously "the greatest monster and miracle in the world" (*CR*, 68) and she rarely saw its merely miraculous side either in herself or other people. Like Goncharov, Woolf was a deeply private person and dreaded the feeling of being exposed. "Oh but why did I read this egotistic sentimental trash!" Woolf characteristically lamented after reading to her friends in 1920 a very candid essay on her relationship with George Duckworth. "What possessed me to lay bare my soul!" (*D*, II, 26).[7]

It was at the time of writing *Jacob's Room*, her first novel with strong autobiographical overtones, that Woolf became particularly sensitized to issues of "egotism" in fiction.[8] She had read so many autobiographical novels that, in her opinion, were purely egotistic and self-serving that she often asked herself whether she might be committing the same sin. "I wonder . . . whether I too deal thus openly in autobiography and call it fiction?" Woolf mused in her diary on January 14, 1920 (*D*, II, 7), and a week later she developed her thought further: "I suppose the danger is the damned egotistical self; which ruins Joyce [*Portrait*] and [Dorothy] Richardson [*Pilgrimage*] to my mind: is one pliant and rich enough to provide a wall for the book from oneself without its becoming as in Joyce and Richardson, narrowing and restricting? My hope is that I've learnt my business sufficiently now to provide all sorts of entertainments" (*D*, II, 14). This belief in her powers as a craftsman appears to have been what reconciled Woolf to using autobiography not only in *Jacob's Room* but also in her subsequent novels. "I think writing must be formal," she wrote in 1924, restating again her faith in the possibility of careful artistic control. "The art must be respected. . . . [I]f one lets the mind run loose, it becomes egotistic and personal, which I detest" (*D*, II, 321). Like Goncharov almost a century before her, Woolf equated authorial control over the subjectiveness of one's materials with the phenomenon of artistic detachment, and she wanted to practice it religiously.

She did, indeed, worship detachment. That someone possessed it in full measure was the highest praise she could bestow on writers: from Milton, with his "sublime aloofness and impersonality of the emotions" (*D*, I, 192), through Jane Austen, whose "genius compelled her to absent herself" (*GR*, 116), to Proust, whose "mind . . . lies open with the sympathy of a poet and the detachment of a scientist to everything that it has the power to feel" (*GR*, 125). Conversely, the writers who usually suffer the harshest treatment in Woolf's hands are the ones who, in her opinion, sadly lack this wonderful quality of being able to distance themselves. "Mrs. Browning," wrote Woolf in her article "Aurora Leigh," "could no more conceal herself than she could control herself, a sign no doubt of imperfection in an artist, but a sign also that life has impinged upon art more than life should" (*2CR*, 185). Woolf could be rather doctrinaire about her belief in detachment not only with writers but also with painters. Thus after Mark Gertler complained to her that "the shapes and objects have tortured him," she "advised him, for art's sake, to keep sane; to grasp, and not exaggerate, and put sheets of glass between him and his matter" (*D*, I, 176).

She always prided herself on being able to put those "sheets of glass" between herself and her "matter" even if her raw material was personal and subjective. And yet the years of writing *To the Lighthouse*, this most autobiographical of all her fictional works, were full of self-doubt as to whether she *was* actually a good enough artist to overwhelm the immensely powerful autobiographical element in her novel. At the very beginning of her work on *To the Lighthouse* she kept asking herself: "What theme have I? Shan't I be held up for personal reason? It will be too like father, or mother: and, oddly, I know so little of my own powers" (*D*, III, 49); and as she was finishing her novel a year later she was still worried about the same possibility of her work being too personal: "I go in dread of 'sentimentality.' Is the whole theme open to that charge?" (*D*, III, 110).

As in Goncharov's case, Woolf's use of a split autobiographical self instead of a more traditional single character appears to have gone a long way to allay her fears. To begin with, she was much less recognizable in two characters than she would have been in one. But, most importantly, by skillfully manipulating her past and present fictional selves Woolf could also perfect her art of detachment. For while it is true, as J. H. Buckley points out, that "Lily Briscoe, observing the family circle from the outside, represents the detached artist who was her creator,"[9] it is also important to remember that Woolf is not merely detached *through* Lily, but detached *from* Lily and Lily's "vision," and that this enables her to make her own art even more "impersonal" and "aloof."

For in order to be detached from the past one needs to be detached from the present—that is what Woolf says again and again in her writings. "[T]o feel the present sliding over the depths of the past, peace is necessary. The present must be smooth, habitual" (*MB*, 98), she wrote in "A Sketch of the Past." Besides her fear of self-exposure and dread of narcissism, this lack of double detachment might have kept Woolf from being content with writing her autobiographical novel in a more traditional way, with a mature self as a narrator rather than a protagonist. To her, such a choice would have meant rendering both experiences meaningless: the present, because the narrator is living it rather than artistically re-creating it, and the past, because without the impersonal peacefulness of the present it cannot assume the essential quality of being "transparent enough to reflect the light of our life, and yet steady, tranquil, composed with the aloofness of a work of art" (*D*, I, 266).

Thus, in *David Copperfield,* for example, the mature self, unobserved, is watching the growth of the younger self, and even if we think that the "real" author *is* ironically observing the "assumed" one, the possible evidence for that lies totally outside of the literary text, for it depends on our knowledge of Dickens as a person. But in *To the Lighthouse,* as in *A Common Story,* the mature self, while watching the younger self, is at the same time being observed by a truly impersonal narrator who exists outside of any temporal frame. For while, given its multiple narrators among the characters, Woolf's work may easily give an impression of a novel almost without an authorial voice (with the exception of the brief "Time Passes" segment), it is only an impression. According to Leaska's statistical study of the novel, the omniscient narrator accounts for 17, 76, and 10 percent, respectively, of all narration in the three sections of the book.[10] And if in the first section we do, indeed, often see Woolf's characters through the eyes of each other, in the final section of the novel the outside information we get about Lily Briscoe, Woolf's "present self," comes almost exclusively from the omniscient narrator. It can hardly be otherwise, for there is no one on the lawn with Lily as she is completing her painting except for Mr. Carmichael, who is hardly an observer, immersed as he is in his habitual opium-induced oblivion.

It is the authorial voice—and Woolf puts the long passage quoted below between parentheses as if even to separate it graphically from

Lily's "narrated monologue"[11]—that, for example, highlights for us Lily's contradictory feelings about love and marriage:

> What was this mania of [Mrs. Ramsay's] for marriage? Lily wondered, stepping to and fro from her easel.
>
> (Suddenly, as suddenly as a star slides in the sky, a reddish light seemed to burn in her mind, covering Paul Rayley, issuing from him. It rose like a fire sent up in token of some celebration by savages on a distant beach. She heard the roar and the crackle. The whole sea for miles round ran red and gold. . . . And the roar and the crackle repelled her with fear and disgust, as if while she saw its splendour and power she saw too how it fed on the treasure of the house greedily, disgustingly, and she loathed it . . .)
>
> She had only escaped by the skin of her teeth, though, she thought. (261–62)

The shifts in diction are striking and unmistakable. Framed on both sides by Lily's colloquialisms—"What was this mania"; "by the skin of her teeth"—the text in the parenthesis is saturated with poetic tropes: similes, metaphors, hyperbole. This rich allegorical language lifts Lily's experience out of the realm of the ordinary and gives it a particular quality that is simultaneously individual and general. It is individual because Lily's own and thus unique artistic nature shines through the complexity of the passage's imagery, but by likening love to the savage's fire which feeds on "the treasure of the house," the author also makes a gigantic step toward generalizing her protagonist's inner conflicts.

Needless to say, Woolf could not have managed that effect if she had not reserved for herself the role of an impersonal narrator capable of observing not only her past but also her present fictional self. As in Goncharov, the strategy of a split, rather than single, autobiographical self gives Woolf not only the protection of privacy and certain guarantees against excessive narcissism; it also leads to this peculiarly double nature of the book which is well captured in Phyllis Rose's appraisal: "[A]t her most autobiographical and personal, Woolf writes the novel that, of all her work, is the most universal."[12] And, like Goncharov, that was exactly the result Woolf was trying to achieve. When people failed to see it, she was angry: "I did not mean to paint an exact portrait of my father in Mr

Ramsay," she wrote in 1927 to a reviewer who interpreted her book as a mere fictional portrayal of her parents. "A book makes everything into itself and the portrait became changed to fit it as I wrote" (*L,* VI, 517). That was, Woolf thought, what made her different from Mrs. Browning: in her own writings art always came before life.

But Woolf's crafty use of a split autobiographical self even goes significantly beyond the already magnificent achievement of a detached, "aloof" presentation that transforms her personal material into a universal novel. As in the case of *A Common Story,* the same strategy also allows Woolf to reject not only the traditional single character of most autobiographical novels, but also their very format—that of a bildungsroman. However, while Goncharov's novel largely parodies a bildungsroman by mimicking it, Woolf's work avoids the traditional form altogether and instead offers a viable alternative to it. In her use of a split autobiographical self as a tool for an unorthodox novel of education, Woolf may have been guided by the example of Joyce's *Ulysses,* which reduced the traditional time span of a subjective novel of education from years to twenty-four hours,[13] yet, regardless of whether Woolf was indebted to Joyce or not, her own achievement is quite remarkable and deserves our full attention.

While not, strictly speaking, a twenty-four-hour novel, *To the Lighthouse* presents us with events that essentially happen within a span of slightly more than twenty-four hours: morning, afternoon, evening of the "Window" section of the novel, the ten-year-long night of "Time Passes," and again the morning and early afternoon of the "Lighthouse" chapter. The temporal scheme here is largely dramatic—one is reminded of a two-act play where the second act is separated from the first by a long interval.[14] Several critics have commented on Woolf's talent for "compressing"—what Alex Zwerdling calls her "technique of descriptive economy."[15] "To speak of measuring one's time by days or months, rather than years, has urgency," writes Harold Bloom in his introduction to a book of critical essays on Virginia Woolf, "and this urgency increases when the fiction of duration embraces only hours."[16]

Before Joyce and Woolf, few people would have believed that a short-span novel could successfully replace the traditional bildungsroman as a vehicle for a many-sided representation of human life. And yet the overwhelming critical consensus now seems to be that the modernist writers' alternative was not only as good as its traditional counterpart but even better. Thus, writing specifically about *Ulysses* and *To the Lighthouse,* Erich Auerbach discovered that

> There is greater confidence in syntheses gained through full exploitation of an everyday occurrence than in a chronologically well-ordered total treatment which accompanies the subject from beginning to end, attempts not to omit anything externally important, and emphasizes the great turning points of destiny. . . . He who represents the course of a human life or a sequence of events extending over a prolonged period of time and represents it from beginning to end, must prune and isolate arbitrarily. . . . But the things that happen to a few individuals in the course of a few minutes, hours, or possibly even days—those one can hope to report with reasonable completeness.[17]

Avrom Fleishman also concludes that *To the Lighthouse* can, paradoxically, be more "complete" than huge chronological family sagas: "Although *To the Lighthouse* does not follow the individual's career from birth to death . . . it is as universal a symbol of family life as we possess, ranging from courtship and marriage, through child-raising and children's life at various stages, to the deaths of parents and children and the readjustment of family relations in their wake." "In English literature, at least," he continues, "it is hard to think of a more systematic ordering of the patterns of the generations. . . ."[18] Woolf's achievement becomes more remarkable if we remember that her novel gives a complete cycle not just of human life in general, but of her own life in particular. Completeness is rarely associated with autobiographical novels. Since a single autobiographical protagonist in a traditional subjective bildungsroman is often too closely bound to the author through the lack of detachment, and since the author himself is still in the process of developing, such an autobiography is doomed, to use J. H. Buckley's words, to "remain to some degree incomplete and ambiguous."[19]

The strategy of splitting oneself into two fictional characters is what makes possible both the "urgency" in Woolf's novel and its completeness. Instead of following the development of a single protagonist from youth to maturity, Woolf presents two characters who largely embody those major stages of human life. That allows her, a strong believer in "moments of being" rather than in linear chronology as the only meaningful measure of one's time, to free herself from needing the grandiose time span of traditional autobiographical novels and to concentrate on two days in the lives of her characters. Her talent does the rest: it packs those two days with so much of what is essential in our lives that her very personal and lyrical novel becomes an epic of human existence.

We walk through ourselves,
meeting robbers, ghosts, old
men, young men, wives, widows,
brothers-in-love, but always
meeting ourselves.

Ulysses

7

Impersonalizing the Personal: Joyce's *Ulysses*

Insofar as Woolf's novel can be interpreted as a child's attempt to come to terms with a surrogate parent, *To the Lighthouse* may be close thematically to Joyce's *Ulysses.* But the most pronounced link between the two modernist novels lies in the way both writers chose to express their inner duality in an autobiographical novel through not one but two fictionalized selves. The parallel quests of Stephen Dedalus as a son in search of a surrogate father, and Leopold Bloom as a father in search of a surrogate son, are among the most discussed themes in this century's literary criticism, and Joyce's use of a fictionalized split self has obviously been established in critical thought much more firmly than either Woolf's or Goncharov's. Nonetheless, the significance of Joyce's technique for artistic purposes has been generally overlooked. And yet, there can hardly be a better novel to illustrate the use of a dual character as a means for impersonalizing the personal. As Michael Groden convincingly argues in *"Ulysses" in Progress,* Joyce's novel has dual "human" and "symbolic" tendencies, and any critic who chooses to subordinate one to the other robs the work of its rich complexity.[1] Compared with Goncharov's *A Common Story* and Woolf's *To the Lighthouse,* which, as we saw earlier, are similarly dual, *Ulysses* goes several steps further in both the personal and impersonal directions. It is more candid and more minutely autobiographical than either Goncharov's or Woolf's works and it also reaches even higher summits of detached, symbolic presentation.

It is, of course, very well known that Joyce, like Goncharov and Woolf, considered an impersonal creator a sine qua non for a good novel. He was barely twenty years old and hardly yet a writer when his imagination was captivated by Flaubert's description of the artist who "in his work must be like God in his creation, invisible and all-powerful."[2] Joyce disagreed with Goncharov and Woolf's belief that in literature an author's preoccupation with his or her own life is excessive narcissism. He felt that no apologies were necessary for any amount of autobiographical material in one's work; to him, one's life was not just a legitimate subject for literature, it was, in fact, the only meaningful one. "To recreate life out of life,"[3] "to forge literature out of [one's] experience, and not out of a conceived idea, or a temporary emotion,"[4] was for him as necessary a prerequisite for a successful work as detachment.

"What can a man know but what passes inside his own head?" he once asked his brother. To Stanislaus Joyce's angry question as to whether he really believed that "the only novel is the egomaniac's," the writer, without a minute's hesitation, replied in the affirmative.[5] "My own mind," Joyce made his protagonist say in *Stephen Hero,* "is more interesting to me than the entire country" (*SH,* 248). Perhaps it was only inevitable that Woolf would find the frequent exhibition of Joyce's "damned egotistical self" on the pages of *A Portrait of the Artist as a Young Man* rather distasteful,[6] yet to Joyce "egoism" was not an insult but a term of praise. "[S]ubtle egoism" was, he thought, a true sign of "the modern mind" (*CDD,* 54), and he delighted in finding its traces not only in himself but in his favorite writers: in William Blake, to whom Joyce attributed "unlimited egoism" (*CW,* 217), or in the idol of his youth, Henrik Ibsen, whom he labeled "an egoarch" (*L,* II, 205).

It is important to bear in mind, however, that the differences between Joyce's, Woolf's, and Goncharov's perceptions of egotism may have been less a matter of different personalities than of different experiences. With Joyce the firm belief in one's right to extreme individualism came largely as a result of an intellectual conviction, a strong reaction against the theories of humility and personal sacrifice that had dominated his Jesuit youth. He always viewed the two systems of beliefs as directly opposed to each other and sadly regretted when adherents to secular individualism succumbed to guilt fostered, he thought, by the Catholic church. "He died a Roman Catholic," wrote Joyce of Oscar Wilde, one of the more famous examples of such a conversion, "adding another facet to his public life by the repudiation of his wild doctrine. After having mocked the idols of the market place, he bent his knees, sad and repentant that he had once been the singer of the divinity of joy, and closed the book of his spirit's rebellion with an act of spiritual dedication" (*CW,* 203). Neither Woolf, brought up in an atmosphere totally devoid of any religious fervor, nor Goncharov, who, while deeply aware of his culture's taboo against personal pride, was by no means as devout a Russian Orthodox as young Joyce was a Jesuit, was as likely to develop an equally rebellious response to the powerful dogma of self-denial in the service of one's God.

"[N]o writer in English since Sterne," writes Stanislaus Joyce in *My Brother's Keeper,* "has exploited the minute, unpromising material of his immediate experience so thoroughly as my brother did, using it in order to delineate a character or complete his picture of an environment" (*MBK,* 32). Stanislaus Joyce's comment is hardly an overstatement. Joyce's phenomenal memory retained, among other things, that which to many would have been the most insignificant and utterly forgettable moments of one's everyday existence. Furthermore, not quite satisfied with the generous offerings of his own recollections, Joyce frequently turned the two most intelligent members of his family, his aunt Josephine Murray and his brother Stanislaus, into his assistants.

But the fact that Joyce, unlike Woolf or Goncharov, believed in autobiography as the most legitimate subject for fiction should not obscure the profound similarities between him and the other two writers. He was first of all an artist, and the demands of his craft overpowered the demands of his ego.[7] Like Woolf and Goncharov, Joyce felt that he had to make himself, in his brother's words, "free to create artistically, unhampered by the shackles of autobiography" (*MBK,* 148). To study the development of Joyce's prose over the years is to study the same subject matter—himself—being presented with a progressive degree of distance from one novel to the next.

He started his quest for a successful autobiographical novel with *Stephen Hero* in 1903, the same year he formulated his notion of the "three conditions of art: the lyrical, the epical and the dramatic": "That art is lyrical whereby the artist sets forth the image in immediate relation to himself; that art is epical whereby the artist sets forth the image in mediate relation to himself and to others; that art is dramatic whereby the artist sets forth the image in immediate relation to others" (*WD*, 54).

Joyce's tripartite progression of art here is strikingly similar to the last three levels of consciousness in theosophy: human or "I-am-I"; universal or "I-am-thee-and-thou-art-I"; and Divine, which united all consciousnesses into one. In 1903, Joyce, like many of his friends, was still intrigued by Madame Blavatsky's theosophical theories. His fascination did not last very long—"She was a nice old bag of tricks," his J. J. O'Molloy says about "that Blavatsky woman" in *Ulysses* (*U*, 115)—but it did leave its imprint even on many of his later works, including, of course, *Finnegans Wake*.[8]

Stephen Hero in its complete form was "lyrical" (or "human"). Stephen Daedalus (he was yet to lose his diphthongal vowel) definitely stood in immediate relation to his creator. It was, perhaps, even "epical," for Joyce, mostly by his use of third- rather than first-person narration, did establish some sort of a "mediate relation" between himself and the others. Yet, as became more and more apparent to its author, the work never approached its final, "dramatic" mode. Too obviously personal and frequently too serious and adolescent, the novel failed to achieve the "divine" dimension—the "immediate relation to others" that would virtually obscure the author—that Joyce had hoped his work could reach.

In 1908 Joyce ventured to approach his subject one more time. He kept as the book's focus the same protagonist, most of the same events, and many of the same characters. He also kept the third-person narration but tried to make sure that the author's identification with Stephen was less perceivable than in the earlier version. For that purpose he abandoned the somewhat traditional omniscient narrator of the first version and opted for a truer incarnation of Flaubert's "invisible and all-powerful" author. *Portrait* was also to feature Joyce's now all-too-famous description of such a "divine" creator who manages, to use theosophical terms, to unite all consciousnesses into one:

> The dramatic form is reached when the vitality which has flowed and eddied round each person fills every person with such vital force that he or she assumes a proper and intangible esthetic life. The personality of the artist, at first a cry or a cadence or a mood

> and then a fluid and lambent narrative, finally refines itself out of existence, impersonalises itself, so to speak. The esthetic image in the dramatic form is life purified in and reprojected from the human imagination. The mystery of esthetic like that of material creation is accomplished. The artist, like the God of creation, remains within or behind or beyond or above his handiwork, invisible, refined out of existence, indifferent, paring his fingernails. (*P*, 215)

But to understand Joyce's purposes in the novel, it is equally important, it seems to me, to remember what immediately follows Stephen's tirade: "'Trying to refine them [i.e. his nails] also out of existence,' said Lynch" (*P*, 215). It was not just the invisible author but also this note of undercutting irony that, I believe, were to separate the deadly serious *Stephen Hero* from *A Portrait of the Artist as a Young Man*. And yet the two purposes were often at odds with each other.

The criticism of Joyce's first published novel provides proof that that may have been the case. While some critics believe that Joyce's work mostly shares with *Stephen Hero* a complete solemnity about the plight of the young protagonist, others tend to see Joyce's view of Stephen as quite ironic.[9] And there are also those who, like Wayne Booth, wonder whether Joyce himself quite knew what he was doing: "Is [Stephen's] rejection of priesthood a triumph, a tragedy, or merely a comedy of errors?. . . Are we to smile at Stephen or pity him in his tortured longing? Are we to marvel at his artistry, or scoff at his conceit?"[10] With the hindsight of *Ulysses*, one is often tempted to answer "all of the above." But interpreting one novel through another that did not even exist at the time, is not, of course, what Joyce could have hoped his critics would do.

I believe that Joyce's portrayal of his young self in *Portrait* was to be mildly ironic and that, despite his intentions, Joyce did not quite succeed in creating a proper vehicle for his irony. Having refined the implied author almost totally out of existence by limiting his remarks to mere stage directions, Joyce had no choice but to rely on other characters, primarily Lynch and Cranly, as his agents. The difficulty with that approach was, however, that Joyce also wanted to show that Dedalus's friends were rapidly becoming his traitors since Joyce felt that their real-life prototypes (Vincent Cosgrave and John Francis Byrne) had betrayed him. As such the characters could only have been appropriate conductors of malicious rather than benign irony.

Joyce must have perceived those limitations of his *Portrait.* While the book, unlike *Stephen Hero,* largely succeeded in reaching the final, "dramatic" condition of art by making "the Artist" of the title into "an artist" symbolizing all creative minds in search of means of self-expression, Joyce nevertheless decided to write the continuation of Stephen Dedalus's quest in a very different way. Thus he abandoned the format of a bildungsroman[11]—his new novel was to concentrate on but one day in Stephen's life. Within that one day, Stephen, the undisputed solo performer of *Portrait,* now had to share the stage with another character—Leopold Bloom, a Dublin Jew and a commercial traveler. While a significant part of the narration was still to be done through interior monologues, as it was in *Portrait,* Joyce decided against an almost totally suppressed authorial voice. Instead he chose a set of dramatized semiomniscient narrators and an aloof, Ariel-like presence that could ironically observe the humans, mimic their language, and parody their civilization.

"I feel like an engineer boring through a mountain from two sides," Joyce told a friend once. "If my calculations are correct we shall meet in the middle" (*MU,* 320). He was allegedly talking about *Finnegans Wake,* but his description is even more appropriate for his method in *Ulysses.* Joyce's idea of consciousness was truly eclectic: he borrowed something from theosophy, something from the nineteenth-century psychologists, something from Freud. Like Woolf, he never wholly subscribed to any particular school of thought either in this or in anything else. Even when he appears to be echoing someone else—as in his Flaubert-inspired definition of detachment—he always adds a peculiar twist of his own. That also happens when, in *Ulysses,* Stephen at first appears to parallel Freud's notion of the "repressed" but ends up, instead, contradicting it: "Secrets, silent, stony sit in dark palaces of . . . our hearts: secrets weary of their tyranny: tyrants willing to be dethroned" (24). The idea of the dark secrets willing, without any outside pressure, "to be dethroned" is very far from what Freud and his followers believed. Frank Budgen quotes Joyce as saying to him once: "Why all this fuss and bother about the mystery of the unconscious? What about the mystery of the conscious?

What do they know about that?" (*MU,* 320). That simple remark captures, it seems to me, what may have been in Joyce's mind when he decided to split his fictional alter ego into two in *Ulysses.* Joyce *was* interested in "the mystery of the conscious," and, like Woolf and Goncharov, he chose to fictionalize in his novel two equally co-conscious parts of his nature.

In his 1959 article, "A Portrait of the Artist as Blephen-Stoom," Julian Kaye painstakingly builds an argument that Joyce did, in fact, fully intend Stephen and Bloom as his "fictional representatives."[12] Kaye comments on similarities in ages, dates, and names that could not have been mere coincidences as used by a writer who liked to play with numbers and for whom names (most of them real) were very important. Thus Stephen's age in 1904—twenty-two—corresponds to Joyce's own in the same year; Bloom's age—thirty-eight—is emphasized in the "Circe" section of *Ulysses* ("Stephen: . . . I am twentytwo. Sixteen years ago he [Bloom] was twentytwo too" [459]) which Joyce was writing in 1920, when he himself was thirty-eight. The date given for the marriage of Bloom and Molly is October 8 (605), which is the date on which Joyce eloped with Nora and left Ireland. Further examples of autobiographical "vital statistics" include Stephen's mother's name, May (Mary), which she inherited from Joyce's own mother, and the name of Bloom's mother, Ellen, which corresponds to that of Joyce's paternal grandmother.[13]

Like Goncharov, Joyce obviously had a lot of fun dividing bits and pieces of his personal history among his protagonists, and a list of the events and characteristics he shared with Stephen, Bloom, and Molly could go on and on, running the risk of turning into unimaginative cataloguing. But the relation of Joyce's protagonists to their creator is a much better-charted territory than that of Goncharov's and Woolf's to their characters, and reviewing all the instances of this interconnection is hardly necessary. Instead, for the purposes of this study, it is much more useful to distinguish between the different quality of autobiography in Stephen and in Bloom, and to concentrate on those aspects of their relationship to Joyce that are most pertinent to our discussion.

Robert Scholes once summarized the difference of autobiography in Stephen and Bloom as follows: "[I]t is not enough to say that Stephen is a young Joyce and Bloom is a mature Joyce. Stephen 'is' Joyce in a different way from the way Bloom 'is' Joyce. Stephen is Joyce in his skin, with all the significant features that would make him recognizable. And with no features that Joyce himself did not possess. . . . But Bloom contains large elements of Joyce's neural circuitry without being recognizable as Joyce; and at some important levels of experience he is a 'truer' representation of Joyce than Stephen."[14] Like Stephen, Joyce was born in Dublin in 1882, one of numerous children in an impoverished Catholic family, and he also received a mostly Jesuit education. Like Stephen, he broke with the church before he turned twenty and went to Paris only to be called back to Dublin by his father's telegram that his mother was dying. Like Stephen on the day depicted in *Ulysses,* he spent several days (but in September, not June, of 1904) living at the Martello tower at Sandycove with a friend, who, he thought, was fast becoming his enemy.

Joyce's "neural circuitry," like Bloom's, included a strong tendency toward sexual masochism (Bloom, after all, even shares his first name with Leopold von Sacher-Masoch): he appears to have enjoyed perversely the feeling of being "cuckolded" and, like the Dublin Jew, tortured himself by imagining someone else making love to his wife. Not quite satisfied with what he thought could be Nora's past "infidelities," Joyce instigated his wife to pursue new ones: her husband, Nora told a friend, wanted her to "go with other men so that he would have something to write about."[15] While she was not quite ready to do that, she nevertheless tried to meet her husband halfway and not interfere with his fantasy. For that purpose she even saluted him in a letter once as "Dear Cuckold."[16]

But Joyce apparently needed more thrills, and, similarly to Bloom, he wrote letters with Greek "ε's" to a largely fantasized mistress, Marthe Fleischmann, that encouraged her to dwell on how she would punish him when they met. Also like Bloom, who examines the statues of Greek goddesses in the National Museum in order to see whether they have an anal opening (thus making Mulligan suspect him of homosexuality: "O, I fear me, he is Greeker than the Greeks" [165]), Joyce had what Ezra Pound wittily called an "arsthetic obsession."[17] "[Arse] is a word that is scarcely ever out of Jim's mouth," Stanislaus wrote in 1904. "He has been remarked for it and *playfully* accused of being a bugger because of the way he pronounces it" (*CDD,* 49–50; his emphasis).

There is an interesting parallel between *To the Lighthouse* and *Ulysses* in the possible tint of homosexuality added to the protagonists' relationship. Buck Mulligan is convinced that Bloom is sexually attracted to Stephen: "He looked upon you to lust after you" (179), and Joyce himself did not deny that such could well be the case. "You see an undercurrent of homosexuality in Bloom . . . and no doubt you are right," he once told Budgen (*MU,* 315). But as in Woolf's novel, where homosexual overtones may exist in Lily's attitude toward Mrs. Ramsay, this undercurrent fits within a larger surrogate parent/surrogate child framework. For Bloom, whose only son died eleven days after birth,[18] Stephen's main appeal lies in his "sonhood"; Stephen, who is repelled by and attracted to figures of paternity, recognizes Bloom's fatherly instincts.[19] There is, however, a substantial difference between Woolf's projection of her search for a surrogate parent in *To the Lighthouse* and Joyce's treatment of a similar theme in *Ulysses.* Cam Ramsay and Lily Briscoe may be different when it comes to age and maturity, yet they both remain essentially "children" who are in need of maternal protection. The difference between Stephen Dedalus and Leopold Bloom, on the other hand, lies not only in age and maturity but also in the fact that one is still a son while the other is already a father. Whereas childless Woolf was looking for a mother outside of herself, Joyce, who at the time of writing the novel had two children, is looking for a father within himself: Stephen's seemingly paradoxical search for a father while Simon Dedalus is still very much alive should be interpreted as his anticipation of his own future fatherhood rather than his seeking, as Lily does, a substitute for a real parent.

This is not to say that Joyce was not interested in surrogate parenthood. He was—but, like Woolf, he felt need for *maternal* protection, and it was his late mother, not his father, whom he sought to replace. It was May Joyce's "*Amor matris,* subjective and objective genitive, [which] may be the only true thing in life" (170) that her son was trying to find or re-create in his wife. "My little mother," Joyce characteristically wrote to Nora in 1909, "take me into the dark sanctuary of your womb. Shelter me, dear, from harm!" (*SL,* 195). In another letter written the same year he makes his hope for all-forgiving motherly love from his wife even more distinct: "Oh my darling be only a little kinder to me, bear with me a little even if I am inconsiderate and unmanageable and believe me we will be happy together" (*SL,* 175). In the novel, while Bloom and Stephen are at opposite points of a father/son relationship, they, not unlike Cam and Lily, appear to share the same desire, unmitigated by age or experience, for maternal love and protection.

Ironically, Joyce's problem was very similar to Woolf's not only because he missed "amor matris" but also because he appears to have regretted that he himself could not be a mother. By now, largely due to Richard Ellmann, we are aware of numerous paradoxes in Joyce's personality, but the contrast between his condescension to women, which he never took pains to conceal either in life or in fiction, and his highest esteem for motherhood is one of the starkest. The same person who believed that a new fur coat would keep his wife content or even cure his daughter of depression ("I think that will do her inferiority complex more good than a visit to a psycho-analyst," he wrote to a friend in 1932 [*L*, I, 326]) was capable of the truest moments of metaphorical couvade. Bloom's imaginary pregnancy in the "Circe" episode of *Ulysses* ("O, I so want to be a mother" [403]) is not mere buffoonery, for it underscores Joyce's lifelong envy of the permanent bond that he thought existed only between mothers and their children. "Only a mother and a deadborn child ever buried in the one coffin," reflects Bloom at Dignam's funeral. "I see what it means. I see. To protect him as long as possible even in the earth" (90). "Fatherhood, in the sense of conscious begetting, is unknown to man," Joyce makes Stephen say in the "Library" scene. "Paternity may be a legal fiction. Who is the father of any son that any son should love him or he any son?" (170). That Stephen's sentiment was fully shared by Joyce is made obvious in a letter he sent to his brother soon after the birth of Joyce and Nora's first child: "Paternity *is* a legal fiction" (*L*, II, 108; my emphasis).

Joyce appears to have indeed envied Nora her pregnancies. "[I'm] thinking of the book I have written," he wrote to her about *Dubliners*, "the child which I have carried for years and years in the womb of the imagination as you carried in your womb the children you love" (*L*, II, 308). Speaking of one's books as children is obviously a cliché, yet Joyce's extended simile is much more elaborate than the usual comparison; he was also to repeat this image in *Portrait*: "O! In the virgin womb of the imagination the word was made flesh" (*P*, 217). In September of 1909, Joyce, preparing to go back to Trieste after a rather traumatic visit to Ireland, even asked his wife not to "bring onions or garlic into the house.

You will think I'm going to have a child. It is not that but I don't know what to do I am so upset and excited" (*SL,* 171–72). The seriousness with which Joyce says "It is not that" makes one almost wonder whether he did not, in fact, entertain hopes that, like Bloom in "Circe," he might one day find himself "about to have a baby" (403). Later in his life, burdened by enormous love for his daughter yet helpless to cure her schizophrenia, Joyce thought he came close to the intensity of the mother-child relationship, and, according to Maria Jolas, often "talked of fatherhood as if it were motherhood."[20]

At least partially, perhaps, Joyce's veneration for motherhood had its roots in his youthful devotion to the Virgin Mary, and already in one of his early epiphanies the image of the Virgin Mary naturally blends with the image of his earthly mother, also Mary:

> She comes at night when the city is still; invisible, inaudible, all unsummoned. She comes from her ancient seat to visit the least of her children, mother most venerable, as though he had never been alien to her. She knows the inmost heart; therefore she is gentle, nothing exacting; saying I am susceptible of change, an imaginative influence in the hearts of my children. Who has pity for you when you are sad among the strangers? Years and years I loved you when you lay in my womb. (*Ep,* 68)[21]

Several years after recording the epiphany, Joyce wrote to his brother about the English teacher at the Berlitz school in Trieste who had said that Joyce would "die a Catholic because I am always moping in and out of the Greek Churches and am a believer at heart: whereas in my opinion I am incapable of belief of any kind" (*L,* II, 89). But to his critics, as to Joyce's Berlitz colleague, the writer often appears to have been overly optimistic about his clean break with the Church.

8

Ulysses' Body and Soul

Whereas Goncharov and Woolf were most preoccupied with the conflicts of their hearts and minds, Joyce affected to find that dichotomy rather meaningless. When Frank Budgen in a conversation with Joyce once used the word "heart" in its conventional sense, the writer quickly replied: "The seat of the affections lies lower down, I think" (*MU*, 13). Similarly, when another friend alluded to the conventional opposition of the "intellectual" to the "sensual," Joyce allegedly responded: "I do not think I know exactly what you mean when you say 'sensual'."[1] Yet despite Joyce's objection to traditional juxtapositions, his own particular conflict was different from Woolf's and Goncharov's not in the degree of commonness but merely in nature: while the other two writers' perception of the divisions between their hearts and minds betrayed the largely secular character of their concerns, Joyce's preoccupation with the body and the soul reveals the emotional ties he still had with the religiosity of his youth.

As late as 1912 Joyce could still sound like a good Catholic when he talked about the conflict between spirit and flesh: "We might say indeed that modern man has an epidermis rather than a soul. The sensory power of his body has developed enormously, but it has developed to the detriment of the spiritual faculty" (*JJP*, 21). As Theoharis Constantine Theoharis emphasizes in *Joyce's "Ulysses": An Anatomy of the Soul,* young Joyce's theoretical concept of the soul was a complex conglomeration of, among others, Aquinas, Aristotle, Bruno, Dante, and Mathew Arnold.[2] Yet there is nothing too intricate about the juxtapositions of body and soul as Joyce employs them in his early notebooks or letters to his wife. In fact, they appear almost as stark as Goncharov's. "All men are brutes, dearest," Joyce wrote to Nora in December of 1909, when he was in Dublin and she back in Trieste, "but at least in me there is also something higher at times. Yes, I too have felt at moments the burning in my soul of that pure and sacred fire which burns for ever on the altar of my love's heart" (*SL,* 187). On another occasion, after getting a response from Nora that appeared to acknowledge a similar division in her own personality, Joyce exclaimed: "Are you too, then, like me, one moment high as stars, the next lower than the lowest wretches?" (*SL,* 167). He also often explained to his common-law wife how this double nature affected his feelings for her: "One moment I see you like a virgin or madonna the next moment I see you shameless, insolent, half-naked and obscene!" (*SL,* 166–67).

But even at this early stage, Joyce was much too realistic to try to suppress his "low" side into a state of oblivion. Instead, he sought within himself that which he obviously sought in his relationship with his wife—a certain harmony between body and soul. "My body soon will penetrate into yours, O that my soul could too!" (*SL,* 169), he wrote to Nora in September of 1909. "I want you to read over and over all I have written to you," he wrote to her after a series of sexually explicit letters. "Some of it is ugly, obscene and bestial, some of it is pure and holy and spiritual: all of it is myself" (*SL,* 169).

By the time he came to write *Ulysses,* Joyce appears to have significantly softened his dichotomy. Thus his juxtaposition of Stephen and Bloom in the novel is never quite as clear-cut as the divisions he draws in his letters to Nora. There is spirituality in Bloom and Stephen is not altogether "holy." Yet Joyce makes obvious from the start his intention to contrast Stephen's preoccupation with his soul to Bloom's constant awareness of his body. Each chapter's subject outlines, first published in the Stuart Gilbert study of *Ulysses* written under Joyce's supervision, make a point of the contrast. Whereas they specify only a "scene . . . hour . . . art . . . symbol . . . technic . . ." in Stephen's part of the book, they add an "organ" as soon as Bloom takes over the narration in the fourth episode of the novel. For example, the outline for the first episode, "Telemachus," reads as follows: "Scene: The Tower; Hour: 8 a.m.; Art: Theology; Symbol: Heir; Technic: Narrative (young)"; in contrast the outline for the fourth episode, "Calypso," reads "Scene: The House; Hour: 8 a.m.; Organ:

Kidney; Art: Economics; Symbol: Nymph; Technic: Narrative (mature)."[3] Thus Stephen's inorganic nature is opposed to Bloom's organic one as clearly as the youthfulness of one is opposed to the maturity of the other.

"My soul walks with me, form of forms," reflects Stephen, in the "Proteus" chapter of *Ulysses* (37). "This is my body," says Bloom to himself at the close of "Lotus-Eaters," anticipating the bath he is going to take with a newly acquired scented soap (71). Like much in *Ulysses,* both interior utterances are echoes or direct borrowings from other sources. Stephen's reflection on his soul closely follows Aristotle's "the soul is the form of forms" (*De Anima,* III, 432a), while Bloom is reproducing verbatim Jesus' famous words at the Last Supper: "This is my body which is given for you: this do in remembrance of me" (Luke 22:19). The Eucharistic image of the body and blood of Christ had always been a strong theme in Joyce's writings. In *Portrait* he used it as a metaphor for an artist—"a priest of eternal imagination, transmuting the daily bread of experience into the radiant body of everliving life" (*P,* 221); in *Ulysses* it is featured, deflated of its lofty meaning, on the very first page of the book in Buck Mulligan's parody of a preacher: "For this, O dearly beloved, is the genuine christine: body and soul and blood and ouns. Slow music, please. Shut your eyes, gents. One moment. A little trouble about those white corpuscles. Silence, all" (3).[4]

At first glance, Bloom, an aging Jew of Hungarian ancestry, and Stephen, an Irishman and an ex-Catholic, are very unlikely doubles. Stephen, as seen through Bloom's eyes, is "a lithe young man, clad in mourning" (73), a description that echoes Joyce's earlier portrayal of himself in one of the epiphanies written soon after his mother's death: "He runs out darkly-clad, lithe and serious" (*Ep.,* 86). Stephen *is* young—he is twenty-two years old and has yet to experience a sexual relationship with a woman other than a prostitute. His body in that sense is virtually virginal, for Joyce did not consider sex with a prostitute as differing much from an act of masturbation. But Stephen's soul is a different matter. "The soul like the body may have a virginity," wrote Joyce in his notes to *Exiles* (*E,* 113), and Stephen's soul definitely lost his when it broke away from Catholicism. Consequently, Stephen is much more knowledgeable about the mysteries of the soul than the secrets of the body. On the day we meet him, he may be even further alienated from his body by the simple reason that he cannot see it well. As Joyce seems to suggest in the "Circe" episode, Stephen has broken his glasses a day before and his "sight is somewhat troubled" (454); the main problem with his vision being, as Stephen tells his companions in Nighttown, that "[t]he eye sees all flat" (456). His inner eye, of course, does not need any glasses to distinguish the soul, but the flat outward vision would make a multi-dimensional human body a caricature.

Stephen's soul is evoked numerous times in the first three chapters of *Ulysses*. Thus he remembers a dream where his mother came from the grave "to shake and bend my soul" (9), and it is through his soul that he communicates with her apparition: "No, mother! Let me be and let me live. . . . Stephen, still trembling at his soul's cry, heard warm running sunlight and in the air behind him friendly words" (9). At ten in the morning Stephen is shown to be giving his pupils a lesson in history but his mind is wandering off, reflecting on Aristotle's "The soul is in manner all that is: the soul is the form of forms" (21)—the same concept, or, more precisely, two concepts, that occupy his mind later in "Proteus." He also thinks about the souls of others, like the non-Christian medieval interpreters of Aristotle, who were trying to reconcile Aristotle's thought with their own religions, whether Muslim or Jewish: "Gone too from the world, Averroes and Moses Maimonides, dark men in mien and movement, flashing in their mocking mirrors the obscure soul of the world, a darkness shining in brightness which brightness could not comprehend" (23).

As E. L. Epstein has pointed out, "the 'brightness' is that of Stephen's enemies—Garrett Deasy, the pet of the sun, Buck Mulligan 'tripping and sunny like the buck himself . . . ,' Haines with his pale eyes, Private Carr and Compton with their 'blond copper polls' while Stephen himself feels a great affinity for darkness; he has felt it ever since the early chapters of *A Portrait*."[5]

The critic also suggests that the forces of "darkness" are usually, as in the instance of Rabbi Maimonides, associated with the Jews, and cites, as another example, Mr. Deasy's remark that the Jews "sinned against the light" (28). Stephen's somewhat surprising "affinity for darkness" is manifest both in his appearance and in his thoughts. In mourning for his mother, he wears dark clothes, and while conducting an imaginary conversation with an imaginary female companion he notes that his darkness goes beyond the mere surface: "You find my words dark. Darkness is in our souls do you not think?" (40).

When a dark Jew—Bloom is also wearing mourning clothes, for later that morning he has to go to Paddy Dignam's funeral—makes his appearance in the fourth chapter of *Ulysses,* a perceptive reader is well prepared for the event. He is equally prepared to learn that before the day is over, this Jew is going to wander all over Dublin. Darkness and wandering are quite connected, at least according to Mr. Deasy: "They sinned against the light, Mr Deasy said gravely. And you can see the darkness in their eyes. And that is why they are wanderers on the earth to this day" (28). A reader might further expect that, like Maimonides, dark Bloom would "flash . . . in [his] mocking mirror the obscure soul of the world." But here he would be wrong because, ironically, Bloom is mostly body.

In a conversation with Stephen later that day, Bloom, in fact, shows a bit of uncertainty about what "the soul" actually means: "You as a good catholic, he observed, talking of body and soul, believe in the soul. Or do you mean the intelligence, the brainpower as such, as distinct from any outside object, the table, let us say, that cup" (518). In his hesitancy in formulating the meaning of the word "soul," which parallels Stephen's lack of familiarity with his own body, Bloom is supposed to be a truer representative of his ancient tribe than Rabbi Maimonides, for he is one of those numerous Jews the likes of whom Stephen saw in Paris: "Their eyes knew their years of wandering and, patient, knew the dishonours of their flesh" (28). Joyce emphasizes further Bloom's patience with "the dishonours" of his flesh through a subtle use of the Eucharistic image, making sure that, unlike Stephen, who is a heavy drinker (Christ's "blood and ouns"), Bloom should be interested primarily in food (Christ's "body"), with an occasional exception for "a good burgundy which he was a staunch believer in" (503) merely to enhance his meals. "I am a stickler for solid food," Bloom explains to Stephen towards the end of the day in the cabman's shelter. "You ought to eat more solid food. You would feel a different man." To which Stephen, whose teeth are in such bad shape that it is hard for him to chew, replies: "Liquids I can eat" (519).

It is not surprising therefore that the "Calypso" chapter opens with the famous description of Bloom's eating habits: "Mr Leopold Bloom ate with relish the inner organs of beasts and fowls. He liked thick giblet soup, nutty gizzards, a stuffed roast heart, liverslices fried with crust-crumbs, fried hencod's roes. Most of all he liked grilled mutton kidneys which gave to his palate a fine tang of faintly scented urine" (45). Food is obviously Bloom's passion and the reader gets a double exposure to his gastronomic tastes at each meal: he plans his meals as deliberately as he eats them. One could even say that Bloom is quite an artist (Joyce-like) at conceptualizing his feasts, but here we may run the same risk of overstretching the word's meaning as some critics do when they define Mrs. Ramsay's fine cooking as artistry. If Bloom is an "artist"—"There's a touch of the artist about old Bloom," says C. P. M'Coy (193)—he, like Mrs. Ramsay, is not one because of food.

Thus Ellmann notes, for example, that Bloom's attempt "to try jotting down on my cuff what [Molly] said dressing" (56) reveals "a crude resemblance to the inch-by-inch naturalism which Stephen Dedalus at moments practices, and also to the jumpiness of the internal monologue."[6] The method is also reminiscent of Stephen's (and Joyce's) epiphanies, the written records of memorable language and scenes, even though they were more professionally done and written not on cuffs but on "green oval leaves" (34). William Schutte finds Bloom's artistic touch not in anything he wrote or tried to write but in his very personality:

> What are the qualities traditionally required of the literary artist? An interest in words and in language, certainly. . . . Keen perception of events and of meanings which underlie them. . . . Compassion for his fellow men and an understanding of the nature of their strength and weaknesses. And finally, architectonic skill, the ability to shape his perception with the aid of the "right" words into a unified and meaningful whole. This last skill Bloom manifestly does not have. . . . But . . . he is as keenly interested in words as Stephen, his perceptions about the world around him are usually penetrating and often unconventional, and his compassion encompasses not only his acquaintances but all mankind.[7]

And not only "all mankind," one should add, but also the animal world: cats, "a dog (breed unknown) with a lame paw" (537), gulls, horses.

Schutte, however, overlooks another important artistic quality that

Bloom possesses in full: the Keatsian "sympathetic imagination." In the "Lestrygonians" episode, after revealing "compassion for his fellow men" by helping a blind man across the street, Bloom actually closes his eyes to find out what it feels like not to see: "With a gentle finger he felt ever so slowly the hair combed back above his ears. Again. Fibres of fine straw. Then gently his finger felt the skin of his right cheek. Downy hair there too. . . . Want to try in the dark to see. . . . Poor fellow! Quite a boy. Terrible" (149). As Mrs. Ramsay's tendency to exaggerate can reveal certain artistic inclinations, so Bloom's desire to get into someone else's skin points to an artist's mentality. Another important artistic attribute in Bloom is his knack for observing little details—a capability that Stephen lacks, at least temporarily, if he has indeed broken his glasses. But Schutte is quite right in emphasizing Bloom's deficiency in the most important professional skill of shaping the material of his observation into a literary form. The only character in *Ulysses* who is likely to become a *real* artist is, of course, not Bloom but Stephen. And yet, as many critics rightly indicate, it is only through the communion with Bloom's cruder yet more humane artistic sensibility that Stephen can reach that goal. Only by adding Bloom's experienced body to his sophisticated soul can Stephen eventually become a Joyce.

While Joyce's fictional presentation of his selves thus appears to be similar to Goncharov's, inasmuch as Joyce also relies almost wholly on two interacting characters to embody the complementary sides of his personality (as opposed to Woolf's more complex schema and little physical interaction), it is worthwhile to pursue the comparison further. Goncharov was also quite realistic in having accepted the splits in his personality as a necessary evil. But whereas Goncharov projects a strong note of regret over the inevitable loss of idealism that comes with maturity, Joyce, by the time he was wrapping up *Ulysses,* did not lament much the loss of his youthful dreams. "I live in soul and body," Joyce wrote in his notes to *Exiles* in 1914 (*E,* 118), but as he was progressing with his novel body seems to have been taking over. "I took Homer's work and placed in its framework my nice little people, with their bodies and souls. Their bodies—*Ulysses* is more an epic of the body than of the human spirit," he reportedly explained to Jan Parandowski.[8] He also put it in a similar way to Budgen: "Among other things . . . my book is the epic of the human body. . . . In my book the body lives in and moves through space and is the home of a full human personality" (*MU,* 21).

Bloom is "a full human personality" or a "complete man," as Joyce characterized his protagonist (and Homer's Odysseus) (*MU,* 16), because he is not just a son but also a father, not just an inexperienced boy with an abstract notion of love but a husband and a lover—and Joyce appears to have preferred this portrait of the artist as a complete man to a portrait of the artist as a young man. The writers' different attitudes toward their lost illusions consequently affected the roles their dual fictional selves play in the novels. In *A Common Story* young Aleksandr Aduev remains the unchallenged hero of the novel while the mature Piotr's role is largely secondary; in *Ulysses* the narration also opens with a younger alter ego but then the mature Bloom takes over the book in "Calypso" and never really relinquishes his grip on it.

"I have just got a letter asking me why I don't give Bloom a rest," he confided to Budgen as the novel was serialized in the *Little Review.* "The writer of it [Ezra Pound] wants more Stephen. But Stephen no longer interests me to the same extent. He has a shape that can't be changed" (*MU,* 105). Bloom was in many ways an ideal character for Joyce. Bloom's mature body is obviously more capable of change than Stephen's youthful soul, which even a wish of his dying mother could not "bend" (9). Furthermore, a wandering Jew naturally has to be more flexible in a largely hostile environment than an Irishman as yet living in his own country. Like Woolf's Lily Briscoe, who by virtue of being an outsider and a painter is a natural observer, Bloom, whom most Gentiles will forever consider a foreigner even though he was born in their country and even baptized, is also a perfect spectator and can be an amused commentator on the culture and civilization from which neither Stephen nor young Joyce could be sufficiently detached.

But there is much more to Bloom's being Jewish than that. First, there is an interesting connection between Jews and "egotism" that was developed by Stanislaus Joyce in his Dublin diary and that Joyce, in the habit of reading his brother's journal without his permission, undoubtedly read: "[The Jews] were the original egoists and from them men have learnt the first principles of a religion which their masculine energy has pushed to such admirable excesses. . . . They have a talent for living on the surface and yet being happy" (*CDD,* 114). Secondly, and more importantly, Bloom also appears to embody Jewish emotionalism as opposed to Stephen's largely Greek rationalism:

> [Jews and Irish] were alike, [Joyce] declared, in being impulsive, given to fantasy, addicted to associative thinking, wanting in rational discipline. He held, perhaps with Arnold's 'Hebraism and Hellenism' in mind, that there were two basically different ways of thinking, the Greek and the Jewish, and that the Greek was logical and rational. One day he and Weiss [Joyce's Jewish friend in Zurich] were walking and met a Greek, with whom they talked for a long time. Afterwards Joyce remarked, 'It's strange—you spoke like a Greek and he spoke like a Jew.' (*JJ,* 395)[9]

One does not have to be overly perceptive to realize that Joyce's juxtaposition along the lines of "rational" and "impulsive" thinking is but a variation on the same old mind/heart, rational/emotional conflict which, when couched in its traditional terms, Joyce refused to accept as a meaningful dichotomy. Curiously enough, Goncharov also had pet ideas about different nationalities embodying rationality and emotionalism as their national traits. Like Joyce, he identified impulsiveness and lack of systematic thinking with his own people (Aleksandr Aduev, Oblomov) while logic and rationality were attributes of the English (Aduev Sr. is an Anglophile) and the German (Shtolz in *Oblomov*). But unlike Goncharov who, in the somewhat exaggerated "romantic" fashion, lumped impulsive thinking and idealism together in one category and rational thought and pragmatism in the other, Joyce draws a distinction between rationality and pragmatism: thus he makes Stephen a rationalist *and* an idealist, and it is the largely impulsive Bloom who truly embodies pragmatism and common sense.

In a recent article, Gordon Tweedie has suggested that there was "a creative contradiction in the character of Joyce himself, between his negative attitude towards ordinary common sense and his stated belief that ordinary, commonplace experience is a proper subject for art, between the abstract idealism implied by his notations on esthetics and the practicality, the *pragma* of art-making, between his early refutation of the worth of pragmatic thinking and its appearance in his own mature work" (his emphasis).[10] As we all know by now, Joyce was full of contradictions, and Tweedie's observation rings quite true. And yet, as Tweedie himself indirectly implies by associating Bloom's pragmatism not with any garden variety but with William James's, Joyce's apparent ambivalence may be a reflection of the ambivalence in the term itself.

Thus for Goncharov "pragmatism" obviously meant a "practical approach to life," and, as was discussed earlier, he would have definitely preferred to remain an idealist for the rest of his life were it not for the "hostile" world which, he felt, doomed him to either become a "realist" or perish. Therefore for him pragmatism was the reverse of idealism simply because he assumed that, like himself, most pragmatists were but disillusioned idealists. But Joyce's more "modern" mind discerned different nuances of pragmatism. There was the pragmatism of William James to which Joyce appears to have objected for philosophical reasons because he believed, whether rightly or wrongly, that it directly opposed idealism by "show[ing] the absurdity of pure thought" (*CW,* 135). There was also, he thought, a "vulgar" common sense of the "crowd" striving towards loss of identity, conformity, and compromise as means of safe existence—and this kind of pragmatism he definitely loathed. "He dreaded the sea that would drown his body and the crowd that would drown his soul," Joyce wrote in his Trieste Notebook (*WD,* 95).

Yet Bloom's pragmatism, in my opinion, is neither Jamesian nor that of the crowd. It is also not the pragmatism of a disillusioned idealist. In Joyce's eyes, Bloom may be pragmatic for the same reason for which he is emotional—simply because he is a Jew. It is, after all, a rather common stereotype that Jewishness and practicality go hand in hand. What may have made this "Jewish" brand of pragmatism attractive to Joyce was that despite having to compromise in order to survive, Jews, by the virtue of their different religion and appearance, could still never totally conform and be assimilated by or "drowned" in an alien crowd. To Joyce that capability of bending without breaking, of living in a crowd yet being distinct, was a positive sign of completeness and maturity both in Bloom and, I believe, in his older self.

Joyce's identification of the youthful side of his personality with the Greeks does not come as a surprise: after all it is mostly in Aristotelian terms that young Joyce thought about his soul, and Joyce never stopped viewing ancient Greece as "the most cultured nation."[11] But Joyce's identification of his more mature, pragmatic, emotional, and "bodily" side with the Jews is less readily explainable. He came from a country where Jews were extremely rare for the simple reason that, as Mr. Daisy points out, Ireland "never let them in" (30). Though Ireland, like the rest of Great Britain, had but few Jews, it had a strong tradition of anti-Semitism, which is dutifully reflected on the pages of *Ulysses* in virtually everyone's reaction to Bloom. Yet as early as 1906 Joyce already had a cuckolded Dublin Jew in mind for a protagonist, and in his letters home kept asking his relatives for newspapers with articles pertaining to Irish Jews, like the ones about Mr. Harris, the jeweler whose non-Jewish wife, accused by her husband of adultery, was seeking divorce from him on the grounds of cruelty (*L,* II, 194), or Alfred H. Hunter, who, although not a Jew, was believed to be one, and who was also rumored to have an unfaithful wife (*L,* II, 168). We can only speculate, of course, as to how Joyce developed his interest in Jews. It may have been the combination of a rebellious reaction against the mentality that surrounded him and his feeling of being a foreigner in his own country: "A strange place this is to me," Joyce wrote to Nora in 1909 when visiting Ireland, "though I was born in it and bear one of its old names" (*SL,* 179). As Marilyn Reizbaum succinctly sums it up, in Joyce's eyes the Jew, because of his "condition and . . . nature . . . had contained within him all the ambiguities which Joyce perceived in himself: exile, wanderer, assimilator, achiever, survivor, equally at home and a stranger in every country in the world."[12]

But Joyce probably also associated his fictional "body" with Jews because his real body often lusted after their women. His attraction could have initially stemmed from the same combination of early intense feelings for the Virgin Mary as the prototype for all mothers and his own desire for motherly protection in the women he was attracted to. That is at least what a letter he sent to Marthe Fleischmann (with Greek "ε's" and all), whom he erroneously took for a Jew, seems to imply: "If I am wrong, you must not be offended. Jesus Christ put on his human body in the womb of a Jewish woman" (*L,* II, 432). In Trieste, soon before World War I broke out, he fell in love with his young Jewish student, who became the subject of his reflections in a notebook now known as *Giacomo Joyce.* He describes her as "[r]ounded and ripened: rounded by the lathe of intermarriage and ripened in the forcing-house of the seclusion of her race" (*GJ,* 2), and attributes to her people "owl's eyes and owl's wisdom" (*GJ,* 8). Through his attraction to the girl, whose identity is not quite clear,[13] Joyce seems to have come one step further to identifying himself with Jews. He went to the Jewish cemetery in Trieste and was struck by the specter of what he thought (not altogether correctly) was the Jewish refusal to believe in the afterlife: "Corpses of Jews lie about rooting in the mould of their holy field. . . . The tomb of her people and hers: black stone, silence without hope: and all is ready. Do not die!" (*GJ,* 6). His own rejection of the Christian notion of the soul's immortality must have made him feel as much "without hope" as he thought Jews were, and his desperate cry "Do not die!" was most likely addressed not only to the young girl he cared for, but also to himself.[14]

In the best Aristotelian tradition of the inseparability of the soul and the body, "Greek" Stephen and Jewish Bloom are almost supernaturally interlinked from the very beginning of the novel. Thus, like Cam and Lily, Bloom and Stephen regularly "antiphone" (Joyce's verb, 169), and on occasion they do so even before they meet face to face. Stephen, for example, reflects on the water from Cock (a real name) Lake which "flows purling, widely flowing, floating foampool, flower unfurling" in "Proteus" (41), and Bloom echoes him in "Lotus-Eaters" while anticipating his own "cock" lake in the foamy bath: "[Bloom] saw the dark tangled curls of his bush floating, floating hair of the stream around the limp father of thousands, a languid floating flower" (71). But in *Ulysses* the instances of the protagonists' echoing each others' thoughts are spread much further apart than in *To the Lighthouse* and also sustained throughout the whole novel. Thus they both think of death and ghosts, Hamlet and Shakespeare, Aristotle (in Bloom's case, the "pseudo Aristotle" of *Aristotle's Masterpiece,* a mild bit of pornography dating from the seventeenth century), AE, foot and mouth disease, and so forth.

There are further examples of the strong telepathic connection between Joyce's characters already after they meet. At one point Bloom literally reads his younger companion's mind. It occurs when, in the middle of their conversation about Mulligan, Stephen falls silent, his "mind's eye being too busily engaged in repicturing his family hearth the last time he saw it with his sister sitting by the ingle . . . waiting for some weak Trinidad shell cocoa . . . so that she and he could drink it with the oatmealwater for milk after the Friday herrings they had eaten at two a penny with an egg apiece for Maggy, Boody and Katey. . . ." Stephen's family's lack of food has not come up in their conversation prior to Stephen's thoughts (although Bloom is obviously aware of their situation, having seen one of Stephen's sisters auctioning off the remnants of their furniture and books earlier in the day), yet Bloom's next remark about Mulligan appears to be a direct response to Stephen's recollections: "He knows which side his bread is buttered on though in all probability he never realised what it is to be without regular meals" (507).

If Nabokov is right, "on the night of 15 June to 16 June, Stephen Dedalus in his tower at Sandycove, and Mr. Bloom in the connubial bed in his house on Eccles Street" even "dream the same dream."[15] A similar one, at any rate—both have an Oriental motif. It is more likely, as Nabokov and Stuart Gilbert point out,[16] that Stephen dreams a prophetic dream, anticipating the appearance in his life of Bloom and Molly: "That man led me, spoke. I was not afraid. The melon he had he held against my face. . . . That was the rule, said. In. Come. Red carpet spread. You will see who. . . . With woman steps she followed. . . . Spoils slung at her back. . . . When night hides her body's flaws. . . ." (39).

When Bloom, after running into Stephen and observing him closely the whole afternoon, finally finds himself later in a position to take care of young Dedalus, he obviously makes the most out of the situation. At one point, as he stands guard over Stephen's drunken, prostrate body in Nighttown, the older man lifts his eyes and beholds the vision of his late son, Rudy, who, by his presence, seems to sanctify Bloom's new fatherly relationship to Stephen. That Stephen is drunk and thus almost as helpless as a baby, or as Rudy was before he died, makes Bloom's parental role so much more likely, and Stephen at first appears to follow the older man around rather obediently, obviously relieved that someone is making all the decisions for him. Bloom pours out all the paternal care he cannot exercise on the son he lost eleven years ago. He lectures Stephen on the dangers of liquor and prostitutes, saves Stephen's money by making sure he does not leave it all in the brothel, protects him from the ire of Bella Cohen and the two privates on the street, takes him to a cabman's shelter for coffee, worries about his poor eating habits ("The melon he had he held against my face," with obvious sexual overtones in "the melon"), and, finally, brings him home to Eccles Street ("In. Come. Red carpet spread"). He even urges Stephen to spend the night and seems to contemplate, among other things, a professional as well as sexual liaison between the younger character and Molly ("That was the rule, said. . . . You will see who"). If that smacks of incest—Molly, being the wife of Stephen's surrogate father, is, after all, his surrogate mother—the incestuous overtones are fully intended; Joyce, as was mentioned earlier, often fantasized about being taken back into the motherly "womb."

In the "Circe" episode, Lynch's "cap" makes the following comment on Bloom meeting Stephen: "Jewgreek is greekjew. Extremes meet" (411). Extremes did meet in Joyce: his "sonhood" blended into his "fatherhood," his soul apparently learned to live with his body, and his "Greek" and "Jewish" sides meshed. Joyce felt it was through his experience with Nora that he discovered the parts of himself that were dormant while he was young. He discovered his body because it longed after hers, he developed the impulsive "Jewish" side because strong feelings defy rationality, he became a father because she bore his children. Joyce believed in reconciliation of the extremes: he loved Blake for his ability to marry Heaven and Hell and he admired Bruno for the same reason. "Giordano Bruno . . . says," Joyce wrote in 1912, "that every power, whether in nature or in the spirit, must create an opposite power, without which it cannot fulfill itself, and he adds that in each such separation there is a tendency toward reunion" (*JJP,* 20).

It is very tempting to interpret the novel along the same lines, as the "opposite powers" reuniting, as Bloom and Stephen blending first into "Stoom . . . Blethen" (558) and then into their creator. After all, while it is important to know that Stephen and Bloom are Joyce's own age in 1904 and 1920 respectively, it is equally important to realize that the sixteen years that separate Bloom (and the mature Joyce) from Stephen (and the young Joyce) are the sixteen years of marriage (Molly and Bloom were married in 1888). The action in the novel takes place on June 16, 1904 (188), which, of course, was the date Joyce took his first walk with Nora. It was that "sacred day," Ellmann tells us, "that divided Stephen Dedalus, the insurgent youth, from Leopold Bloom, the complaisant husband" (*JJ,* 156).

This interpretation is so much more attractive because Molly obviously bears a strong resemblance to Joyce's perception of Nora. Even Molly's Spanish blood brings her close in Joyce's mind to his own Galway-born Irish wife. "The lazy Dubliner," wrote Joyce, referring to himself in an article for an Italian newspaper about Ireland, "who travels little and knows his own country only by hearsay, believes that the inhabitants of Galway are descendants of Spanish stock, and you can't go four steps . . . without meeting the true Spanish type . . ." (*CW,* 229). But most importantly, in Joyce's mind Nora and Molly shared the bare essence of what to him constituted a "woman": "body of white, a flute alive" (234) and womb. The latter is prominent among Bloom's fleeting thoughts right before he falls asleep next to Molly's warm body, having quite reconciled himself to her marital transgressions, secure in the thought that others come and go yet he can share her bed "till death do us part": "Womb? Weary? He rests. He has travelled" (606).

As was mentioned earlier, Joyce's notion of women was not particularly enlightened. In his notes to *Exiles,* for example, he warned an actor who was to play Richard Rowan that the character "must not appear as a champion of woman's right. His language at times must be nearer to that of Schopenhauer against women and he must show at times a deep contempt for the long haired, short-legged sex" (*E,* 120). "After all," he wrote to Stanislaus soon after he eloped with Nora, "it is only Skeffington [Joyce's erstwhile friend and a convinced feminist], and fellows like him, who think that woman is man's equal" (*L,* II, 96).[17] "He knows nothing at all about women," Nora reportedly said of her husband to Samuel Beckett once, and she was most likely right.[18] Yet, for his own purposes, he knew about women as much as he needed. He was, after all, incurably self-centered, and all he had to know was how their presence affected *him.* Consequently, Molly's importance, too, lies largely in her impact on Bloom and her potential impact on Stephen, for it is through an experience with a Molly (or even Molly herself, as we are at times led to suspect by her husband) that Stephen too can become a "complete man"—a father, a husband, and also a cuckold.

There are numerous indications that Joyce *does* intend his fictionalized selves to "fuse." "[T]he ingredients will not fuse until they have reached a certain temperature," he wrote to Pound about his work on *Ulysses* in

1917 (unpublished, quoted in *JJ*, 416). At the end of "Eumaeus," as Stephen and Bloom are walking away from the cab which has brought them near Bloom's house, and the driver watches "the two figures . . . , both black, one full, one lean, walk towards the railway bridge, 'to be *married* by Father Maher'" (543, my emphasis), it appears that the right temperature is about to be reached.[19] The beginning of "Ithaca" develops the theme of the marriage of the "opposite powers" even further: we learn that while Bloom and Stephen represent two different temperaments, "The scientific. The artistic" (558), they take an interest in each other's special fields. Bloom is "sensitive to artistic impressions," Stephen is willing to converse on "the influence of gaslight or the light of arc and glowlamps on the growth of adjoining paraheliotropic trees" (544).[20]

We further learn that they were baptized by the same priest in the same church, and Bloom even recognizes in Stephen "the predestination of a future" (565). The theme of metempsychosis, or "transmigration of souls," as Bloom explains the word to Molly in the morning (52), is picked up again in connection with "Greek and Irish and Hebrew characters" (here "linguistic symbols" but the double meaning is intended) and Molly is shown to be the person who helps to bring all those different elements together: "In disoccupied moments she had more than once covered a sheet of paper with signs and hieroglyphics which she stated were Greek and Irish and Hebrew characters. . . . Unusual polysyllables of foreign origin she interpreted phonetically . . . : metempsychosis (met him pike hoses)" (562). Molly's interpretation makes more sense than appears at first: it is the "met him" part (Stephen meeting Bloom, Bloom, Stephen) that is all that matters in the metempsychosis taking place in the book. When Bloom is about to propose to Stephen that he spend the night in his house, he thinks of the "various advantages [that] would or might have resulted from a prolongation of such an extemporisation": "For the guest: security of domicile and seclusion of study. For the host: rejuvenation of intelligence, vicarious satisfaction. For the hostess: disintegration of obsession, acquisition of correct Italian pronunciation" (570). Here, in a nutshell, is exactly what, in Joyce's view, happened to him and Nora when his selves merged into one: for Joyce it was "security of domicile" and rejuvenated intelligence, enriched by carnal, not just spiritual, knowledge. For Nora, who assisted the fusion, the process meant "disintegration of obsession," that is, loss of her own virginity, and, interestingly enough, "acquisition of correct Italian pronunciation," for, having to elope, they went to Italy and for the rest of their lives spoke Italian at home to their children.

And yet, when invited to stay (and thus "fuse"), Stephen "[p]romptly, inexplicably, with amicability, gratefully" declines the offer (572), making readers like Budgen (and, among others, Hugh Kenner) believe that the protagonists "are like two ships bound for different ports that come within hail and disappear into the night" (*MU*, 259). The end of *Ulysses* thus appears to be not unlike that of *A Common Story* where the protagonists seem all but destined to merge into each other when, at the last moment, the uncle starts moving in a different direction. There is one important difference, though: where Goncharov's break appears quite final, Joyce's is but tentative. While Goncharov feels that a complete integration of conflicting parts is impossible, Joyce appears to suggest that the process is not instantaneous and needs (as it did in him) a "certain temperature" and time to take place. When we watch Stephen walking down Eccles Street "into the night," we cannot assume with Budgen that he is walking away from Bloom forever. He may be just taking a long walk that will eventually bring him back, the kind of walk Bloom has in mind when he says earlier in the novel: "Think you're escaping and run into yourself. Longest way round is the shortest way home" (309).

9

Ulysses as an Alternative to the Autobiographical Bildungsroman

Ulysses, like *To the Lighthouse,* reminds one of a play—in this case, very appropriately, a Greek one. It has three parts and at least two classical unities: that of place (Dublin) and of time (twenty-four hours). Like Woolf, Joyce believed in "moments of being" as the most meaningful measurement of time. "To him," Joyce wrote in 1912 about Blake, and, undoubtedly, about himself, "each moment shorter than a pulse-beat was equivalent in its duration to six thousand years, because in such an infinitely short instant the work of the poet is conceived and born" (*CW,* 222). Joyce became the first English writer to compress the action of a novel to twenty-four hours, and upon hearing of similar attempts (Woolf's *Mrs. Dalloway* and Louis Bromfield's *Twenty-Four Hours,* for example, appeared within five years of *Ulysses*) he used to remark: "The Prince of Wales seems to have passed through here," meaning that, like the Prince, he was a trendsetter.[1] He shared with Blake not only his sense of time but also his preoccupation with the themes of innocence and experience. In his autobiographical novel it was equally important for Joyce to record "an infinitely short instant" in the history of human lives and to reflect major stages of human development. In short, within the format of an un- or even anti-bildungsroman, Joyce wished to do what Bakhtin thought was possible only in traditional novels of education—to make "the hero himself . . . a variable."

One may actually argue that the dual protagonist of Joyce's non-bildungsroman, "Blephen-Stoom," becomes "a variable" to a much larger degree than Stephen Dedalus did alone in Joyce's earlier novel of education, for *Ulysses* replaces a few drastic developments within the one hero of *Por-*

trait with the more minute but also more numerous changes that the two deeply interconnected protagonists experience both independently and as a result of their connection. Furthermore, when Stephen Dedalus comes dangerously close to becoming "the ready-made hero" with the "shape that can't be changed," Joyce is much better equipped than he was in his previous novel to avoid the stasis by focusing on Stephen's more mature "double," whose nature and "shape" allow for more variety and flexibility. Having thus moved away from the monology of *Portrait* toward what Bakhtin might have called the "dialogism" of *Ulysses,* Joyce also gave himself more room to perfect his art of detachment.

Unlike *A Portrait of the Artist as a Young Man, Ulysses* does not feature lengthy and elaborate discussions on the essence of artistic distance. If anything, at one point it even lampoons Stephen's earlier treatment of the subject by presenting in Bloom a parody of "the God of creation . . . paring his fingernails." When Bloom sees Boylan from the carriage that is taking him and his companions to Dignam's funeral, he is anxious not to betray his feelings in front of the other men and attempts to "detach" himself from the painful subject: "Mr Bloom reviewed the nails of his left hand, then those of his right hand. The nails, yes. Is there anything more in him that they she [Molly] sees? Fascination. Worst man in Dublin. That keeps him alive. They sometimes feel what a person is. Instinct. But a type like that. My nails. I am just looking at them: well pared" (76). The trick does not work, and Bloom is, of course, obsessed with thoughts about Boylan and Molly for the rest of the day.

Whereas in *Portrait* Joyce appears to have interpreted Flaubert's invisible author too literally, many chapters of *Ulysses* do in fact have a strong authorial voice. Although the initial chapters of the novel are still dominated by Stephen's interior monologue, "Calypso" and "Lotus-Eaters" immediately transform the book into a dialogue. Furthermore, since almost every chapter after "Lotus-Eaters" has a different narrative strategy and often a whole set of different dramatized narrators, the narrative technique of *Ulysses* rapidly becomes not only "dialogic" but, to use Bakhtin's terminology once more, truly "polyphonous."

As we have seen in the previous chapter, Woolf performs a similar feat in *To the Lighthouse* by mixing the voices of her multiple internal narrators with the voice of the omniscient author. But Joyce's narrative arsenal in *Ulysses* is much larger than Woolf's. While his interior narrators (Stephen, Bloom, Molly, Gerty MacDowell, etc.) may be similar in number to Woolf's, he also adds scores of dramatized semiomniscient narrators mimicking particular literary and even musical styles (the various narrators in "Eumaneus," "Ithaca," "Aeolus," Cyclops," and "Sirens") and thus removes himself even further from the abundant autobiographical material that went into the construction of his novel.[2] All this "heteroglossia"[3] could create a total chaos if there were no larger authorial persona present in *Ulysses.*

David Hayman calls this larger authorial presence in the novel the "arranger" "to designate a figure who can be identified neither with the author nor with his narrators, but who exercises an increasing degree of overt control over his increasingly challenging materials."[4] Hayman's notion has been adopted and modified by many critics. Hugh Kenner, who likes to capitalize the word (the "Arranger") to emphasize his importance, discusses the Arranger's performance at length in both *Joyce's Voices* and *"Ulysses".*[5] Other critics prefer different designations: Sheldon Brivic, for example, describes that same authorial persona in Freudian/Lacanian terms as "the Other of *Ulysses,*"[6] and Weldon Thornton uses the term "Presenter" to stress that the figure's "authority extends only to form, not to content."[7] In a recent book, *"Ulysses" and Justice,* James McMichael even replaces the other critics' impersonal designations with the familiar "Jamesy" because, as he explains, "[i]t is a word that Molly Bloom may or may not be using to address the intelligence behind *Ulysses*" (as in "O Jamesy, let me up out of this pooh sweets of sin . . ." [*U,* 633]).[8] But regardless of the label the reader gives it, the supreme narrative authority in the novel is, of course, none other than Joyce's "God of creation," who is not merely evoked here, as he was in *Portrait,* but appears as an active force. He is that illusive Ariel-like spirit of *Ulysses* who, by pulling the right strings, is in full control of the narration done by his more visible agents, and he is that brilliant conductor who, while on an elevated podium with his back to the audience, successfully fuses each musician's individual effort into one harmonic whole.

Thus it seems to me that it is in *Ulysses* that Joyce fully reaches the "dramatic form," which was formulated by Stephen in *Portrait.* He does so by finally finding a proper vehicle for this supreme impersonal authority who can first disperse "the vitality which has flown and eddied round each person," and then "fill . . . every person with such vital force that he or she assumes a proper and intangible esthetic life." Having achieved this "esthetic life" and thus having become not only actors in their own story but also its heterogeneous narrators, Joyce's main protagonists and numerous narrators assist their creator in "refining" himself "out of existence" and advancing to the only place where, according to Joyce's belief, a true artist belongs—"behind or beyond or above his handiwork."

"*A Portrait of the Artist* necessarily precedes *Ulysses,*" writes J. H. Buckley in his article on English bildungsromane,[9] implying that the writer had to try his hand in a more traditional form and see for himself its strengths and weaknesses before he felt compelled to unleash his artistic daring any further. As this chapter has intended to show, it was largely by replacing the single autobiographical self of the earlier novel with the split autobiographical self of *Ulysses* that Joyce could make his new novel surpass *Portrait* both as autobiography and a truly "dramatic" literary "handiwork."

A man who died long ago to ordinary life may be forgiven a certain boldness. He, for whom the world is becoming an illusion, has greater rights. He, who has discovered a second reality in life, is beyond its laws . . .

Andrei Bely

10

Beyond Goncharov, Woolf, and Joyce: Co-Consciousness in *Don Quixote, Pamela,* and *Petersburg*

The purpose of this chapter is to probe the phenomenon of the autobiographical novel of co-consciousness further by exploring, albeit briefly, other works where one can find similar "divided-they-stand" fictional beings who represent their creators' autobiographies. On the surface, it may appear that there are quite a number of novels where more than one character shoulders the burden of the writer's "inner" or "outer" autobiography in an "active," seemingly co-conscious way. But the examples are not as numerous as one may think.

There are, to be sure, quite a few novels where autobiographical duality of some sort is strongly felt.[1] In American literature alone, for example, one can think of such obviously "dual" presentations as Faulkner's *The Sound and the Fury,* Fitzgerald's *The Great Gatsby,* Steinbeck's *Of Mice and Men,* Nabokov's *Ada,* and Cather's *My Ántonia.* Yet none of these works fit the pattern of the autobiographical novel of co-consciousness that I have tried to establish here in relation to Goncharov, Woolf, and Joyce.

To begin with, these novels do not feature "younger" and "older" selves who, in their totality, re-create not only the "inner" but also the "chronological," "changeable" autobiography of their creators. Instead, they present either brothers and sisters who are just a few years apart (*Ada, The Sound and the Fury*) or friends who are each other's contemporaries (*Of Mice and Men, The Great Gatsby, My Ántonia*). Furthermore, two of these novels—*The Great Gatsby* and *My Ántonia*—are also first-person renditions (as *The Sound and the Fury* is to a large extent, but there the narrative system is much more complex since we have several first-person narrators throughout the book and an impersonal third-person narrator at the very end), and the presence of one of the "divided selves" as the narrator of the book brings them closer to the numerous "simulated" autobiographies briefly discussed in chapter 3 (*David Copperfield,* for example) than to *A Common Story, To the Lighthouse,* or *Ulysses.*

The Sound and the Fury, The Great Gatsby, and *Of Mice and Men* are vastly different from *A Common Story, Ulysses,* and *To the Lighthouse* for yet another, and much more crucial, reason. Faulkner's, Steinbeck's, and Fitzgerald's "doubles" definitely belong to the more traditional "divided-they-fall" variety of the literary doppelgänger: Benjy's and Lennie's mental retardation, the disintegration of the whole Compson family, Quentin's suicide, and Jay Gatsby's rapid unraveling and eventual death are more than sufficient testimony to that. Describing his own mental breakdown in 1936, Fitzgerald alluded to the capacity "to hold two opposed ideas in the mind at the same time, and still retain the ability to function" as "a test of a first-rate intelligence."[2] It is obvious that, according to Fitzgerald's design in the novel, Nick Carraway and Jay Gatsby, while largely representing these "two opposed ideas," are *not* able to function in tandem and thus fail the test (as, Fitzgerald thought, he himself often did). Steinbeck develops this concept more dramatically while bringing it even closer to the classical stories of the doppelgänger by making a "rational" self (George) kill the "irrational" one (Lennie) because, like so many of its nineteenth-century literary counterparts, the irrational self has turned murderous. Needless to say, all this is very unlike what happens to the Aduevs, Cam and Lily, or Stephen and Bloom, who do not only survive the experience of their authors' fictional *Ichspaltung* but who also seek integration.

But while these American works are some examples of possible "dual" autobiographies that do *not* fit the Goncharov/Woolf/Joyce approach to inner duality, there are several novels I am aware of that fit the pattern much better, or come very close to fitting it. Among them are Cervantes' *Don Quixote,* Richardson's *Pamela,* and, most of all, Andrei Bely's *Petersburg.*

Don Quixote

There is a more-than-obvious duality in *Don Quixote,* and at least one critic, Marthe Robert, makes a strong and convincing case that Don Quixote and Sancho Panza are literary doubles who mirror the inner splits of Cervantes himself. Robert presents a complicated thesis of numerous doublings not only between the two characters but also within the two characters, yet she believes that the main split occurs along the lines of the "embarrassing flesh," or "the body" (Sancho) and the idealistic, artistic spirit (Quixote).

The critic draws a shrewd distinction between the classical tradition of the double and Cervantes' use of the theme. She points out that Cervantes presents us not with an "academic quarrel where purely allegorical figures are assigned stereotypical roles" but with a "very real, agonizing, and largely insoluble conflict divided among various characters so that it can be seen from every possible angle." Robert also gives a formulation of Cervantes' approach to duality that is very similar to my attempt to define the phenomenon of co-consciousness in Goncharov, Woolf, and Joyce. According to her, in *Don Quixote* we can see "contradictory tendencies, deep-rooted and equally active, which can neither suppress nor mutually accept each other, and therefore ask us to respect them together and, if possible, to set them free."[3]

We should not, however, exaggerate the similarities that exist between the techniques used by Cervantes and the three writers in this study. While he did appear to have shared their belief in "the mystery of the conscious" or co-consciousness, Cervantes stops short of putting his coactive doubles to the same *artistic* use. Thus Don Quixote and Sancho Panza do *not* represent the developmental stages of the changeable protagonist; furthermore, they are still rather "extreme" (even if not "allegorical") embodiments of their "stereotypical roles" and as such create only a grotesque and exaggerated form of Cervantes' autobiography. One can obviously argue that so are the Aduevs—yet the two never really reach the same level of caricature that Cervantes' characters do.[4]

Sancho and Don Quixote are also not sufficiently independent of each other to be comparable to the Aduevs, Cam and Lily, or Stephen and Bloom. While it is true that, like Sancho, Piotr Aduev and Cam Ramsay are not as fully developed as their counterparts, they are, nevertheless, independent characters who have definite fictional lives of their own. As Vladimir Nabokov points out in *Lectures on Don Quixote,* Sancho often "only plays up to his master," and when the two characters get separated in the second part of the book, "[t]he switches are very crude, as the author shuttles self-consciously between Sancho's island and Don Quixote's castle, and it is a positive relief to everybody concerned—authors, characters, and reader—when the two get together again and revert to their natural knight-and-squire combination."[5]

Pamela

Even though *Pamela* is a first-person narrative, being largely an epistolary novel, it differs from other "simulated" autobiographies mentioned here (such as Defoe's *Robinson Crusoe* and Sterne's *Tristram Shandy*) by the strong presence of the "arranger," who, for most part, stays hidden behind the scenes but makes sure that Pamela's point of view is not necessarily the only one by including the letters of others within her own. Pamela also functions as a convenient (although not very plausible) agent of a hidden omniscient author by recording verbatim all her conversations with Mr. B. The effect of all of this manipulation is that even though Pamela still predominates the narration, Mr. B. achieves a perceivable voice of his own.

Pamela (as well as *Clarissa*) may be as much about androgyny as it is about morality. The best characterization of the nature of duality in *Pamela* belongs to Ian Watt, who described it as "a work that could be praised from the pulpit and yet attacked as pornography, a work that gratified the reading public with the combined attractions of a sermon and a striptease."[6] The same description can obviously fit *Clarissa*. The real difference between the two novels lies in how Richardson manipulates the conflict between the two opposing genders and their different attitudes towards sex. In *Pamela* there is a clear-cut reconciliation of the opposites that leads to a marriage; in *Clarissa* the same conflict is not resolved and leads to the heroine's death. Between the two of them, *Pamela* and *Clarissa* present two contrary approaches to duality: that of integration (or "divided-they-stand") and that of disintegration (or "divided-they-fall"). Since *Clarissa* was written several years after *Pamela,* one could assume that Richardson moved from one view to the other, but it is equally plausible, it seems to me, that his views constantly alternated.

How much of this tension between the two attitudes toward sexuality is Richardson's own is an open question, since we simply do not know as much about his life and innermost thoughts as we do about Joyce's, Woolf's, or even Goncharov's. But many critics do note what one of them recently labeled as Richardson's "almost instinctive association with women."[7] Watt, for one, believes that Richardson's "deep personal identification with the opposite sex . . . went far beyond social preference or cultural rapport."[8] Some critics also suggest that in an act of such "deep personal identification" with Clarissa Harlowe the writer may have even given this character his own birthday—July 24.[9] In *Pamela,* there are also interesting incidents of cross-gender dressing which are markedly distinct from those in, say, Shakespeare's plays, where women usually dress as men, in that Richardson's novels feature male protagonists who dress as women in order to deceive and thus seduce the heroines. It is not my intention here to speculate on the nature of Richardson's sexuality, but I do believe that it is logical to suppose that at least a part of the conflict he depicts in both *Pamela* and *Clarissa* points back to his own personality, given the extraordinary dualism of his novels and what little we do know about his life.

This reaction seems even more justified when we realize that for Richardson the conflict between the "feminine" and "masculine" notions of sexuality is a part of a larger conflict between one's body (usually represented by nonvirginal men) and one's soul (mostly represented by female virgins, who are supposedly not driven by the whims of their flesh, yet since Richardson apparently believed that virginity prior to marriage was almost as desirable in men as it was in women, it is quite possible that a virgin of either sex could be the embodiment of "soul"[10]). In this *Pamela* can be seen as a novel that highlights the same tension as *Ulysses,* and, to a lesser extent, *Don Quixote.* It does not take any stretch of the imagination to assume that, like Joyce and Cervantes, Richardson was no stranger to that particular duality.

As with *Don Quixote,* however, we should not exaggerate the similarities that may exist between *Pamela* and the novels by Goncharov, Woolf, and Joyce. Even if Pamela and Mr. B. do contain two reconciled halves of their androgynous creator, the "changeable" quality of the protagonist is still not present here since the characters do not represent the writer's "younger" and "older" selves, unless we choose to interpret Richardson's references to the "shyness and bashfulness" of his youth as somehow connected with the same qualities in Pamela.[11] Despite managing to acquire his own individual voice against the odds of a one-person narrative, Mr. B. still remains much less developed than Pamela. His role in the novel is in fact quite similar to that of Sancho in *Don Quixote* inasmuch as he is Pamela's constant consort (undesired during sinful pursuits but quite welcomed after marriage) and only acts in connection with her.

Petersburg

Bely's *Petersburg,* which is often compared with Joyce's *Ulysses* and which was first published several years prior to it in 1916,[12] is close to Joyce's novel not only in its strong modernist tendencies and its depiction of a big city but also in its treatment of inner duality. Like Woolf, Bely attributed his duality to heredity. He was the only child of the prominent Moscow mathematician Nikolai Bugaev, who was a strong proponent of rational thought, and of a highly emotional and artistically inclined mother. Kenneth M. Brostrom's description of the possible influence of his parents on Bely is a good summary of Bely's own reflections on the subject: "A precocious, impressionable child, Bely was often both victim and prize in family frays, as his loving and possessive parents sought to shape him in their own image. As an adult Bely was both quirky and capable of sustained, concentrated labor, both emotionally volatile and intellectually gifted, in many ways a predictable and yet altogether unusual amalgam of these parental impresses."[13] His parents' inability to reconcile their differences and enjoy their marriage also probably resulted in Bely's skepticism about the possibility of "human," as opposed to "divine," reconciliation.

The Ableukhovs, father and son of *Petersburg,* embody between the two of them many of the conflicts that Bely perceived both in himself and in Russian society as a whole (the novel takes place in 1905). Despite the highly sophisticated nature of Bely's text—and I will obviously not be able to do full justice to it here since I am going to concentrate on just the contours of one major theme in the novel—his juxtapositions are often stark and simple, and in that it is even closer to Goncharov's than to Joyce's or Woolf's. Thus Ableukhov Sr., who is "head of a Government Institution"[14] as well as a senator, is a strong supporter of the political status quo. His son Nikolai Apollonovich, a lapsed university student, is (or rather thinks he is) a sympathizer with the radical left. Ableukhov Sr. shares with his obvious literary and real-life predecessors, Aleksei Karenin, Piotr Aduev, and Bely's own father,[15] a belief in moderation and common sense. His son is highly emotional, considers himself "a truly creative being" (28), and is given to wild mood swings. Apollon Apollonovich (who also inherited Gogol's Akakii Akakievich as his literary predecessor) is always particular about his dress and wears well-cut European suits. Nikolai spends his lazy mornings in his "oriental drawing room," wearing "Tartar slippers" and "a Bukhara dressing gown" (27). Apollon Ableukhov likes "proportionality and symmetry" (10) as well as closed spaces and straight lines. Nikolai Ableukhov prefers the infinity of the universe of which he deems himself to be "the sole center . . . conceivable and inconceivable" (28).

Like the Aduevs, however, the Ableukhovs are from the very beginning as remarkably similar as they are pointedly different. They both feel abandoned by the same woman, Anna Petrovna, Apollon's wife and Nikolai's mother, who, like her famous literary namesake and propagator, ran off with another man, leaving a husband and a son behind. (In Anna Ableukhov's case, the man was not a Russian aristocrat but an Italian singer.) Both father and son surround themselves with satin, probably reminiscent of Anna Ableukhov's silky dresses: Apollon in his womblike carriage, Nikolai in his womblike bedroom. We also learn that "Nikolai Apollonovich, just like Apollon Apollonovich, talked to himself. His movements were abrupt, like his papa's movements. Like Apollon Apollonovich, he was distinguished by an unprepossessing stature and by restless eyes set in a smiling face" (27). In short, the father and the son are virtual twins. Toward the end of the novel Apollon, just like Piotr Aduev before him, begins to lose faith in his old ways, retires, and—probably accepting the "wild," "Asian" part of his complicated Russian heritage (his great-great-grandfather was, after all, Mirza Ab-Lai of the Kirghiz-Kaisak Horde)—even starts wearing a "tattered dressing gown" (240) that is not unlike his son's "Bukhara" one.[16]

The plot appears to be an obvious play on the theme of the double. Because of his left-wing sympathies, Nikolai gets involved in a plot to kill an important government official who turns out to be his father. Nikolai eventually decides against killing his father: blood is thicker than the veneer of radicalism that he has so fashionably acquired. In fact, since his father is obviously his second (and in many ways much truer) self, for Nikolai patricide may amount to suicide. But, as Bely seems to be implying, each of us must bear at least some consequences for our beliefs, no matter how thin or fleeting, and therefore before Nikolai can get rid of the bomb with which he is supposed to kill his father, Apollon, being, after all, Nikolai's alter ego, acts for him. He carries the bomb, hidden in a sardine tin, to his study, the one place where he can almost always be found, thus making sure Nikolai will fulfill his original promise to the terrorists. But fate is merciful, and the explosion fails to kill Apollon Ableukhov.

After the explosion, Nikolai and his father never see each other again: while Nikolai lies unconscious, Apollon leaves for the country and arranges a passport for his son to go abroad. Nikolai, we are told at the end of the last chapter, "did not return to Russia until the demise of his father" (290). This is not, however, the end of the novel. The epilogue places us within the period that occurred between Nikolai's departure and his father's death. In a technique reminiscent of Woolf's and Joyce's, Bely shifts from one protagonist to the other, making them "antiphone." First we visit with Nikolai in "a coastal village near Tunis," where he is remembering and imagining his father. Then we find ourselves in a Russian countryside where Apollon Apollonovich, who is sitting in a room surrounded by oval family portraits, is "penning his memoirs." From there we go back to Nikolai who is already in Egypt, "sitting before the Sphinx," contemplating "the fate of Egypt in the twentieth century," and "doing research" (292). Next stop is the Russian countryside again, where the proud and almost totally senile father is trying to remember the title of the book Nikolai has just published. Nikolai, we are informed, is in

Nazareth. The very last segment of this "antiphony" takes us back to the future. It is 1913, Nikolai's parents are both dead, and he himself is said to have changed: "His voice had grown harsher. . . . His quickness of movement has disappeared. He lived all alone. He never invited anyone, and never visited anyone. He was seen in church. Of late he had been reading the philosopher Skovoroda" (293).

"We must resist a natural inclination to simplify," write Robert A. Maguire and John E. Malmstad in the introduction to their English translation of Bely's novel:

> We will not get very far if we succumb to the temptation . . . of assuming that Bely's world is built on a system of dualities that amounts to a set of viable alternatives: east/west, animate/inanimate, revolutionary/reactionary, present/past, Christ/Satan. . . . There are no real alternatives for Bely. Revolution and reaction are equally incompetent to deal with reality . . . ; east and west are so intermingled in the Russian character that they cannot possibly be separated; there is no meaningful division between present and past. . . . The most useful rhetorical model for this novel is not either/or, but both/and.[17]

And yet the critics who tell us to resist simplification appear to fall into the very same trap they warn the reader about when they tell us about the "reconciliation" that supposedly crowns the book: "In Chapter VIII, Anna Petrovna comes back to the Ableukhov household; the family is reunited; everything suggests that a fresh start is being made. . . . father and son experience true reconciliation."[18] But all that happens *prior* to the incident with the bomb, after which the "true reconciliation" probably goes up in the explosion's smoke. As in Goncharov's *A Common Story,* and, some would argue, in *Ulysses,* the two selves appear to be on the brink of merging into one—and yet something stops them short of doing so.

Like the other three writers, Bely does most likely believe in the possibility of some sort of eventual resolution; its nature, however, is significantly different from theirs. Bely's reconciliation is distinctly "divine"; it is achieved not due to the humans but mainly despite them. In Bely's system of beliefs one cannot really be both a "revolutionary" and a "reactionary," an "oriental" and a "European," or, like his parents, a pragmatist and an artist, unless a stronger superhuman force intervenes and merges all otherwise irreconcilable opposites into one universal "I-am-thee-and-thou-art-I" consciousness. For while Joyce never took theosophy seriously, Bely did.

He was an attentive student of both Helena Blavatsky and of Vladimir Solov'ev, a Russian turn-of-the-century religious philosopher who, like Blavatsky, believed that all cataclysms and conflicts would be eventually resolved by the "all-in-oneness" (*vseedinstvo*) of the divine consciousness. In 1912, while working on *Petersburg,* Bely turned to yet another similar religio-philosophical movement, Rudolf Steiner's anthroposophy, which began as an outgrowth of Madame Blavatsky's theosophy. Much of *Petersburg* is, in fact, colored by Bely's newly found affinity with Steiner's thought. It is in all probability the divine "cosmic" force of anthroposophy that creates the "antiphony" at the end of the novel and powerfully blends two divided consciousnesses into one. Bely's affinity with Steiner (and with Solov'ev and Blavatsky before him) also goes a long way toward explaining why in the epilogue Nikolai chooses to live such a solitary existence: in becoming a part of the larger consciousness around him which produces the only true *coincidentia oppositorum,* the protagonist is compelled to reject the "world [of] illusion" and accept, instead, "a second reality," which is "beyond [the] laws" of "ordinary life."[19]

Vladimir Alexandrov is definitely right when he suggests that "[a]n awareness of Steiner's influence on *Petersburg* adds weight to the argument against understanding the novel as a mere metaphor for Bely's own purely psychological quandaries."[20] We can still probably talk about the Ableukhovs as co-conscious literary characters who between them share many aspects of Bely's own autobiography, but we have to bear in mind that, unlike the Aduevs, Cam and Lily, or Stephen and Bloom—the creations of largely secular authors—Apollon and Nikolai Ableukhov, despite their occasional premonitions of the existence of the "second space" (93), are not sufficient in themselves to reconstruct an essential part of their creator's view of his "split" being—his "second reality." This "second reality" also affects the very core of the novel as an artifice: while Joyce and Woolf, and, to a certain extent, Goncharov, felt that in their works they were the ultimate "arrangers," or "Gods of creation," Bely thought that he was guided by a much higher creative force. Bely's profound belief in "cosmic" consciousness, the belief that found its way into the novel and influenced not only the actions of the protagonists but also the strategies of the narrator, creates a crucial difference between him and the other three writers. It was for that reason that in this book I did not choose to feature Andrei Bely together with Goncharov, Woolf, and Joyce as one of the "mainstream" practitioners of "the autobiographical novel of co-consciousness."

This being said, we should still be able to appreciate the similarities between Bely's uses of co-consciousness, limited as it may be in his case, and Goncharov's, Woolf's, and Joyce's. Like *Ulysses, To the Lighthouse,* and *A Common Story,* and unlike the other novels discussed in this chapter, *Petersburg* does feature an older and a younger self who can represent not only the psychological but also the chronological autobiography of the author. In 1912, when Bely was actively working on the novel, he was of course still a relatively young man of thirty-two and thus nowhere near the age of Ableukhov Sr. Yet being already in his thirties, the age that is conventionally associated with "maturity," the writer probably considered himself closer to the father than to the son, whose confused, turbulent, and rather juvenile love affair in the novel is modeled after young Bely's tortuous relationship with Liubov' Blok, which had also started in 1905 and which, by 1912, the writer was quite relieved to have largely behind him.

Conclusion

There are topics so huge and vague that one often wonders whether they should even be touched. Both duality and autobiography are among them. Yet when careful and craft-conscious writers approach vague and broad themes they inevitably mold them into discernible artistic shapes. *A Common Story, To the Lighthouse,* and *Ulysses* are, in my opinion, obvious products of such skillful and consistent "molding," and it makes analyzing them a more palatable and rewarding task.

Goncharov, Woolf, and Joyce used their duality and autobiography to produce a highly controlled and original shape—an autobiographical novel where discordance is often viewed not only as unsettling ambiguity but also as richness. Their novels are no longer satisfied with the linear development of a traditional autobiographical bildungsroman; instead they opt for a more suggestive and more complex "in-the-beginning-is-my-end" circularity, even if this circularity is, as in Goncharov, quite vicious.

As with most autobiographies, whether fictional or nonfictional, *A Common Story, To the Lighthouse,* and *Ulysses* strive, to borrow Spengemann's description again, "to discover, through a fictive action, some ground upon which conflicting aspects of the writer's own nature might be reconciled in complete being." But in their case, the process of attempted reconciliation is more concrete and more graphic than in many other autobiographical novels. The physical presence of two characters who represent the "conflicting aspects," and the importance attached to their interaction or meeting, highlight both the process of reconciliation and its result. The protagonists are truly made to play out their creators' views on whether "complete being" is a mere phantom or reality.

I believe that the autobiographical novel of co-consciousness is a distinct genre of autobiographical fiction. It is not limited to Goncharov,

Woolf, and Joyce, but they did provide us with particularly masterful and discernible variants of this genre, and analyzing their works may make it easier to see similar tendencies in other fiction. In chapter 10 I attempted to take it beyond the three writers in this study but obviously did not even come close to exhausting all possible sources of literary co-consciousness. Thus several people who read the manuscript urged me to take a closer look at Thomas Mann, André Gide, and Christa Wolf. I could have also followed Marthe Robert's lead and examined duality not only in Cervantes but also in Franz Kafka. I am sure every reader of this book will have his or her candidates to add to this list. Yet I had to stop somewhere, lest the chaos of an impossibly broad and vague theme, which Goncharov, Woolf, and Joyce had so conveniently and accommodatingly "tamed" for my purposes, would engulf and consume me.

Notes

Introduction

1. Rosenfield, "The Shadow Within," 328.

2. Swift, *Gulliver's Travels,* 215–16, 214.

3. Bakhtin, *Speech Genres,* 21.

4. Freud, "The Relation of the Poet to Day-Dreaming," in *Collected Papers,* 4:180.

5. Rosenfield, "The Shadow Within," 326.

6. William Blake, "The Voice of the Devil," in "The Marriage of Heaven and Hell" (1793).

7. Joyce, *Ulysses,* 168.

8. D. H. Lawrence, "'The Grand Inquisitor' by F. M. Dostoievsky," in *Selected Literary Criticism,* 233–34.

9. Simon Lesser, *Fiction and the Unconscious,* 202.

10. These six identities are "Twin Brother," "Pursuer," "Tempter," "Vision of Horror," "Saviour," and "The Beloved." Keppler, *The Literature of the Second Self.*

11. Rogers's categories are "The Mirror Image," "The Secret Sharer," "The Opposing Self," and "Fair Maid and Femme Fatale." Rogers, *The Psychoanalytic Study of the Double in Literature.*

12. See, for example, Rank, *The Double: A Psychoanalytic Study,* and Guerard, "Concepts of the Double," in *Stories of the Double.*

13. See, for example, Wain, "The Double in Romantic Narrative," and Waldeck, *The Split Self from Goethe to Broch.*

14. Clifford Hallam, "Toward a Definition of Doppelgänger," in Crook, *Fearful Symmetry,* 12–13.

15. Waldeck's statement that "The split self in its broadest sense is universal in literature, yet at the same time only spottingly acknowledged in literary criticism" (*The Split Self,* 15) is typical in this respect.

16. Jung, *Modern Man in Search of a Soul,* 117.

Chapter 1

1. Belinsky, "Vzgliad na russkuiu literaturu 1847 goda," in Poliakov, *I. A. Goncharov v russkoi kritike,* 32. As noted in the Preface, all translations from Russian of primary and secondary sources are mine unless otherwise stated.

2. V. P. Ostrogorsky, in Pokrovsky, *Ivan Goncharov: ego zhizn' i sochineniia,* 358.

3. Tseitlin, *I. A. Goncharov,* 438. For other instances of the same view see, for example, Dmitry Merezhkovsky, "Goncharov," in *Polnoe sobranie sochinenii,* 18:33–57; Vsevolod Setchkarev's *Ivan Goncharov: His Life and His Works;* and Mechtild Russell's *Untersuchungen zur Theorie und Praxis der Typisierung bei I. A. Gončarov.* Among more recent works, the view that Goncharov was a mainstream realist who was primarily interested in depicting social "types" can be also found in Edmund Heier's "Direct Literary Portraiture in I. A. Goncharov's *The Precipice*" and in Friedrich Scholz's "Gončarovs Roman *Oblomov* Und Der Russishe Realismus," both in Thiergen, *I. A. Gončarov: Beiträge zu Werk und Wirkung,* 31–55 and 135–52, respectively. On Goncharov as an "ultimate realist," see also Blot, *Ivan Gontcharov: Ou le Réalisme Impossible.*

4. Stilman, "Oblomovka Revisited," 49.

5. Lyngstad and Lyngstad, *Ivan Goncharov,* 17.

6. Ibid., 178.

7. Goncharov, "Avtobiografiia" (1858), in *Sobranie sochinenii,* 8:240.

8. Goncharov, "Avtobiografiia" (1874), in *Sobranie,* 8:246.

9. Goncharov, *The Same Old Story,* 41. All subsequent citations are to this edition and will be incorporated into the text.

10. In apparent response to a letter from Goncharov that did not survive, V. A. Solonitsyn wrote on April 25, 1844, that "You are wrong when you maintain that you have seen and observed too little of life yet"; quoted in Tseitlin, *Goncharov,* 52.

11. Goncharov, "Better Late Than Never," *SOS,* 439.

12. Quoted in A. F. Koni, "Ivan Aleksandrovich Goncharov," in Piksanov, *Goncharov v vospominaniiakh sovremennikov,* 242.

13. "Better Late Than Never," *SOS,* 439

14. In *The Russian Religious Mind: Kievan Christianity—the Tenth to the Thirteenth Centuries,* G. P. Fedotov attributes this drastic change of ideals to moral and spiritual reasons while Gail Lenhoff suggests in *The Martyred Princes Boris and Gleb: A Socio-Cultural Study of the Cult and the Texts* that the canonization was also a political act directed at stopping Russian princes from warring against each other.

15. It should be noted here that some scholars question the authenticity of Grozny's and Kurbsky's letters. Thus in *The Kurbskii-Groznyi Apocrypha,* Edward L. Keenan argues that Grozny's and Kurbsky's letters were forgeries from the first half of the seventeenth century and served as "political allegories" (5) for discussing the rule of the Romanovs.

16. For more on early Russian autobiographies, see Zenkovsky, "Der Mönch Epifanij und die Entstehung der altrussischen Autobiographie" and Mintslov, *Obzor zapisok, dnevnikov, vospominanii, pisem i puteshestvii, otnosiashchikhsia k istorii Rossii i napechatannykh na russkom iazyke.* Most of the autobiographies mentioned in this chapter are also available in reprints with new English introductions in the "Memoir Series" published by Columbia University and edited by Marc Raef.

17. Wachtel, *The Battle for Childhood,* 3.

18. Wachtel does not do Bolotov's autobiography justice when he describes it as a work "with minimal description of childhood" (43). He clarifies his statement in a footnote by remarking that while "Bolotov does describe the years when he was a child . . . he cannot be said to discuss childhood [because he] never tries to recreate the child's perception of the world" (217n.54). Such an explanation is highly unconvincing, though. A particular point of view by itself does not create or negate "a discussion of childhood."

19. The word "autobiografiia"—later "avtobiografiia"—was first introduced into Russian by A. I. Turgenev, a collector of old autobiographical manuscripts, in 1817, eight years after Robert Southey coined the word "autobiography" in English.

20. Wachtel, *Battle,* 17.

21. See Eikhenbaum, "Molodoi Tolstoy," in *O literature,* 72–74.

22. Wachtel does mention Karamzin's novel but only in a footnote, calling it an "unfinished story" (209n.1). There are other examples of the pre-Tolstoy use of the myth of happy childhood in Russian literature as well. Nikolai Polevoi freely used the convention in 1830 when he declared that "on the banks of Angara the days of my childhood flew by carelessly, joyfully, and quickly" ("Sokhatyi," 172–76), and frequently eighteenth-century women—among them Dolgorukaia and Labzina—contrasted a happy childhood with an unhappy adulthood in their autobiographies. It is also important to bear in mind that even "Oblomov's Dream" was published several years prior to Tolstoy's *Childhood.*

23. Goncharov, "Avtobiografiia" (1858), in *Sobranie,* 8:241.

24. A letter to L. A. Polonsky, May 20, 1880, in *Sobranie,* 8:470. He never idolized Karamzin quite as much as he did Pushkin. Thus in a letter to A. and M. A. Iazykov dated December 15, 1853, Goncharov writes: "From childhood

[Pushkin] has been my idol, and only he alone" (*Sobranie* 8:286). Yet Nikolai Karamzin was, at least in Goncharov's youth, a very close second.

25. Goncharov, "Predislovie k romanu 'Obryv'," in *Sobranie,* 8:121. On Karamzin's life in letters see, for example, Cross, *N. M. Karamzin: A Study of His Literary Career (1783–1803).*

26. July 13, 1849; *Sobranie* 8:271–74.

27. See note 24.

28. For more on Belinsky and his opposition to romanticism, see Ginzburg's "Belinskii and the Emergence of Realism," in *On Psychological Prose,* 58–101.

29. In a letter to Ivan Turgenev, February 27, 1866, quoted in Rybasov, *I. A. Goncharov,* 11.

30. In a letter to A. F. Marks and V. P. Ostrogorsky, October 29, 1887, in *Sobranie,* 8:499.

31. In a letter to A. F. Koni, June 26, 1887, in *Sobranie,* 8:494. Also see N. I. Barsov's "Vospominanie ob I. A. Goncharove," where he writes: "What Goncharov talked about with indignation and even repugnance were writers' autobiographical stories, their memoirs about their childhood and their past." In Piksanov, *Goncharov v vospominaniiakh,* 154.

32. See, for example, his letter to A. A. Fet, November 19, 1888, in *Sobranie,* 8:511–12. During this later period of his life, while he was working on *Obryv* (*The Precipice*), Goncharov was generally very suspicious about other people's actions and motifs. His celebrated feud with Turgenev over Turgenev's alleged plagiarism of Goncharov's third novel was quite characteristic of the writer's state of mind in those years. For Goncharov's account of the feud, see "Neobyknovennaia istoriia" (*An Uncommon Story,* 1876), in *Sobranie,* 8:249–62. For a general discussion of the controversy and reasons for it, see Ehre, *Oblomov and His Creator,* 54–62.

33. Goncharov, "Narushenie voli," in *Sobranie,* 8:185. "Home" is written in English.

34. Koni, "Ivan Aleksandrovich Goncharov," in Piksanov, *Goncharov v vospominaniiakh,* 254.

Chapter 2

1. Goncharov, "Luchshe pozdno, chem nikogda," in *Sobranie,* 8:142.

2. Liatsky, *Roman i zhizn',* 104.

3. Goncharov, "Vospominaniia: na rodine," in *Sobranie,* 7:287.

4. Potanin, "Vospominaniia ob I. A. Goncharove," in Piksanov, *Goncharov v vospominaniiakh,* 24.

5. A letter to I. I. L'khovsky, ca. July 2, 1853, in *Sobranie,* 8:285.

6. See Goncharov's "Vospominaniia: v universitete," in *Sobranie,* 7:244–70.

7. See Beisov, *Goncharov i rodnoi krai,* 54–55, and Goncharov's own description in "Vospominaniia: na rodine," in *Sobranie,* 7:339–40.

8. See Alekseev, *Letopis' zhizni i tvorchestva I. A. Goncharova,* 20.

9. For descriptions of Goncharov's relationship with Annushka, see Potanin, "Vospominaniia," and M. V. Kirmalov, "Vospominaniia ob I. A. Goncharove," in Piksanov, *Goncharov v vospominaniiakh,* 40 and 113, respectively. For his city habits, see his letter to the Maikovs, June 13, 1849, in *Sobranie,* 8:274, where he writes that his family in Simbirsk "is horrified by my not going to church." The best description of his fishing expeditions with Petersburg friends is given in his short story "Likhaia bolezn'" ("Severe Illness"), written in the late 1830s but not published until many years after his death (*Sobranie* 7:370–403).

10. "Luchshe pozdno," in *Sobranie,* 7:136.

11. Ehre, *Oblomov and His Creator,* 38. The "two Goncharovs" Ehre is talking about here are not Piotr and Aleksandr Aduev, but Piotr Aduev and Oblomov.

12. Quoted in Liatsky, *Roman i zhizn',* 119–20.

13. In a letter to Grand Duke Konstantin Romanov, April 1, 1887; quoted in Tseitlin, *I. A. Goncharov,* 55, where, perhaps in order to obscure the identity of the tsar's brother, the addressee is constantly referred to as "poet Romanov."

14. In a letter to E. P. Maikova, May 16, 1866, in *Sobranie,* 8:346.

15. A letter to A. F. Koni, July 11, 1888, in *Sobranie,* 8:508.

16. See, for example, the reminiscences of A. V. Starchevsky in Piksanov, *Goncharov v vospominaniiakh,* 51–55. A rather simplistic view, based on the observations of Starchevsky and others that the Solonitsyns, and especially the uncle, were the direct prototypes for the Aduevs, can be found in several works on the writer published in the Soviet Union and abroad. For instance, in *Goncharov: Studies in the Modern European Literature and Thought,* Janko Lavrin writes: "Even the models for some of his figures are known to us. The practical worldly-wise uncle Aduev, for instance, is supposed to have been a certain N. A. [sic] Solonitzyn, one of Goncharov's chiefs in the civil service" (24). See also Evgen'ev-Maksimov, *I. A. Goncharov: zhizn', lichnost', tvorchestvo* and Lotshits, *Goncharov.*

17. See *Sobranie,* 7:404–36.

18. On Goncharov's juxtaposition of the city and the countryside, see the chapter "Landt und Stadt" in Lohff, *Die Bildlichkeit in den Romanen Ivan Aleksandrovič Gončarovs.* See also Klein's "Gončarov und die Idylle."

19. Paperno, *Chernyshevsky and the Age of Realism,* 68.

20. For more on Belinsky's philosophical views, see Ginzburg's excellent discussion in "Belinskii and the Emergence of Realism" in *On Psychological Prose.*

21. Quoted in A. Ia. Panaeva, "Iz 'Vospominanii'," in Piksanov, *Goncharov v vospominaniiakh,* 48.

22. Goncharov, "Neobyknovennaia istoriia," in *Sobranie,* 8:251.

23. Goncharov, *Obryv,* in *Sobranie,* 3:5.

24. A letter to Iu. D. Efremova, August 20, 1849, in *Sobranie,* 8:275.

25. A letter to S. S. Nikitenko, August 21, 1866, in *Sobranie,* 8:356.

26. Grigorovich, "Iz 'Literaturnykh vospominanii'," in Piksanov, *Goncharov v vospominaniiakh,* 56. Interestingly, Goncharov, in his turn, considered Grigorovich "cold" and "vain": see his letter to A. F. Koni, August 10, 1880, in *Sobranie,* 8:471.

27. A letter from Nekrasov to V. G. Belinsky, fall 1846, quoted in *Pis'ma V. G. Belinskogo,* 3:359.

28. A letter from Belinsky to V. P. Botkin, March 4, 1847, ibid., 194.

29. Aikhenval'd, "Goncharov," in *Siluety russkikh pisatelei,* 150.

30. A letter to I. I. L'khovsky, ca. July 20, 1853, in *Sobranie,* 8:284.

31. "Pushkin's devil" and "Pushkin's Demon" are closely related but they come from different poems. The first appears in Pushkin's "Angel" (1827) where the devil sees an angel standing at the gates of Paradise and is emotionally moved by the sight. The second gives the title to another short poem, "Demon" (1823), in which the Demon presents himself to a young and idealistic poet and "pour[s] cold poison into the soul" by mocking beauty, inspiration, and love as mere phantoms of one's imagination. The poem is, of course, very appropriate for describing the Aduevs' relationship and a perfect paradigm for a confrontation between "innocence" and "experience" in general.

32. Liatsky, *Goncharov,* 370.

33. See, for example, Goncharov's article "Zametki o lichnosti Belinskogo" ("Notes on Belinsky's Personality"), where Goncharov directly alludes to Polevoi's autobiographical narrative in *Ocherki.* In *Sobranie,* 8:97.

34. Polevoi, *Ocherki russkoi litteratury,* xli. Spelling "litteratura" with two "t"s, as in Latin and French, was widely practiced in nineteenth-century Russia but viewed by many as a sign of pretentiousness. Nabokov makes fun of this trend in *The Gift* when he describes Nikolai Nadezhdin, Goncharov's favorite professor at Moscow University (and Polevoi's contemporary, fellow critic, and editor), as a "seminarist . . . who used to write 'literature' with three 't's" (266).

35. Polevoi, *Ocherki,* xxxiii.

36. In *Ocherki,* Polevoi lamented his lack of formal education much in the same way in which Goncharov came to lament his; *Ocherki,* xxxiv–xxxvii.

37. Joyce, *Portrait,* 215.

38. Goncharov's statement here is also reminiscent of Thomas Mann's descrip-

tion of an ideal writer in *Tonio Kröger* (1903), a short novel that is not dissimilar to *A Common Story* in its main theme ("business" and "common life" vs. "art") as well as in its strong expression of the writer's own inner duality: "The artist must be unhuman, extra-human; he must stand in a queer aloof relationship to our humanity; only so is he in a position, I ought to say only so would he be tempted, to represent it, to portray it to good effect" (Mann, *Stories of Three Decades,* 103). Like Joyce's—and, obviously, unlike Goncharov's—Mann's formulation was influenced by Flaubert, whose notion of the author's impersonality is briefly discussed in chapters 7 and 8 in connection with Joyce. On Flaubert's influence on Mann, see an interestingly personal essay by D. H. Lawrence, "Thomas Mann," where Lawrence also discusses Mann's portrayal of himself as a young man in *Tonio Kröger* (in *Selected Literary Criticism,* 260–65).

39. A review in *Severnaiia pchela,* April 1847, by L. Brandt. Quoted in Liatsky, *Roman i zhizn',* 155.

40. Belinsky, "Vzgliad na russkuiu literaturu 1847 goda," in Poliakov, 32.

41. Pisarev, "'Oblomov': roman I. A. Goncharova," in Poliakov, 120.

42. Skabichevsky, "Staraia pravda," in Poliakov, 279–80.

43. Quoted in Liatsky, *Roman i zhizn',* 156.

44. From the anonymous review that appeared on March 8, 1847, in *Vedomosti S.-Peterburgskoi gorodskoi politsii,* quoted in Alekseev, *Letopis',* 28

45. Liatsky, *Goncharov,* 1.

46. "Luchshe pozdno," in *Sobranie,* 7:138.

47. Belinsky, "Vzgliad," in *Pisma,* 51.

48. "Better Late," *SOS,* 437.

49. Aikhenval'd, *Siluety,* 150.

50. "Better Late," *SOS,* 439.

51. Ibid., 434.

Chapter 3

1. From a biography by Otto Klinke; quoted in Rank's *The Double,* 35.

2. From a biography by Gaston Vorberg; quoted in Rank, *The Double,* 39. Vorberg's emphasis.

3. Rank, "The Double as Immortal Self," in *Beyond Psychology,* 81–82.

4. Vladimir Nabokov, who, as we all know, took great pleasure in frustrating his readers' expectations, plays on this traditional assumption that literary doubles have to be twin images of each other when at the end of *Despair* he surprises us by revealing that Hermann's alleged double did not look anything like him. In Fastbinder's movie from the novel, the surprise—which is essential to *Despair*—

is unfortunately no longer there since the viewer can see from the very beginning that Felix and Hermann do not resemble each other.

5. Tymms, *Doubles in Literary Psychology,* 29.

6. Miyoshi, *The Divided Self,* xii.

7. Freud, *The Ego and the Id,* 15. All other citation to *The Ego and the Id* will be incorporated into the text.

8. Prince, *Psychotherapy and Multiple Personality,* 201.

9. Slonim, *The Epic of Russian Literature,* 280.

10. As Whyte points out in *The Unconscious before Freud,* "by 1870–1880 the general conception of the unconscious mind was a European commonplace, and . . . many special applications of this general idea had been vigorously discussed for several decades" (169–70).

11. Co-authored by Simon P. Goodhart.

12. Interestingly enough, James Joyce was quite familiar with Prince's work, which he even used as a sourcebook for *Finnegans Wake.*

13. Hilgard, *Divided Consciousness,* 18.

14. The Russian writer's interest in clinical cases of divided consciousness is, in fact, well documented. In *Podrostok* (*The Adolescent,* 1875), for example, Dostoevsky himself makes his interest in the subject quite apparent when he makes Arkady quote from a work by "an expert": "What is a 'double,' really? A double, at least according to a medical book written by an expert that I read . . . , is nothing else but the first stage of some serious psychological disorder that may lead to a rather bad end. . . . [It is] a 'split' between one's feelings and one's will" (from the epilogue). We also know that Dostoevsky read C. G. Carus's *Psyche,* which appeared in the same year as *The Double* (1846). He was so impressed with the work that he even intended to translate it from German. For more on that, see Simmons, *Dostoevski: The Making of a Novelist,* 76–77.

15. Freud, "The 'Uncanny,'" in *Collected Papers,* 4:388.

16. Goncharov's scandalous accusation that Turgenev appropriated many of his own ideas is one of the most vivid examples of Goncharov's suspiciousness, which at times was almost manic in its nature. See note 32 of chapter 1.

17. Prince, *The Dissociation of a Personality,* 530.

18. Sidis and Goodhart, *Multiple Personality,* 364.

19. Jung, *Psychological Types,* 590.

20. Prince, *Psychotherapy and Multiple Personality,* 210.

21. Hilgard, 18.

22. Jung, *Psychological Types,* 590.

23. Quoted in Mattoon, *Jungian Psychology in Perspective,* 29.

24. There actually exists a Jungian study on Goncharov—Nathalie Baratoff's *Oblomov: A Jungian Approach. A Literary Image of the Mother Complex*—but the author limits herself only to manifestations of what she diagnoses as Oblomov's "severe mother complex" (7).

25. Sidis, *Multiple,* 364, 365.

26. Quoted in Northridge, *Modern Theories of the Unconscious,* 82.

27. Freud, "The 'Uncanny,'" 388.

28. Quoted in Pope and Singer, *The Stream of Consciousness,* 162.

29. Ibid., 163. The 1990s have been witnessing an even stronger surge of studies on the functions of the two hemispheres of a human brain. It has been largely spurred and facilitated by highly sophisticated scanners called M.R.I. (Magnetic Resonance Imaging) machines which, when used in conjunction with computers, can actually pinpoint the area of activity when a certain mental process is taking place. For a popular description of the technique involved and some of the preliminary results, see Sandra Blakeslee, "Scanner Pinpoints Site of Thought as Brain Sees or Speaks," *New York Times,* June 1, 1993, B5–B6.

30. Pope and Singer, *The Stream of Consciousness,* 163.

31. Pilling, *Autobiography and Imagination: Studies in Self-Scrutiny,* 1–2.

32. Nabokov, *Mary,* xiv.

33. Buckley, *The Turning Key,* 115.

34. Frye, *Anatomy of Criticism,* 307.

35. Cuddon, *A Dictionary of Literary Terms,* 42.

36. Bruss, *Autobiographical Acts,* 8.

37. Spengemann, *The Forms of Autobiography,* 132.

38. Ibid., 122.

39. Buckley, *The Turning Key,* 39–40.

40. Fleishman, *Figures of Autobiography,* 16, 18–19. Fleishman's introduction to the book is an excellent survey of different theories and views on autobiography.

41. Frye, *The Educated Imagination,* 29.

42. Fleishman, *Figures,* 39.

43. Buckley, *The Turning Key,* 40.

44. Holman, *Handbook to Literature,* 49; Cuddon, 664.

45. Dickens, *David Copperfield,* 13.

46. Of the European and Russian "simulated" autobiographies that Goncharov was likely to have known, only in Sterne's *Tristram Shandy* does the narrator assume a very active role, but he does so, of course, largely at the expense of the protagonist, who is not allowed to develop beyond his first hours.

47. Bakhtin, *Speech Genres,* 22.

Chapter 4

1. Woolf, "The Russian Point of View," in *The Common Reader,* 179. All subsequent citations of Virginia Woolf's critical and autobiographical materials will be incorporated into the text using the following abbreviations:

CDB	*The Captain's Death Bed and Other Essays*
CR	*The Common Reader*
2CR	*The Second Common Reader*
D	*The Diary of Virginia Woolf*
DM	*The Death of the Moth and Other Essays*
GR	*Granite and Rainbow: Essays*
L	*The Letters of Virginia Woolf*
MB	*Moments of Being* (2d ed.)
1MB	*Moments of Being: Unpublished Autobiographical Writings.* Used for variants that do not appear in the second edition.

2. Buckley, *The Turning Key,* 47.

3. Woolf, *"To the Lighthouse": The Original Holograph Draft,* 3.

4. Ibid., 29.

5. Woolf, *To the Lighthouse,* 42. All subsequent citations will be incorporated into the text.

6. See Leaska, *Virginia Woolf's "Lighthouse,"* 208. Leaska estimates that, of the number of lines attributable to different narrators in the novel, Lily has roughly 150 more lines than Mrs. Ramsay.

7. Guiguet, *Virginia Woolf,* 257.

8. Rose, *Woman of Letters,* 112.

9. Leslie Stephen, *The Mausoleum Book,* 30.

10. Julia Duckworth Stephen, *Stories for Children, Essays for Adults,* 47.

11. Julia Duckworth Stephen, *Stories,* 47. In his early biography of Leslie Stephen, Noel Annan observed that Woolf "inherited from her mother much of her sensibility and even an echo of her style" (quoted in Beja, *"To the Lighthouse": A Casebook,* 42). This statement is absent from Annan's newly revised edition of the biography, *Leslie Stephen: The Godless Victorian.* Rosamond Lehmann, who was most likely not familiar with Julia Stephen's writings, noted that in Woolf's novels "her dialogue is so simple as almost to seem written for a child" (in Noble, *Recollections of Virginia Woolf,* 64). For more on Woolf and her literary inheritance from her mother, see Diane F. Gillespie's introduction to Julia Stephen's *Stories* and Jane Marcus's "Thinking Back through Our Mothers," in Marcus, *New Feminist Essays on Virginia Woolf,* 1–30. On possible traumatic aspects of the Virginia Woolf/Julia Stephen relationship, see Jane Marcus's "Virginia Woolf

and Her Violin: Mothering, Madness and Music" and Martine Stemerick's, "Virginia Woolf and Julia Stephen: The Distaff Side of History," in Ginsberg, *Virginia Woolf: Centennial Essays,* 27–49 and 51–80, respectively. For a more general study on Woolf and her mother, see also Rosenman, *The Invisible Presence: Virginia Woolf and the Mother-Daughter Relationship.*

12. Julia Duckworth Stephen, *Stories,* 219.

13. Lily's concept of Ramsay's work is, after all, not much more advanced than Mrs. Ramsay's "the influence of somebody upon something" (101).

14. Fleishman, *Virginia Woolf,* 106–7n.6.

15. See Guiguet, *Virginia Woolf,* 258.

16. For an analysis of Woolf's dependence on these women which, as Kushen believes, stemmed from "the catastrophic failure of the relation between [Woolf] and her mother" (3), see Kushen, *Virginia Woolf and the Nature of Communion.*

17. Leonard Woolf, *Sowing,* 182.

18. "Mr. Bennett and Mrs. Brown," *CDB,* 102.

19. Quentin Bell in the introduction to *The Diary of Virginia Woolf,* 1:xxvi.

20. Gillespie, *The Sisters' Arts,* 11.

21. Quoted in Quentin Bell, *Virginia Woolf: A Biography,* 2:128.

22. Rose, *Woman of Letters,* 169. Michael Rosenthal in *Virginia Woolf* similarly states: "Of Mrs Ramsay's many considerable talents, none is more important than her skill of creating, from the flux and chaos around her, moments of order . . . The Boeuf en Daube dinner at the end of the first part of the novel is one such moment of creation" (108). But if Rose and Rosenthal suggest that doing her womanly duties well makes Mrs. Ramsay an artist of sorts, there are others who, on the contrary, maintain that Mrs. Ramsay cannot be an artist *because* she is so conventionally feminine. Rosenman, for example, writes: "Stifling her words with a patriarchal fairy tale ["The Fisherman and His Wife"], denying her power, Mrs. Ramsay is not a true artist, but she is an object of art" (*The Invisible Presence,* 97).

23. Zwerdling, *Virginia Woolf and the Real World,* 208.

24. As Peter F. Alexander points out in *Leonard and Virginia Woolf,* Leonard himself may have regretted his decision later in life: "There were . . . signs that he wondered if he had made the right decision in refusing to let her have children. . . . He was very much struck by the childless couple in [Edward Albee's *Who's Afraid of Virginia Woolf*]. . . . Its relevance to Virginia's lifelong childlessness, and its terrible consequences, could not be avoided" (199–200). Leonard Woolf even wrote to Albee and drew his attention to Virginia's story "Lappin and Lapinova," in which another childless woman attempts to live in the world of fantasy in order to escape the terrible void in her life. "The details are quite

different," he noted, "but the theme is the same as that of the imaginary child in your play" (Leonard Woolf, *Letters*, 537).

25. It is interesting that, while the excitement of awaiting the return of the young lovers with the possible news of engagement is very reminiscent of what happened when Virginia and Vanessa waited for the results of a long walk taken by their half-sister Stella Duckworth and her husband-to-be Jack Hills back in 1897, the Rayleys' subsequent marital arrangement is very similar to the Bells': parents to "two little boys" (*To the Lighthouse*, 257), separated but not divorced, friends rather than enemies, free to go their own ways.

26. Zwerdling, *Virginia Woolf*, 175.

27. Gordon, *Virginia Woolf: A Writer's Life*, 11. On Woolf and Victorianism see also Paul, *The Victorian Heritage of Virginia Woolf: The External World in Her Novels*.

28. If we accept Elizabeth Abel's convincing suggestion that the brooch Minta loses, "the sole ornament she possessed" (186), is a symbol of her virginity, then Lily's strong reaction can be also interpreted as her "sisterly" lament for Minta's youth and innocence, which had been irrevocably lost together with the brooch that night on the beach. See Elizabeth Abel, "'Cam the Wicked': Woolf's Portrait of the Artist as Her Father's Daughter," in Marcus, *Virginia Woolf and Bloomsbury: A Centenary Celebration*, 170–94.

Chapter 5

1. Quentin Bell, *Virginia Woolf*, 1:24.

2. See her letter to V. Dickinson, June 5, 1927: "People in the Hebrides are very angry. Is it Cornwall? I'm not as sure as you are" (*L*, III:389). One of those "angry" was Scottish poet Rachel A. Taylor, who wrote in her review for the *Spectator* on May 14, 1927: "But why, when this account of the interaction of 'naked thinking hearts' needs merely a setting of a house and a terrace, some rocks, a bay and a lighthouse, must the house be placed in the Hebrides? Mrs Woolf creates her own atmosphere wherever she takes her people; but to anybody who has been subdued by the magic of Hebridean atmosphere, there is disturbance of impression, a collision of spiritual values." Reprinted in Majumdar, *Virginia Woolf: The Critical Heritage*, 199–200.

3. Nancy was loosely modeled on Vanessa Stephen; of all the children her fictional name is phonetically the closest to Vanessa's nickname, much in use in her family: Nessa. The choice of Nancy to convey Woolf's own feeling for the sea

is rather logical, for Vanessa was, after all, spiritually the closest sibling to Virginia. As was the case with Vanessa and Virginia, Nancy is, most likely, three years older than Cam and thus a more "mature" ten.

4. Cam's meditations about the past seem to echo Mrs. Ramsay's in the first section of the book: "She knew what had happened to [the Mannings], what to her. It was like reading a good book again, for she knew the end of that story, since it had happened twenty years ago, and life, which shot down even from this dining-room table in cascades, heaven knows where, was sealed up there, and lay, like a lake, placidly between its banks" (140).

5. Gordon, *Virginia Woolf,* 199.

6. Woolf, *"The Waves": The Two Holograph Drafts,* 157.

7. Morrell, *Ottoline at Garsington,* 244.

8. *Diary of Virginia Woolf,* II, 193.

9. Abel, "'Cam the Wicked'," in Marcus, *Virginia Woolf and Bloomsbury,* 183. Another critic, Beverly Ann Schlack, goes even further in identifying the father's role in his daughter's development as totally negative. Thus, in "Fathers in General: The Patriarchy in Virginia Woolf's Fiction," Schlack unequivocally states: "Fathers in Woolf's fiction are oppressive or ineffectual. In either case they manage to burden, demean, or disappoint their women" (in Marcus, *Virginia Woolf: A Feminist Slant,* 53). But in the case of Leslie Stephen and Virginia Woolf, some critics believe the opposite. Katherine Hill, for one, maintains that Woolf's father wanted his daughter to inherit his intellectual tradition and therefore "trained her extensively in history and biography to give her the background fundamental to this achievement" ("Virginia Woolf and Leslie Stephen," 351). Whether Leslie Stephen deliberately trained his daughter or merely wisely refrained from discouraging her unconventional pursuits, it is clear that Virginia Woolf was much more ambivalent on the subject of her father—and his fictional representatives—than Schlack would want us to believe. On a related topic, see also Marcus, *Virginia Woolf and the Languages of Patriarchy.*

10. Julia Duckworth Stephen, *Stories,* 241.

11. Quentin Bell in the introduction to *The Diary of Virginia Woolf,* I:xxi–xxii.

12. Leslie Stephen to Julia Stephen, July 29–30, 1893. Unpublished, Berg Collection, New York Public Library; quoted in Zwerdling, *Virginia Woolf,* 184.

13. The first statement belongs to Stephen's friend and first biographer Frederic William Maitland; reprinted in Beja's *"To the Lighthouse": A Casebook,* 36. Stephen's "confession" comes from *The Mausoleum Book,* 76.

14. Temple, "Never Say 'I': 'To the Lighthouse' as Vision and Confession," in Sprague, *Virginia Woolf: A Collection of Critical Essays,* 94.

Chapter 6

1. In a letter to A. F. Koni, July 11, 1988, in *Sobranie,* 8:508.

2. Lily painting the family through the frame of the window creates an ironic double effect of life imitating art and art imitating life. On the one hand, the family—enclosed in the frame of the open window and so anticipating Lily's own finished product—already looks like a painting. On the other, once Lily is ready to frame her picture, she will be merely re-creating the actual scene in which the family is literally framed by the window. This effect may make readers rethink their habitual assumptions about the point at which life stops and art begins. For an illuminating discussion on the literary uses of frames in Woolf's works, see C. Ruth Miller, *Virginia Woolf: The Frames of Art and Life.*

3. See Abel, *Virginia Woolf and the Fictions of Psychoanalysis.* Abel does admit, however, that even though Woolf had "access to the psychoanalytic culture that emerged in London in the 1920s," it is virtually impossible to prove any direct influence and that, at best, one can only talk about "intertexuality" (xvi).

4. Rosamond Lehmann, in *Recollections of Virginia Woolf,* 66. For more on Woolf and consciousness, see Love, *Worlds in Consciousness: Mythopoetic Thought in the Novels of Virginia Woolf.* For a discussion of Woolf's interest in collective consciousness, see also Allen McLaurin, "Consciousness and Group Consciousness in Virginia Woolf," in Warner, *Virginia Woolf: A Centenary Perspective,* 28–40.

5. From Cornwall Diary, August 11, 1905; in Berg Collection, unpublished, quoted in Gordon, *Virginia Woolf,* 14.

6. Characteristically, after Thoby died, Virginia and Adrian Stephen, living together at the time, made a conscious decision not to repress memories of him, however painful those recollections might be. Their decision was based on the unnaturalness of having to suppress, mostly for their father's sake, all casual references to Stella after her death. On Woolf's relationship with George and Gerald Duckworth, see DeSalvo, *Virginia Woolf: The Impact of Childhood Sexual Abuse on Her Life and Work,* where the author postulates (or, rather, speculates, with very little factual evidence) that Woolf was not only a direct victim of incestuous molestation but also a constant witness of sexual, emotional, and physical abuse being inflicted by men, including her father, on all her female siblings.

7. See "The Memoir Club Contributions: 22 Hyde Park Gate," in *MB,* 164–77.

8. Judy Little is right when she calls *Jacob's Room* "Woolf's parodic 'bildungsroman'" ("'Jacob's Room' as Comedy: Woolf's Parodic 'Bildungsroman,'" in

Marcus, *New Feminist Essays,* 105–24). By imitating the format of the bildungsroman without adopting its essential quality of the hero's emotional and intellectual growth, *Jacob's Room* is quite similar to Goncharov's *A Common Story.*

9. Buckley, *The Turning Key,* 129. Lyndall Gordon is one of many critics who make a similar observation: "Lily Briscoe, composing [the Ramsays'] portrait, enacts the obsessive drama of Virginia Woolf, the transforming of personal memory into impersonal art" (*Virginia Woolf,* 7).

10. Leaska, *Virginia Woolf's "Lighthouse"*, 208.

11. The term is Dorrit Cohn's; see *Transparent Minds,* 99–126.

12. Rose, *Woman of Letters,* 172.

13. *Ulysses* is not the first work to drastically reduce the traditional time span of an autobiographical novel. Thus Tolstoy's *Childhood,* for example, focuses on only two crucial days in the life of the young protagonist. But, as will be discussed in chapter 7, *Ulysses,* like *To the Lighthouse,* attempts to achieve the changeable quality of a bildungsroman without having to expand its temporal limits, while Tolstoy's novel is but the first installment in an autobiographical trilogy, *Childhood—Boyhood—Youth* (originally conceived as a tetralogy, *The Four Ages of Development*). It thus leaves the subsequent stages of the protagonist's development for the later parts which, together with the first three segments, would have functioned as one bildungsroman.

14. On the "dramatic" quality of Woolf's novels, see Wheare, *Virginia Woolf: Dramatic Novelist.*

15. Zwerdling, *Virginia Woolf,* 21.

16. Harold Bloom, introduction to *Modern Critical Views: Virginia Woolf,* 2.

17. Auerbach, *Mimesis,* 484–85.

18. Fleishman, *Virginia Woolf,* 121–22.

19. Buckley, "Autobiography in the English Bildungsroman," 97.

Chapter 7

1. Groden, *"Ulysses" in Progress,* 20.

2. A letter to Mlle. Leroyer de Chantepie, March 18, 1857, in Flaubert, *Letters. 1830–1857,* 230. Also see his letter to Louise Colet, December 9, 1852: "An author in his book must be like God in the universe, present everywhere and visible nowhere" (173).

3. Joyce, *Portrait,* 172. All subsequent citations of James Joyce's works and autobiographical materials, as well as some works about him, will be incorporated into the text using the following abbreviations:

CDD Stanislaus Joyce, *The Complete Dublin Diary*
CW *The Critical Writings*
E *Exiles*
Ep *Epifanie*
FW *Finnegans Wake*
GJ *Giacomo Joyce*
JJ Ellmann, *James Joyce*
JJP *James Joyce in Padua*
L *Letters of James Joyce* Volume numbers will be given in Roman numerals.
MBK Stanislaus Joyce, *My Brother's Keeper: James Joyce's Early Years*
MU Budgen, *James Joyce and the Making of "Ulysses"*
P *A Portrait of the Artist as a Young Man*
SH *Stephen Hero*
SL *Selected Letters of James Joyce*
WD Scholes and Kain, *The Workshop of Daedalus: James Joyce and the Raw Materials for "A Portrait of the Artist as a Young Man"*

4. In Power, *Conversations,* 36.

5. Quoted in *JJ,* 265.

6. Woolf, *The Diary,* II:14. For more on Woolf's reaction to Joyce, see Jean Guiguet, "Virginia Woolf et James Joyce: un problème de dates et de tempéraments," in Bonnerot, *"Ulysses" Cinquante Ans Après,* 23–31; and Suzette A. Henke, "Virginia Woolf Reads James Joyce," in Beja, *James Joyce,* 39–42. For an interesting recent study analyzing Woolf's and Joyce's affinities, see Fogel, *Covert Relations: James Joyce, Virginia Woolf, and Henry James.*

7. "He is an artist first. He has too much talent to be anything else" (*CDD,* 52).

8. For more on Irish theosophists, see, among others, Boyd, *Ireland's Literary Renaissance,* 212–53. See also the chapter entitled "From Yeats to Thornton Wilder and Beyond" in Sylvia Cranston's 1993 biography, *HPB: The Extraordinary Life and Influence of Helena Blavatsky,* where she devotes a brief section to Joyce (473–76). A critical study of Blavatsky and her movement can be found in Maria Carlson's new book, *No Religion Higher than Truth: A History of the Theosophical Movement in Russia, 1875–1922.*

9. See, for example, Kenner, *Dublin's Joyce,* or Levin, *James Joyce.* For the opposite view, see Noon, *Joyce and Aquinas.*

10. Booth, *The Rhetoric of Fiction,* 329.

11. At least one critic, Peter Costello, believes that Joyce abandoned this format even earlier, when *Portrait* evolved from *Stephen Hero:* "*Stephen Hero* had been a traditional *bildungsroman,* paralleled in fact by contemporary novels such as *The Way of All Flesh* or *Buddenbrooks.* The massive social data and the extended

treatment no longer appealed to Joyce after the concise achievement of 'The Dead'" (*James Joyce,* 275). But while Joyce's *Portrait* is not a totally "traditional bildungsroman," it still retains most of the main features of such a novel. It starts with the protagonist's childhood and early schooling and takes him to a point where he begins to mature both as an artist and as a man.

12. Kaye, "A Portrait of the Artist as Blephen-Stoom," in Magalaner, *A James Joyce 'Miscellanny,'* 80.

13. Joyce, *Ulysses,* 257. All subsequent citations to the novel will be incorporated into the text. The citations are to Hans Gabler's revised edition—not as a matter of preference but simply because when I started writing this chapter back in 1987, Gabler's "corrected text" was generally believed to have supplanted the older 1961 edition. The material I quote here is virtually the same in both editions; thus, in this particular case, the difference between the two is irrelevant. For one version of the controversy surrounding the older and the newer editions of the novel, see Bruce Arnold's *The Scandal of "Ulysses."*

14. Robert Scholes, "'Ulysses': A Structuralist Perspective," in Staley, *"Ulysses": Fifty Years,* 164–65. Reprinted in Scholes, *In Search of James Joyce,* 117–43.

15. Budgen, *Myselves When Young,* 188.

16. Letter unpublished, quoted in *JJ,* 445. On what she calls Joyce's "yearnings toward [his wife's] adultery" (157), see Brenda Maddox, *Nora: The Real Life of Molly Bloom.*

17. Quoted in *JJ,* 442.

18. Peter Costello believes that it was Nora's miscarriage in 1908, which Joyce took very hard, that provided the lost son motif for Bloom (*James Joyce,* 276).

19. There are, of course, numerous views on Stephen's reaction to the "Father" in Bloom. Edmund L. Epstein, for example, argues in *The Ordeal of Stephen Dedalus* that Stephen rebels equally against all paternal figures—his biological father, God, and, eventually, Bloom. See also Van der Vat, "Paternity in 'Ulysses'"; Walcott, "The Paternity of James Joyce's Stephen Dedalus"; Sheldon Brivic, "The Father In Joyce," in Benstock, *The Seventh of Joyce,* 74–80; Mary T. Reynolds, "Paternal Figures and Paternity Themes," in Bloom, *James Joyce: Modern Critical Views,* 121–46, and, finally, Karen Lawrence, "Paternity, the Legal Fiction," in Newman, *Joyce's "Ulysses": The Larger Perspective,* 89–97. On Joycean "authorities" in general, see Mahaffey, *Reauthorizing Joyce.*

20. Quoted in *JJ,* 293. The extent to which Joyce was obsessed with his daughter's mental health has been further underscored by two recent publications—Stuart Gilbert's journal, kept in the thirties (*Reflections on James Joyce,* 1993), and the catalogue (and description) of Joyce's and Paul Léon's letters from the same period (*The James Joyce—Paul Léon Papers in the National Library of Ireland,* 1992).

21. On Joyce's reaction to his mother's death see, among others, Mark Shechner, "The Song of the Wandering Aengus: James Joyce and His Mother."

Chapter 8

1. Power, *Conversations,* 106.

2. For related discussion, see also Edmund L. Epstein, "James Joyce and the Body," and Robert Boyle, "Worshipper of the Word: James Joyce and the Trinity," in Epstein, *A Starchamber Quiry,* 73–106 and 109–51, respectively.

3. Gilbert, *James Joyce's "Ulysses,"* 97, 134.

4. For more on the Eucharist in Joyce see Richard Ellmann, *Ulysses on the Liffey,* and Robert Boyle, "Miracle in Black Ink: A Glance at Joyce's Use of His Eucharistic Image," in Staley, *"Ulysses": Fifty Years,* 47–60. See also Tucker, *Stephen and Bloom at Life's Feast.*

5. Edmund L. Epstein, "Nestor," in Hart, *James Joyce's "Ulysses": Critical Essays,* 25. Ironically, young Joyce is often described by friends as being very "bright": "[H]e was a tall slight stripling, with flashing teeth—white as a hound's—pale blue eyes that sometimes had an icy look . . ." (Eugene Sheehy in *WD,* 172). Perhaps to compensate for it, Joyce preferred to wear dark clothes, for which one of his landladies even called him "Herr Satan" (*JJ,* 435)

6. Ellmann, *Liffey,* 31.

7. Schutte, "Leopold Bloom: A Touch of the Artist," in Staley, *"Ulysses": Fifty Years,* 122.

8. Jan Parandowski, "Meeting with Joyce," in Potts, *Portraits of the Artist in Exile,* 159.

9. That Bloom was also "Odysseus" and thus supposedly Greek presented no problems for Joyce. Jacques Mercanton remembers a conversation in which the writer said that "[w]hat struck him most . . . in the character of the Homeric *Ulysses* was how little he resembled the other heroes of the *Odyssey.* For them he was a foreigner" ("The Hours of James Joyce," in Potts, 208). When in 1916 Joyce first learnt of Victor Bérard's turn-of-the-century theory that the *Odyssey* had Semitic origins and that places mentioned there were real and could be traced down by finding Hebrew equivalents to Greek words, the writer, according to Budgen, took it as a confirmation of his own intimations: "There's a lot to be said for the theory that the Odyssey is a Semitic poem," he told his friend (*MU,* 170).

10. Tweedie, "'Common Sense': James to Joyce and the Pragmatic L. Bloom," 357.

11. Quoted in George Borach, "Conversations with James Joyce," in Potts, 71.

12. Reizbaum, "The Jewish Connection, Cont'd," in Benstock, *The Seventh of*

Joyce, 236. Also see in the same volume E. L. Epstein, "Joyce and Judaism," and Morton P. Levitt, "The Humanity of Bloom, The Jewishness of Joyce," 221–24, 225–28 respectively. For a detailed study of Joyce's attitude toward Jews and Judaism see Nadel, *Joyce and the Jews.*

13. Ellmann speculates that the girl was Amalia Popper, whose father's first name was, interestingly enough, Leopoldo. See *JJ,* 342.

14. Joyce's interest in Jewish women was also shared by other male members of his family. Thus his brother, Stanislaus, wrote in his diary in 1905: "I think I shall marry a Jewess, for they seem to me the only people who have a plausible theory of chastity and sexuality" (*CDD,* 150). But it was actually James Joyce's son, Giorgio, who married a Jewess. When he announced his engagement to his family, they (his father included) were apparently not too thrilled. "The family still hostile to Mrs. Fleischman and Jews in general," wrote Stuart Gilbert, Joyce's friend and collaborator, at the time of Giorgio's engagement in 1930 (*Reflections,* 36). Joyce's daughter was also attracted to Jews, even though, if we are to believe Gilbert, she was not above making anti-Semitic remarks (ibid., 35, 49). David Hayman, who reviewed Lucia Joyce's unpublished papers, describes her as having "extreme sensitivity to Jewishness" and "attraction to 'Jewish' males [which] approached the condition of fixation." Because of Joyce's enormous influence on his daughter, Hayman interprets Lucia's feelings about Jews as a "litmus test" for Joyce's own "profound interest in and perhaps identification with Jews" ("Shadow of His Mind: The Papers of Lucia Joyce," in Beja, *James Joyce: The Centennial Symposium,* 197). Ira B. Nadel makes a similar observation in *Joyce and the Jews,* 177–78.

15. Nabokov, *Lectures on Literature,* 328.

16. Gilbert, *James Joyce's "Ulysses,"* 126; Nabokov, *Lectures on Literature,* 328.

17. His position obviously did not change later. Thus Stuart Gilbert recorded in his diary in 1930: "J. J. drank well and was expansive. Believes in long dresses for women: anti-feminist. 'La femme c'est rien' is one of his remarks" (*Reflections,* 34). For a feminist critic's view of Joyce and women, see Bonnie Kime Scott, *Joyce and Feminism* and her *James Joyce* in the Humanities Press International Feminist Reading Series. See also *Women in Joyce,* edited by Suzette Henke and Elaine Unkeless.

18. Quoted in *JJ,* 629.

19. The song that goes through the narrator's mind as he is describing the scene is called "The Low-Backed Car"; the lyric is "as we drove in the low-backed car/ To be married by Father Maher.") See Gifford, *Notes for Joyce,* 459.

20. "The word 'scientific' is always a word of praise in [Jim's] mouth. . . . He wishes to take every advantage of scientific inventions" (*CDD,* 54).

Chapter 9

1. Quoted in Louis Gillet, "The Living Joyce," in Potts, *Portrait of the Artist,* 198.

2. For more on Joyce's narrative strategies see Michael Patrick Gillespie's *Reading the Book of Himself* and Melvyn J. Friedman's "Lestrygonians" and Clive Hart's, "Wandering Rocks" in Hart and Hayman, *James Joyce's "Ulysses": Critical Essays,* 131–46 and 181–216, respectively. See also Weldon Thornton, "Voices and Values in 'Ulysses,'" in Newman and Thornton, *Joyce's "Ulysses": The Larger Perspective,* 244–70, Marilyn French, *The Book as World,* and Karen Lawrence, *The Odyssey of Style in "Ulysses."*

3. Like "dialogic" and "polyphony," "heteroglossia" is, of course, also Bakhtin's term—see Bakhtin, *The Dialogic Imagination.* James Maddox complained in 1987 that "[t]he great relevance of Bakhtin's 'dialogism' to Joyce's narratives, especially *Ulysses* and *Finnegans Wake,* has not yet received the major attention it deserves" ("Mockery in 'Ulysses,'" in Newman and Thornton, *Joyce's Ulysses,* 154n.1). This has been remedied somewhat since then. In 1989, R. B. Kershner devoted a whole book to Joyce and Bakhtin (*Joyce, Bakhtin and Popular Culture: Chronicles of Disorder*), and there is a chapter on them in Neil Cornwell's *James Joyce and the Russians.* Several other Joyce scholars—among them Ira B. Nadel in "'The REAL History of the ERA': Joyce, Lewis and Fascism" (1988), Murray McArthur in *Stolen Writings: Blake's "Milton," Joyce's "Ulysses," and the Nature of Influence* (1988), and Patrick McGee in *Paperspace: Style as Ideology in Joyce's "Ulysses"* (1988)—have also used Bakhtin's terminology to analyze Joyce's prose.

4. Hayman, *"Ulysses": The Mechanics of Meaning,* 70.

5. Kenner, *Joyce's Voices and "Ulysses,"* 61–71.

6. Brivic, "The Other of 'Ulysses,'" in Newman and Thornton, *Joyce's "Ulysses,"* 187–212. Brivic also discusses Joyce's authorial presence in "Joyce's Consubstantiality" in Beja, *James Joyce: The Centennial Symposium,* 149–57.

7. Thornton, "Voices and Values in 'Ulysses,'" in Newman and Thornton, *Joyce's "Ulysses,"* 265. In the same article Thornton also emphasizes Joyce's authorial presence in *Ulysses:* "It is, for example, a fact about *Ulysses* that the paths of Stephen and Bloom cross several times during the day; this crossing of their paths is Joyce's doing, and while we may debate its precise meaning, we cannot deny that it is there and that for some purpose Joyce created this set of events rather than another" (245). Thornton may appear to be stating the obvious, but there are numerous critics who, either because they interpret Joyce's notion of the "invisible" author too literally or respect it too much, still seem reluctant to speak of Joyce's authorial presence in the novel.

8. McMichael, *"Ulysses" and Justice,* 14.
9. Buckley, "Autobiography in the English Bildungsroman," 103.

Chapter 10

1. In a recent book, *The Writer's Divided Self in Bulgakov's "The Master and Margarita,"* Riitta H. Pittman examines what she considers to be clear-cut autobiographical splits as reflected in several characters in Bulgakov's famous novel. But *The Master and Margarita,* which in my opinion often lacks the authorial detachment that Goncharov's, Woolf's, and Joyce's novels exhibit in such abundance, is *not* an example of a "co-conscious" autobiographical novel. Pittman, who treats Bulgakov's "splits" using such (largely Jungian) terms as "rational" versus "irrational," and "conscious" versus "unconscious," would probably agree.
2. Fitzgerald, *The Crack-Up,* 69.
3. Robert, *The Old and the New,* 19, 18.
4. It is interesting that Goncharov's "nemesis," Ivan Turgenev, appropriated Cervantes' character for a dichotomy of his own by juxtaposing Don Quixote with Shakespeare's Hamlet. In his 1860 published lecture, "Hamlet and Don-Quixote," Turgenev contrasted the two along the obvious lines of "action" and "contemplation." Needless to say, this was the very conflict that was highlighted in virtually all of Goncharov's own novels (and particularly in *Oblomov*), and Turgenev's lecture undoubtedly fueled Goncharov's suspicion that the other man was simply feeding off his ideas.
5. Nabokov, *Lectures on Don Quixote,* 10. Nabokov also believed that "Knight and squire are really one" (ibid.).
6. Watt, *The Rise of the Novel,* 173.
7. Rudnik-Smalbraak, *Samuel Richardson,* 41.
8. Watt, *The Rise of the Novel,* 153. There is a very interesting recent study on androgynous "divided selves" in European and American culture—Wendy Lesser's *His Other Half: Men Looking at Women through Art.* Lesser does not, however, discuss Richardson there.
9. See, for example, Margaret Anne Doody and Peter Sabor's introduction to *Samuel Richardson: Tercentenary Essays,* 1. The exact date of Richardson's birth is not known, but it is usually surmised that he was born in the last week of July in 1689.
10. Watt quotes from an anonymous pamphlet according to which Richardson's insistence "that his ideal man, Sir Charles Grandison, was a virgin until marriage" produced "scandalous consternation of some of the ladies" (*The Rise*

of the Novel, 157). As was discussed in the previous chapter, Stephen, the "soul" character of *Ulysses,* was also considered by Joyce to be a virgin.

11. Richardson describes his younger self this way in one of his more revealing letters to Rev. Johannes Stinstra—see *The Richardson-Stinstra Correspondence,* 21–44.

12. The so-called definitive text of the novel, which is often in use now and which resulted from the manuscript's being shortened and revised by Bely after 1916, came out in Berlin around the same time as *Ulysses,* in 1922. For an informative comparison of the two editions, see Elsworth, *Andrey Bely: A Critical Study of the Novels,* 111–16. Differing from many Bely scholars, Elsworth considers the earlier, 1916 edition of the novel to be "the canonical text." He explains his choice by pointing to "[t]he inability of the revised text to stand entirely on its own" as shown by the critics' occasional need "to resort to the original text in order to restore the meaning" (116).

13. Brostrom in Terras, *Handbook of Russian Literature,* 45.

14. Bely, *Petersburg,* 5. All subsequent citations are to this edition and will be incorporated into the text.

15. In *The Dream of Rebirth,* a closely "autobiographical" Freudian interpretation of *Petersburg,* Magnus Ljunggren suggests that, as a father figure, Apollon Apollonovich represents not only Bely's biological father but also his "spiritual" one, Rudolf Steiner. While it is true that Steiner was a paternal figure for Bely, and that there is some evidence in Bely's autobiographical writings that his feelings towards the two men were sometimes similar, given the huge difference of Nikolai Bugaev's and Steiner's life philosophies, one should be very careful about lumping them together.

16. In one of his interviews with Vladimir Nabokov, Alfred Appel Jr. offers an interpretation of *Petersburg* which is very similar to mine: "Although I've never seen it discussed as such, the Ableukhov father-son relationship to me constitutes a doubling, making *Petersburg* one of the most interesting and fantastic permutations of the *Doppelgänger* theme" (in Nabokov, *Strong Opinions,* p. 85).

17. Maguire and Malmstad, translator's introduction, to Bely, *Petersburg,* xix.

18. Ibid., xxii. For a later and much longer version of Maguire and Malmstad's interpretation of *Petersburg,* see their article "Petersburg" in Malmstad, *Andrey Bely: Spirit of Symbolism* (96–144), where they changed significantly their earlier view that the novel is about "beginnings" and "returns" as well as "an affirmation of the life principle" (*Petersburg,* xxi), and, instead, find the opposite to be true. Thus we are told that at the end of the novel the whole Ableukhov family "has come to a sterile end" and that the reader is left not with an affirmation of life but

with the fact of death. They rightfully postulate, however, that, in Bely's system of beliefs, death may eventually lead to "a rebirth" (*Andrey Bely,* 138).

19. From Bely's 1901 letter to Margarita Morozova. Quoted in John Elsworth's introduction to Bely, *The Dramatic Symphony,* 8.

20. Alexandrov, *Andrei Bely: The Major Symbolist Fiction,* 108. See the *Petersburg* chapter (100–152) for an excellent discussion of Steiner's significant effect on the novel.

Bibliography

Abel, Elizabeth. *Virginia Woolf and the Fictions of Psychoanalysis.* Chicago: University of Chicago Press, 1989.

Aikhenval'd, Iuly. *Siluety russkikh pisatelei (The Profiles of Russian Writers).* Moscow: Nauchnoe slovo, 1906.

Alekseev, A. D. *Letopis' zhizni i tvorchestva I. A. Goncharova (The Chronicle of Life and Works of I. A. Goncharov).* Moscow: AN SSSR, 1960.

Alexander, Peter F. *Leonard and Virginia Woolf: A Literary Partnership.* New York: Simon & Schuster, 1992.

Alexandrov, Vladimir E. *Andrei Bely: The Major Symbolist Fiction.* Cambridge: Harvard University Press, 1985.

Annan, Noel. *Leslie Stephen: The Godless Victorian.* New York: Random House, 1984.

Arnold, Bruce. *The Scandal of "Ulysses": The Sensational Life of a Twentieth-Century Masterpiece.* New York: St. Martin's, 1991.

Auerbach, Erich. *Mimesis: The Representation of Reality in Western Literature.* Translated by Willard Trask. New York: Doubleday, 1957.

Bakhtin, M. M. *The Dialogic Imagination: Four Essays.* Translated by Caryl Emerson and Michael Holquist. Edited by Michael Holquist. Austin: University of Texas Press, 1981.

———. *Speech Genres and Other Late Essays.* Translated by Vern W. McGee. Edited by Caryl Emerson and Michael Holquist. Austin: University of Texas Press, 1986.

Baratoff, Nathalie. *Oblomov: A Jungian Approach. A Literary Image of the Mother Complex.* Bern: Peter Lang, 1990.

Beisov, P. S. *Goncharov i rodnoi krai (Goncharov and His Native Region).* Kuibyshev: Kuibyshevskoe knizhnoe izdatel'stvo, 1960.

Beja, Morris, ed. *"To the Lighthouse": A Casebook.* London: Macmillan, 1970.

Beja, Morris, Phillip Herring, Maurice Harmon, and David Norris, eds. *James Joyce: The Centennial Symposium.* Urbana: University of Illinois Press, 1986.

Belinsky, V. G. *Pis'ma (Letters).* Edited by E. A. Liatsky. St. Petersburg: Tipografiia M. M. Stasiulevicha, 1914.

Bell, Clive. *Civilization and Old Friends.* Chicago: University of Chicago Press, 1973.

Bell, Quentin. *Virginia Woolf: A Biography.* 2 vols. New York: Harcourt Brace Jovanovich, 1972.

Bely, Andrei. *The Dramatic Symphony. The Forms of Art.* Translated by Roger Keys, Angela Keys, and John Elsworth. Edinburgh: Polygon, 1986.

———. *Petersburg.* Translated by Robert A. Maguire and John E. Malmstad. Bloomington: Indiana University Press, 1978.

Benstock, Bernard, ed. *The Seventh of Joyce.* Bloomington: Indiana University Press, 1982.

Bloom, Harold. *James Joyce: Modern Critical Views.* New York: Chelsea, 1986.

Bloom, Harold, ed. *Modern Critical Views: Virginia Woolf.* New York: Chelsea, 1986.

Blot, Jean. *Ivan Gontcharov ou Le Réalisme Impossible* (*Ivan Goncharov: Or the Impossible Realism*). Paris: L'Age D'Homme, 1986.

Bonnerot, Louis, ed. *"Ulysses" Cinquante Ans Après* (*Ulysses Fifty Years Later*). Paris: Didier, 1974.

Booth, Wayne C. *The Rhetoric of Fiction.* Chicago: University of Chicago Press, 1961.

Boyd, Ernest A. *Ireland's Literary Renaissance.* Dublin: Maunsel, 1916.

Bruss, Elizabeth W. *Autobiographical Acts: The Changing Situation of a Literary Genre.* Baltimore: Johns Hopkins University Press, 1976.

Buckley, Jerome Hamilton. "Autobiography in the English Bildungsroman." In *The Interpretation of Narrative: Theory and Practice,* edited by Morton Bloomfield. Cambridge: Harvard University Press, 1970.

———. *The Turning Key: Autobiography and the Subjective Impulse since 1800.* Cambridge: Harvard University Press, 1984.

Budgen, Frank. *James Joyce and the Making of "Ulysses."* Bloomington: Indiana University Press, 1960.

———. *Myselves When Young.* London: Oxford University Press, 1970.

Carlson, Maria. *No Religion Higher than Truth: A History of the Theosophical Movement in Russia, 1875–1892.* Princeton: Princeton University Press, 1993.

Cohn, Dorrit. *Transparent Minds.* Princeton: Princeton University Press, 1978.

Cornwell, Neil. *James Joyce and the Russians.* London: Macmillan, 1992.

Costello, Peter. *James Joyce: The Years of Growth. 1882–1915.* New York: Pantheon, 1992.

Cranston, Sylvia. *HPB: The Extraordinary Life and Influence of Helena Blavatsky, Founder of Modern Theosophical Movement.* New York: Putnam, 1993.

Crook, Eugene J., ed. *Fearful Symmetry: Doubles and Doubling in Literature and Film.* Tallahassee: University Presses of Florida, 1981.

Cross, A. G. *N. M. Karamzin: A Study of His Literary Career (1783–1803)*. Carbondale: Southern Illinois University Press, 1971.

Cuddon, J. A. *A Dictionary of Literary Terms*. Harmondsworth: Penguin, 1976.

DeSalvo, Louise. *Virginia Woolf: The Impact of Childhood Sexual Abuse on Her Life and Work*. Boston: Beacon, 1989.

Dickens, Charles. *David Copperfield*. New York: New American Library, 1962.

Doody, Margaret Anne, and Peter Sabor, eds. *Samuel Richardson: Tercentenary Essays*. Cambridge: Cambridge University Press, 1989.

Ehre, Milton. *Oblomov and His Creator*. Princeton: Princeton University Press, 1973.

Eikhenbaum, Boris. *O literature. Raboty raznykh let* (About literature. Works of various years). Moscow: Sovetskii pisatel', 1987.

Ellmann, Richard. *James Joyce*. Rev. ed. Oxford: Oxford University Press, 1983.

———. *Ulysses on the Liffey*. New York: Oxford University Press, 1972.

Elsworth, J. D. *Andrey Bely: A Critical Study of the Novels*. Cambridge: Cambridge University Press, 1983.

Epstein, Edmund L. *The Ordeal of Stephen Dedalus*. Carbondale: Southern Illinois Press, 1971.

———, ed. *A Starchamber Quiry: A James Joyce Centennial, Volume 1882–1982*. London: Methuen, 1982.

Evgen'ev-Maksimov, V. E. *I. A. Goncharov: zhizn', lichnost', tvorchestvo* (*Goncharov: His Life, Personality, Works*). Moscow: Gosizdat, 1925.

Fedotov, G. P. *The Russian Religious Mind: Kievan Christianity—the Tenth to the Thirteenth Centuries*. Cambridge: Harvard University Press, 1946.

Fitzgerald, F. Scott. *The Crack-Up*. Edited by Edmund Wilson. New York: New Directions, 1945.

Flaubert, Gustave. *Letters. 1830–1857*. Translated and edited by Francis Steegmuller. Cambridge: Harvard University Press, 1980.

Fleishman, Avrom. *Figures of Autobiography: The Language of Self-Writing in Victorian and Modern England*. Berkeley and Los Angeles: University of California Press, 1983.

———. *Virginia Woolf: A Critical Reading*. Baltimore: Johns Hopkins University Press, 1975.

Fogel, Daniel Mark. *Covert Relations: James Joyce, Virginia Woolf, and Henry James*. Charlottesville and London: University Press of Virginia, 1990.

French, Marilyn. *The Book as World: James Joyce's "Ulysses."* Cambridge: Harvard University Press, 1976.

Freud, Sigmund. *Collected Papers*. 5 vols. Edited by James Strachey and Alix Strachey. London: Hogarth Press, 1948.

———. *The Ego and the Id.* Translated by Joan Riviere. Edited by James Strachey. New York: Norton, 1960.

Frye, Northrop. *Anatomy of Criticism: Four Essays.* Princeton: Princeton University Press, 1957.

———. *The Educated Imagination.* Toronto: CBC Publications, 1963.

Gifford, Don, and Robert J. Seidman. *Notes for Joyce.* New York: E. P. Dutton, 1974.

Gilbert, Stuart. *James Joyce's "Ulysses." A Study.* New York: Vintage, 1955.

———. *Reflections on James Joyce: Stuart Gilbert's Paris Journal.* Edited by Thomas F. Staley and Randolph Lewis. Austin: University of Texas Press, 1993.

Gillespie, Diane F. *The Sisters' Arts: The Writing and Painting of Virginia Woolf and Vanessa Bell.* Syracuse: Syracuse University Press, 1988.

Gillespie, Michael Patrick. *Reading the Book of Himself: Narrative Strategies in the Works of James Joyce.* Columbus: Ohio University Press, 1989.

Ginsberg, Elaine K., and Laura Moss Gottlieb, eds. *Virginia Woolf: Centennial Essays.* Troy: Whitston, 1983.

Ginzburg, Lidiia. *On Psychological Prose.* Translated and edited by Judson Rosengrant. Princeton: Princeton University Press, 1991.

Goncharov, I. A. *The Same Old Story* (*Obyknovennaia Istoriia*). Alternately translated as *A Common Story.* Translated by Ivy Litvinova. Moscow: Foreign Languages, 1957.

———. *Sobranie sochinenii* (*Collection of Works*). 8 vols. Edited by A. G. Tseitlin. Moscow: Pravda, 1952.

Gordon, Lyndall. *Virginia Woolf: A Writer's Life.* New York: Norton, 1984.

Groden, Michael. *"Ulysses" in Progress.* Princeton: Princeton University Press, 1977.

Guerard, Albert J., ed. *Stories of the Double.* Philadelphia: Lippincott, 1967.

Guiguet, Jean. *Virginia Woolf and Her Works.* Translated by Jean Stewart. New York: Harcourt Brace Jovanovich, 1962.

Hart, Clive, and David Hayman. *James Joyce's "Ulysses": Critical Essays.* Berkeley and Los Angeles: University of California Press, 1974.

Hawthorn, Jeremy. *Multiple Personality and the Disintegration of Literary Character: From Oliver Goldsmith to Sylvia Plath.* London: Edward Arnold, 1983.

Hayman, David. *"Ulysses": The Mechanics of Meaning.* Englewood Cliffs: Prentice-Hall, 1970.

Henke, Suzette, and Elaine Unkeless, eds. *Women in Joyce.* Urbana: University of Illinois Press, 1982.

Hilgard, Ernest R. *Divided Consciousness: Multiple Control in Human Thought and Action.* New York: John Wiley, 1977.

Hill, Katherine C. "Virginia Woolf and Leslie Stephen: History and Literary Revolution." *PMLA* 3 (May 1981): 351–62.

Holman, Hugh C. *Handbook to Literature.* Indianapolis: Bobbs-Merrill, 1972.

Joyce, James. *The Critical Writings.* Edited by Ellsworth Mason and Richard Ellmann. New York: Viking, 1964.

———. *Dubliners.* Harmondsworth: Penguin, 1967.

———. *Epifanie.* Edited by Giorgio Melchiori. Milano: Arnoldo Mondadori, 1982.

———. *Exiles.* New York: Viking, 1951.

———. *Finnegans Wake.* Harmondsworth: Penguin, 1976.

———. *Giacomo Joyce.* Edited by Richard Ellmann. New York: Viking, 1959.

———. *James Joyce in Padua.* Translated and edited by Louis Berrone. New York: Random House, 1977.

———. *Joyce's Notes and Early Drafts for "Ulysses": Selections from the Buffalo Collection.* Edited by Philip F. Herring. Charlottesville: University Press of Virginia, 1977.

———. *Joyce's "Ulysses" Notesheets in the British Museum.* Edited by Phillip F. Herring. Charlottesville: University Press of Virginia, 1972.

———. *Letters.* Vol 1. Edited by Stuart Gilbert. New York: Viking, 1957.

———. *Letters.* Vols. 2 and 3. Edited by Richard Ellmann. New York: Viking, 1966.

———. *A Portrait of the Artist as a Young Man.* Harmondsworth: Penguin, 1976.

———. *Selected Letters of James Joyce.* Edited by Richard Ellmann. New York: Viking, 1975.

———. *Stephen Hero.* New York: New Directions, 1944.

———. *Ulysses: The Corrected Text.* Edited by Hans Walter Gabler with Wolfhand Steppe and Claus Melchior. New York: Random House, 1986.

Joyce, James, and Paul Léon. *The James Joyce and Paul Léon Papers in the National Library of Ireland: A Catalogue.* Compiled by Catherine Fahy. Dublin: National Library of Ireland, 1992.

Joyce, Stanislaus. *The Complete Dublin Diary.* Edited by George H. Healey. Ithaca: Cornell University Press, 1971.

———. *My Brother's Keeper: James Joyce's Early Years.* Edited by Richard Ellmann. New York: Viking, 1958.

Jung, C. G. *Modern Man in Search of a Soul.* Translated by W. S. Dell and Cary F. Baynes. New York: Harcourt Brace Jovanovich, 1933.

———. *Psychological Types; or, the Psychology of Individuation.* Translated by H. Godwin Baynes. London: Routledge & Kegan Paul, 1923.

Keenan, Edward L. *The Kurbskii-Groznyi Apocrypha.* Appendix by Daniel C. Waugh. Cambridge: Harvard University Press, 1971.

Kenner, Hugh. *Dublin's Joyce*. Bloomington: Indiana University Press, 1956.

———. *Joyce's Voices*. Berkeley and Los Angeles: University of California Press, 1978.

———. *"Ulysses."* London: George Allen & Unwin, 1980.

Keppler, C. F. *The Literature of the Second Self.* Tucson: University of Arizona Press, 1972.

Kershner, R. B. *Joyce, Bakhtin, and Popular Literature: Chronicles of Disorder.* Chapel Hill: University of North Carolina Press, 1989.

Klein, Joachim. "Gončarov und die Idylle: 'Obyknovennaja istorija'" (*Goncharov and the Idyl: "A Common Story"*). In *Slavistische Studien zum VIII. Internationalen Slavistenkongress in Zagreb 1978* [Slavic Studies at the Eighth International Congress of Slavists in Zagreb, 1978]. Cologne: Böhlau, 1978.

Kushen, Betty. *Virginia Woolf and the Nature of Communion.* West Orange: Raynor, 1983.

Lavrin, Janko. *Goncharov: Studies in the Modern European Literature and Thought.* New Haven: Yale University Press, 1954.

Lawrence, D. H. *Selected Literary Criticism.* Edited by Anthony Beal. New York: Viking, 1971.

Lawrence, Karen. *The Odyssey of Style in "Ulysses."* Princeton: Princeton University Press, 1981.

Leaska, Mitchell. *Virginia Woolf's "Lighthouse": A Study in Critical Method.* New York: Columbia University Press, 1970.

Lenhoff, Gail. *The Martyred Princes Boris and Gleb: A Socio-Cultural Study of the Cult and the Texts.* Columbus: Slavica, 1989.

Lesser, Simon. *Fiction and the Unconscious.* New York: Random House, 1957.

Lesser, Wendy. *His Other Half: Men Looking at Women through Art.* Cambridge: Harvard University Press, 1991.

Levin, Harry. *James Joyce.* New York: New Directions, 1941.

Liatsky, E. A. *Goncharov: zhizn', lichnost', tvorchestvo* (*Goncharov: His Life, Personality, Works*). Stockholm: Severnye ogni, 1920.

———. *Roman i zhizn': razvitie tvorcheskoi lichnosti Goncharova* (*Fiction and Life: the Development of Goncharov as a Writer*). Prague: Plamia, 1925.

Ljunggren, Magnus. *The Dream of Rebirth: A Study of Andrej Belyj's Novel "Petersburg."* Stockholm: Almqvist & Wiksell, 1982.

Lohff, Ulrich M. *Die Bildlichkeit in den Romanen Ivan Aleksandrovič Gončarovs* (*The Pictorial in the Novels of Ivan Aleksandrovich Goncharov*). Munich: Otto Sagner, 1977.

Lotshits, Iury. *Goncharov.* Moscow: Molodaia Gvardiia, 1977.

Love, Jean O. *Worlds in Consciousness: Mythopoetic Thought in the Novels of Virginia Woolf.* Berkeley and Los Angeles: University of California Press, 1970.

Lyngstad, Alexandra, and Sverre Lyngstad. *Ivan Goncharov.* New York: Twayne, 1971.

McArthur, Murray. *Stolen Writings: Blake's "Milton," Joyce's "Ulysses," and the Nature of Influence.* Ann Arbor: UMI Research Press, 1988.

McGee, Patrick. *Paperspace: Style as Ideology in Joyce's "Ulysses."* Lincoln: University of Nebraska Press, 1988.

McMichael, James. *"Ulysses" and Justice.* Princeton: Princeton University Press, 1991.

Maddox, Brenda. *Nora: The Real Life of Molly Bloom.* Boston: Houghton Mifflin, 1988.

Magalaner, Marvin, ed. *A James Joyce Miscellany. Second Series.* Carbondale: Southern Illinois University Press, 1959.

Mahaffey, Vicki. *Reauthorizing Joyce.* Cambridge: Cambridge University Press, 1988.

Majumdar, Robin, and Allen McLaurin, eds. *Virginia Woolf: The Critical Heritage.* London: Routledge & Kegan Paul, 1975.

Malmstad, John E., ed. *Andrey Bely: Spirit of Symbolism.* Ithaca: Cornell University Press, 1987.

Mann, Thomas. *Stories of Three Decades.* Translated by H. T. Lowe-Porter. New York: Knopf, 1955.

Marcus, Jane. *Virginia Woolf and the Languages of Patriarchy.* Bloomington: Indiana University Press, 1987.

Marcus, Jane, ed. *New Feminist Essays on Virginia Woolf.* Lincoln: University of Nebraska Press, 1981.

———. *Virginia Woolf: A Feminist Slant.* Lincoln: University of Nebraska Press, 1983.

———. *Virginia Woolf and Bloomsbury: A Centenary Celebration.* London: Macmillan, 1987.

Mattoon, Mary Ann. *Jungian Psychology in Perspective.* New York: Free Press, 1981.

Mazon, André. *Un maitre du roman russe: Ivan Gontcharov* (*A Master of the Russian Novel: Ivan Goncharov*). Paris: H. Champion, 1914.

Merezhkovsky, Dmitry. *Polnoe sobranie sochinenii* (*Complete Works*). Moscow: Tipografiia Sytina, 1914.

Miller, C. Ruth. *Virginia Woolf: The Frames of Art and Life.* London: Macmillan, 1988.

Miller, Karl. *Doubles: Studies in Literary History.* London: Oxford University Press, 1985.

Mintslov, S. R. *Obzor zapisok, dnevnikov, vospominanii, pisem i puteshestvii, otnosiashchikhsia k istorii Rossii i napechatannykh na russkom iazyke* (*An Overview of Notes, Diaries, Reminiscences, Letters and Travel Journals Concerning the History of Russia and Published in Russian*). 5 vols. Edited by Marc Raef. New York: Oriental Research Partners (Columbia University), 1972.

Miyoshi, Masao. *The Divided Self: A Perspective on the Literature of the Victorians.* New York: New York University Press, 1969.

Morrell, Lady Ottoline. *Ottoline at Garsington: Memoirs of Lady Ottoline Morrell, 1915–1918.* Edited by Robert Gathorne-Hardy. London: Faber and Faber, 1974.

Morris, William E., and Clifford A. Nault, Jr., eds. *Portraits of an Artist: A Casebook on James Joyce's "A Portrait of the Artist as a Young Man."* New York: Odyssey Press, 1962.

Murphy, Gardner. *Personality: A Biosocial Approach to Origins and Structure.* New York: Harper, 1947.

Nabokov, Vladimir. *The Gift.* New York: Putnam, 1963.

———. *Lectures on "Don Quixote."* Edited by Fredson Bowers. New York: Harcourt Brace Jovanovich, 1983.

———. *Lectures on Literature.* Edited by Fredson Bowers. New York: Harcourt Brace Jovanovich, 1980.

———. *Mary.* New York: McGraw-Hill, 1970.

———. *Strong Opinions.* New York: McGraw-Hill, 1973.

Nadel, Ira B. *Joyce and the Jews: Culture and Texts.* Iowa City: University of Iowa Press, 1989.

———. "'The REAL History of the ERA': Joyce, Lewis and Fascism." *Canadian Journal of Irish Studies* 1 (July 1988): 29–35.

Newman, Robert D., and Weldon Thornton. *Joyce's "Ulysses": The Larger Perspective.* Newark: University of Delaware Press, 1987.

Noble, Joan Russell, ed. *Recollections of Virginia Woolf.* London: Peter Owen, 1972.

Noon, William T. *Joyce and Aquinas.* New Haven: Yale University Press, 1957.

Northridge, W. L. *Modern Theories of the Unconscious.* London: Kegan Paul, Trench, Trubner, 1924.

Paperno, Irina. *Chernyshevsky and the Age of Realism: A Study in the Semiotics of Behavior.* Stanford: Stanford University Press, 1988.

Paul, Janis M. *The Victorian Heritage of Virginia Woolf: The External World in Her Novels.* Norman: Pilgrim, 1987.

Piksanov, N. K., ed. *Goncharov v vospominaniiakh sovremennikov* (*Goncharov in the Reminiscences of His Contemporaries*). Leningrad: Khudozhestvennaia literatura, 1969.

Pilling, John. *Autobiography and Imagination: Studies in Self-Scrutiny.* London: Routledge Kegan & Paul, 1981.

Pittman, Riitta H. *The Writer's Divided Self in Bulgakov's "The Master and Margarita."* New York: St. Martin's, 1991.

Pokrovsky, V. I., ed. *Ivan Goncharov: ego zhizn' i sochineniia* (*Ivan Goncharov: His Life and Works*). Moscow: Magazin V. Spiridonova i A. Mikhailova, 1912.

Polevoi, Nikolai. *Ocherki russkoi litteratury* (*Essays on Russian Literature*). St. Petersburg: Tipographiia Sakharova, 1839.

———. "Sokhatyi: Sibirskaia povest'" ("Sokhatyi: A Siberian tale"). In *Dennitsa,* 172–249, 1830.

Poliakov, M. Ia., and S. A. Trubnikov, eds. *I. A. Goncharov v russkoi kritike* (*I. A. Goncharov in Russian Criticism*). Moscow: Khudozhestvennaia literatura, 1958.

Pope, Kenneth S., and Jerome L. Singer, eds. *The Stream of Consciousness: Scientific Investigations into the Flow of Human Experience.* New York: Plenum, 1978.

Potts, Willard, ed. *Portraits of the Artist in Exile: Recollections of James Joyce by Europeans.* Seattle: University of Washington Press, 1979.

Power, Arthur. *Conversations with James Joyce.* Edited by Clive Hart. New York: Harper and Row, 1974.

Prince, Morton. *The Dissociation of a Personality: A Biographical Study in Abnormal Psychology.* New York: Longmans, Green, 1905.

———. *Psychotherapy and Multiple Personality: Selected Essays.* Edited by Nathan G. Hale, Jr. Cambridge: Harvard University Press, 1975.

Rank, Otto. *Beyond Psychology.* New York: Dover, 1941.

———. *The Double: A Psychoanalytic Study.* Translated and edited by Harry Tucker, Jr. Chapel Hill: University of North Carolina Press, 1971.

Richardson, Samuel, and Johannes Stinstra. *The Richardson-Stinstra Correspondence and Stinstra's Preface to "Clarissa."* Edited by William C. Slattery. Carbondale: Southern Illinois University Press, 1969.

Robert, Marthe. *The Old and the New: From Don Quixote to Kafka.* Translated by Carol Cosman. Berkeley and Los Angeles: University of California Press, 1977.

Rogers, Robert. *The Psychoanalytic Study of the Double in Literature.* Detroit: Wayne State University Press, 1970.

Rose, Phyllis. *Woman of Letters: A Life of Virginia Woolf.* New York: Oxford University Press, 1978.

Rosenfield, Clare. "The Shadow Within." *Daedalus* 2 (Spring 1963): 326–44.

Rosenman, Ellen Bayuk. *The Invisible Presence: Virginia Woolf and the Mother-Daughter Relationship.* Baton Rouge: Louisiana State University Press, 1986.

Rosenthal, Michael. *Virginia Woolf.* New York: Columbia University Press, 1979.

Rudnik-Smalbraak, Marijke. *Samuel Richardson: Minute Particulars within the Large Design.* Leiden: Leiden University Press, 1983.

Russell, Mechtild. *Untersuchungen zur Theorie und Praxis der Typisierung bei I. A. Gončarov (Investigation into Theory and Practice of Typification in I. A. Goncharov).* Munich: Otto Sagner, 1978.

Rybasov, A. *I. A. Goncharov.* Moscow: Molodaia Gvardiia, 1957.

Scholes, Robert. *In Search of James Joyce.* Urbana: University of Illinois Press, 1992.

Scholes, Robert, and Richard M. Kain, eds. *The Workshop of Daedalus: James Joyce and the Raw Materials for "A Portrait of the Artist as a Young Man."* Evanston: Northwestern University Press, 1965.

Scott, Bonnie Kime. *James Joyce.* Feminist Readings Series. Atlantic Highlands: Humanities Press International, 1987.

———. *Joyce and Feminism.* Bloomington: Indiana University Press, 1984.

Setchkarev, Vsevolod. *Ivan Goncharov: His Life and His Works.* Wurzburg: Jal, 1974.

Shechner, Mark. "The Song of the Wandering Aengus: James Joyce and His Mother." *James Joyce Quarterly* 1 (Fall 1972): 73–89.

Sidis, Boris. *Psychopathological Researches: Studies in Mental Dissociation.* New York: Stechert, 1902.

Sidis, Boris, and Simon P. Goodhart. *Multiple Personality: An Experimental Investigation into the Nature of Human Individuality.* London: Sidney Appleton, 1904.

Simmons, Ernest J. *Dostoevski: The Making of a Novelist.* London: Oxford University Press, 1940.

Slonim, Marc. *The Epic of Russian Literature.* New York: Oxford University Press, 1950.

Spengemann, William C. *The Forms of Autobiography: Episodes in the History of a Literary Genre.* New Haven: Yale University Press, 1980.

Sprague, Claire, ed. *Virginia Woolf: A Collection of Critical Essays.* Englewood Cliffs: Prentice-Hall, 1971.

Staley, Thomas F., ed. *"Ulysses": Fifty Years.* Bloomington: Indiana University Press, 1972.

Stephen, Julia Duckworth. *Stories for Children, Essays for Adults.* Edited by Diane F. Gillespie and Elizabeth Steele. Syracuse: Syracuse University Press, 1987.

Stephen, Leslie. *The Mausoleum Book*. Edited by Alan Bell. Oxford: Clarendon Press, 1977.

Stilman, Leon. "Oblomovka Revisited." *American Slavic and East European Review* 7 (1948): 45–77.

Swift, Jonathan. *Gulliver's Travels and Other Writings*. Edited by Louis A. Landa. Boston: Houghton Mifflin, 1960.

Terras, Victor, ed. *Handbook of Russian Literature*. New Haven: Yale University Press, 1985.

Theoharis, Theoharis Constantine. *Joyce's "Ulysses": An Anatomy of the Soul*. Chapel Hill: University of North Carolina Press, 1988.

Thiergen, Peter, ed. *I. A. Gončarov: Beiträge zu Werk und Wirkung*. (*I. A. Goncharov: Contributions on His Works and Influence*). Köln: Böhlau, 1989.

Tseitlin, A. G. *I. A. Goncharov*. Moscow: AN SSSR, 1950.

Tucker, Lindsey. *Stephen and Bloom at Life's Feast: Alimentary Symbolism and the Creative Process in James Joyce's "Ulysses."* Columbus: Ohio State University Press, 1984.

Tweedie, Gordon. "'Common Sense': James to Joyce and the Pragmatic L. Bloom." *James Joyce Quarterly* 3 (Spring 1989): 351–66.

Tymms, Ralph. *Doubles in Literary Psychology*. Cambridge: Bowes and Bowes, 1949.

Van der Vat, D. G. "Paternity in 'Ulysses.'" *English Studies* 19 (August 1937): 145–58.

Wachtel, Andrew. *The Battle for Childhood: Creation of a Russian Myth*. Stanford: Stanford University Press, 1990.

Wain, Marianne. "The Double in Romantic Narrative: A Preliminary Study." *Germanic Review* 4 (December 1961): 258–68.

Walcott, William O. "The Paternity of James Joyce's Stephen Dedalus." *Journal of Analytical Psychology* 10 (January 1965): 77–95.

Waldeck, Peter B. *The Split Self from Goethe to Broch*. London: Associated University Presses, 1979.

Warner, Eric, ed. *Virginia Woolf: A Centenary Perspective*. London: Macmillan, 1984.

Watt, Ian. *The Rise of the Novel: Studies in Defoe, Richardson and Fielding*. Berkeley and Los Angeles: University of California Press, 1974.

Wheare, Jane. *Virginia Woolf: Dramatic Novelist*. London: Macmillan, 1989.

Whyte, L. L. *The Unconscious before Freud*. New York: St. Martin's, 1978.

Woolf, Leonard. *Letters*. Edited by Frederic Spotts. New York: Harcourt Brace Jovanovich, 1989.

———. *Sowing: An Autobiography of the Years 1880 to 1904*. New York: Harcourt Brace Jovanovich, 1960.

Woolf, Virginia. *The Captain's Death Bed and Other Essays.* New York: Harcourt Brace Jovanovich, 1950.

———. *The Common Reader.* New York: Harcourt, Brace, 1925.

———. *The Death of the Moth and Other Essays.* New York: Harcourt Brace Jovanovich, 1942.

———. *The Diary of Virginia Woolf.* 5 vols. Edited by Anne Olivier Bell with Andrew McNeillie. New York: Harcourt Brace Jovanovich, 1977–84.

———. *Granite and Rainbow: Essays.* New York: Harcourt Brace Jovanovich, 1958.

———. *Jacob's Room & The Waves.* New York: Harcourt, Brace, 1959.

———. *The Letters of Virginia Woolf.* 6 vols. Edited by Nigel Nicolson with Joanne Trautman. New York: Harcourt Brace Jovanovich, 1975–80.

———. *Moments of Being: Unpublished Autobiographical Writings.* Edited by Jeanne Schulkind. New York: Harcourt Brace Jovanovich, 1976.

———. *Moments of Being.* 2d ed. Edited by Jeanne Schulkind. New York: Harcourt Brace Jovanovich, 1985.

———. *A Room of One's Own.* St. Albans: Chatto, Bodley Head, and Jonathan Cape, 1977.

———. *The Second Common Reader.* New York: Harcourt, Brace 1932.

———. *To the Lighthouse.* New York: Harcourt, Brace, 1927.

———. *"To the Lighthouse": The Original Holograph Draft.* Transcribed and edited by Susan Dick. Toronto: University of Toronto Press, 1982.

———. *"The Waves": The Two Holograph Drafts.* Transcribed and edited by J. W. Graham. Toronto: University of Toronto Press, 1976.

———. *A Writer's Diary.* Edited by Leonard Woolf. New York: Harcourt Brace Jovanovich, 1953.

Zenkovsky, Serge A. "Der Mönch Epifanij und die Entstehung der altrussischen Autobiographie." (*The Monk Epiphany and the Origin of the Old Russian Autobiography*). *Welt der Slaven: Vierteljahrsschrift fur Slavistic* (*World of Slavs: Slavic Studies Quarterly*). Wiesbaden: Otto Harrassowitz, 1956.

Zwerdling, Alex. *Virginia Woolf and the Real World.* Berkeley and Los Angeles: University of California Press, 1986.

Index